1992

Introduction to the Graphical Kernel System (GKS)

Second Edition
Revised for the International Standard

This is volume 28 in A.P.I.C. Studies in Data Processing
General Editors: Fraser Duncan *and* M. J. R. Shave
A complete list of titles in this series appears at the end of this volume

A.P.I.C. Studies in Data Processing
No. 28

Introduction to the Graphical Kernel System (GKS)

Second Edition
Revised for the International Standard

F. R. A. HOPGOOD
D. A. DUCE
J. R. GALLOP
D. C. SUTCLIFFE

Rutherford Appleton Laboratory, Didcot, UK

1986

ACADEMIC PRESS
Harcourt Brace Jovanovich, Publishers
London   San Diego
New York   Berkeley   Boston   Sydney
Tokyo   Toronto

ACADEMIC PRESS LIMITED
24/28 Oval Road
London NW1 7DX

United States Edition published by
ACADEMIC PRESS, INC.
San Diego, CA92101

British Library Cataloguing in Publication Data
Introduction to the Graphical Kernel System (GKS)—
(Automatic Programming Information Centre studies
in data processing ISSN 0067-2483; 28: 2nd edn)
1. Computer graphics
I. Hopgood, F. R. A.   II. Series
001.64'43   T385

ISBN 0-12-355571-X

Printed in Great Britain

Preface

Standards in computer graphics are long overdue. Whereas *de facto* standards in programming languages were common very early on (FORTRAN and ALGOL 60) and international standards soon followed, there has been a long period of graphics history where, at best, regional de facto standards have existed and no international standards have evolved.

Now, after some nine years work by a highly dedicated international group of graphics experts, this trend has been broken, with the publication of the Graphical Kernel System (GKS) as an International Standard by ISO in 1985.

GKS is a graphics system which allows programs to support a wide variety of graphics devices. It is defined independently of programming languages.

This book aims to provide the application programmer with a good understanding of the principles behind GKS and to serve subsequently as an informal manual for GKS. No knowledge of GKS is assumed, but the reader is expected to have a good understanding of programming and at least a rudimentary knowledge of computer graphics. The book is arranged in two main parts. The background of GKS is described and its essential concepts are introduced in the first part whereas those features more likely to be required by the specialist graphics programmer are described in the second.

The book may be read in two ways. Firstly to discover the whole of GKS, the chapters in Part I, which introduce the essential concepts, should be read in sequence. However, the chapters in Part II may be read more or less independently of each other, although they assume knowledge of the whole of Part I. Alternatively, to first become acquainted with GKS as a graphical output system, Chapters 1 to 4 and 7 from Part I should be read in sequence followed by a selection of Chapters 8, and 10 to 13 from Part II. If required, the remaining chapters can be read to complete the picture.

Examples are expressed in a dialect of FORTRAN 77 described in the introductory section on Notation. As an aid to understanding, names greater than 6 characters are allowed. The correspondence between the names actually used and those in the FORTRAN 77 language binding for GKS is given in an appendix.

Part I begins with a chapter which outlines the historical background of graphics standards and the emergence of GKS. In Chapters 2 and 3, output primitives of GKS and their attributes and the coordinate systems, in which they are specified, are described. Chapter 4 describes how pictures may be divided into segments and how these segments may be manipulated. The segment attributes are introduced. GKS is not only concerned with graphical output but also with graphical input. Its powerful input facilities are covered in Chapters 5 and 6. Chapter 7 concludes Part I with a description of the workstation concept which is the central concept in GKS promoting program portability.

The GKS environment and the more advanced facilities are discussed in Part II. Chapter 8 describes the GKS environment, which includes initialisation of GKS, the GKS data structures, the level structure and error handling. Chapter 9 describes the control of input devices. In Chapter 10, more advanced segmentation facilities (system wide segment storage) are considered and Chapter 11 describes the GKS metafile, a means of transporting graphical information between graphics installations. Chapters 12 and 13 describe the output primitives not covered in Chapter 2 and say more about attribute handling.

The authors of the book were the editors of the GKS document. Although that document is quite readable, we felt there was a need for a more descriptive introduction to GKS illustrated with many examples. This book is our answer to that need. We believe it will be useful to all application programmers with an interest in computer graphics.

The first edition was published in 1983. Since then GKS has been published as an International Standard and this book has now been updated and revised.

Finally, we would like to thank all those who have participated, in any way, in the standardization process, which has lasted a number of years at national and international levels. Our thanks must also go to wives, families and friends, who have borne with us during both the standardization process and the writing of this book.

Feast of the Epiphany 1986

Notation

It is inevitable, in a technical work such as this, that a number of abbreviations are used. The more important ones are defined as they are introduced but, for completeness, all the abbreviations are defined in Appendix A.

GKS, itself, is defined independently of a programming language. Before it can be used from a particular language, a *language binding* must be defined for that language. In this book, GKS is presented in terms of the Draft International Standard FORTRAN language binding (FORTRAN 77), details of which are listed in Appendix B.

Since a language binding must obey the conventions of a language, all the subroutine names in the FORTRAN 77 language binding are restricted to be at most six characters. To make this book more readable, each subroutine name has been replaced by the full function name from the GKS document (ISO 7942). Both names are listed in Appendix B. For example, the name of the subroutine for line drawing is GPL but in this book we use the GKS name POLYLINE.

The examples in this book are given in a dialect of FORTRAN 77. In the interests of illustrating the subject matter, some liberties have been taken. In particular, no restrictions are placed on the length of identifiers and the word 'CALL' is omitted from CALL statements.

Thus, using the example above, in FORTRAN 77 we would use:

```
CALL GPL(N, X, Y)
```

to draw a line but here this is written as:

```
POLYLINE(N, X, Y)
```

INTEGER and REAL values are mixed indiscriminately (for example, where a subroutine requires a REAL parameter, an INTEGER or REAL actual parameter may be used). Parameters specifying one of a number of options, which in Pascal would be of enumeration type, are written as variable names, with the assumption that the appropriate settings have been made elsewhere. For example, the GKS function to specify the

CLIP (rather than NOCLIP) option for the clipping indicator will be written as:

SET CLIPPING INDICATOR(CLIP)

In the FORTRAN 77 language binding, names have been defined for these values. These should be made available, by means of PARAME-TER or DATA statements, for inclusion in application programs (in an installation dependent manner). Thus to set the clipping indicator to CLIP requires:

CALL GSCLIP(GCLIP)

Contents

Part I

1 Introduction

A ski lodge 6000 feet up Mount Hood in Oregon was the setting for the announcement in July 1985 that the Graphical Kernel System (GKS) was finally to be published by the International Organization for Standardization (ISO) as International Standard 7942. Why has it taken until 1985 for an International Standard for computer graphics to emerge? After all, *de facto* standards in programming languages have existed for more than twenty years and international standards soon followed. At first sight it might be thought that this was due to the relative infancy of computer graphics, but the origins of computer graphics can be traced back almost to the advent of digital computers.

On the MIT Whirlwind, dual 16 inch displays were available as early as 1951; plotters were in use by 1953 and at least one high speed microfilm recorder was available in 1958. Input devices emerged later, yet lightpens can be traced back to 1958 and the RAND tablet made its debut in 1964. Colour displays appeared in 1962 and by 1965 most of the hardware facilities which we now take for granted had appeared.

However, despite the existence of the technology, the number of display systems installed worldwide by 1964 is believed to be only about 100. Predictably these came from a number of different manufacturers and different graphics packages were written to capitalize on the features of each. There is a parallel here with the early history of programming languages. In that field, however, the availability of FORTRAN on a widely marketed range of IBM machines led to the emergence of a *de facto* standard.

Some standard approaches began to appear in computer graphics, accepted techniques in the use of stand-alone and satellite refresh display systems were emerging in the late 1960's and it is possible that had developments continued in this manner, a standard would have emerged.

Likewise, patterns were apparent in the use of plotters and the GINO and GHOST packages began to be more widely used in the UK in the early 1970's.

1.1 THE CHANGING SCENE

Until the late 1960's, interactive graphics required an expensive refresh display and dedicated host computer. A total cost of $400,000 was not uncommon and thus such systems were only available to a few.

The advent of timesharing systems at about the same time that the storage tube display emerged (at a fraction of the cost, say $4,000 against $80,000 for a refresh display) had a dramatic impact. Interactive graphics was now possible for a large number of people. The storage tube did not allow changes to be made to the picture without completely redrawing it (which was unattractive because of the low bandwidth typically available to the mainframe) but at the same time allowed a large amount of information to be displayed flicker free. Consequently, users developed new and different techniques for graphics with this type of display.

The changes did not stop there. In recent years, the cost of raster displays has plummetted and so low cost raster displays have appeared as competitors to the storage tube. These displays, like storage tubes, do not flicker when storing a large amount of information but in addition provide selective erasure, and other attractive features such as colour and area fill.

One might ask whether these changes will continue and whether there will ever be a time for standardization in computer graphics. The cautious prophet would argue that such rapid changes in both hardware and patterns of usage are unlikely to be repeated in the near future. There are now extensive investments in software (and hardware) mitigating against rapid change. We are, though, seeing the advent of high powered, low cost, single user systems, which is ironic when one recalls that it all started with dedicated systems! New input devices (for example, voice) are also on the horizon. As more and more graphics devices contain embedded microprocessors, more facilities are being put into hardware. It is possible, though obviously undesirable, for widely differing facilities to be put into different devices. Standards will provide guidance on what facilities should be performed in devices and will help to guard against this unproductive diversity.

1.2 SEILLAC I

In August 1974, at an IFIP WG5.2 meeting in Malmo, Sweden, Richard Guedj (France) was asked to initiate an active programme directed towards establishing standards for computer graphics. At a meeting in Bellinglise, it was agreed to organize what later turned out to be a seminal event in computer graphics standardization, the Seillac I workshop at Château de Seillac in the Loire Valley, France. Held in May 1976, the workshop was attended by a number of experts from the computer graphics field (Bob Hopgood was one of the UK delegates) and aimed to reveal the underlying concepts of computer graphics which earlier discussions had shown to be ill-understood.

Topics studied at Seillac ranged over the reasons for standardization as well as the scope and requirements of a standard. There was agreement that both output and input should be included. Standardization of the former was considered easy. However, as subsequent events showed, even the standardization of the 'easy' can generate much debate!

The requirements for a standard received much attention. To agree that the standard should serve the areas of, for example, cartography, schematics, engineering drawing and animation was easy, but it was more difficult to decide whether image processing and high quality typesetting should be included. A standard should be in line with current practice and should answer the needs of the user community. It should not be in conflict with other standards in, say, character sets, and programming languages. A standard is only likely to gain acceptance if its design reflects a high level of expertise.

The graphics system must be at the right level. It should not include features specific to single applications, but at the same time must not be so low as to be device dependent. By this time, it was generally agreed that any standard would specify a set of virtual input and output functions which would be realized in terms of the functions of actual devices.

One of the major debates revolved around both the concept of current position and also its behaviour with respect to transformations. One of the problems was that existing packages did not distinguish between transformations for viewing the picture and those used for constructing the picture out of smaller items (referred to as modelling). Seillac I resolved that there should be a clear distinction between these two types of transformation and that an initial core, or kernel, graphics system should be designed which would only use transformations for viewing a previously constructed picture.

Originally there had been no intention to publish the proceedings of Seillac I, but at the request of IFIP, the working papers were edited some two years later and subsequently published [1]. The Seillac I volume is, therefore, not a polished document, but is invaluable in revealing the seeds from which future activities and ideas grew.

1.3 DEVELOPMENTS

The graphics experts at Seillac I included representatives of the USA and West Germany. Some of those from the USA were members of the Graphic Standards Planning Committee (GSPC), formed two years earlier under the auspices of the ACM Special Interest Group on Computer Graphics (SIGGRAPH). Previously, progress had been slow but Seillac I generated enthusiasm which had led GSPC to work towards the specification of a core graphics system to fulfill one of the Seillac goals. After a large amount of work by GSPC, a first public draft of a core graphics system (often referred to as the Core) was published in 1977 [2]. A whole issue of ACM Computing Surveys in 1978 [3] was devoted to describing the GSPC Core, the major issues that had to be resolved, and examples of use of the GSPC Core. A further version of the Core was published in 1979 [4] which included some raster extensions. Whilst raster graphics had been dismissed in the early version, as being different from vector graphics and only available to a few, the dramatic drop in cost meant that raster graphics had to be considered in the 1979 proposal. The Core is a full 3D graphics system and a number of implementations have been produced in the USA.

Inspired by Seillac I, members of the West German standards organization (DIN) had also been active in defining a core graphics system. The most obvious difference between the German Graphical Kernel System (GKS) and the GSPC Core was that the former was only a 2D system, and, consequently, was significantly smaller.

Meanwhile, a proposal had been made in 1976 to ISO by the Standards Committee of the British Computer Society that the British GINO-F graphics package should become an international standard. At the time there was not a specific working group to deal with computer graphics, and so the programming language subcommittee ISO/TC97/SC5, within whose remit computer graphics lay, organized a working party in London in February 1977. The meeting resolved that no existing graphics package would be a suitable candidate for a graphics standard. It also recommended that a working group of SC5 should be established to deal with standardization of computer graphics and that the specification of a core graphics system should be an early target.

What was intended to be the first meeting of the new working group (ISO/TC97/SC5/WG2 - Graphics) was held in Toronto in August 1977. However, a procedural point actually prevented it being a formal meeting. Whilst the focal point of the discussion was the GSPC Core report of 1977, it became clear that other core systems were under development. In particular, the graphics working group of DIN (UA5.9), chaired by Jose

Encarnacao, were working on the specification of a core graphics system to become a German Standard. The meeting resolved that the Germans and Americans should work towards a common specification of a core graphics system.

1.4 THE ISO GRAPHICS WORKING GROUP

The first formal meeting of WG2 (the graphics working group) was held in Bologna in September 1978. A report of GSPC activities was received and the DIN group reported on GKS, detailing timescales for a DIN standard to be approved in 1981. Norway indicated their intention to propose IDIGS as a Norwegian standard; IDIGS was to be a successor to GPGS, a graphics system in widespread use in Norway and the Netherlands. In order that a single standard proposal might be possible, an Editorial Board was set up to compare the various proposals and recommend changes so that the three proposals might converge or at least be compatible.

The Editorial Board, chaired by Paul ten Hagen (WG2 convenor) and Bob Hopgood, met in Amsterdam in February 1979 and was presented with GKS Version 3 (a document of 46 pages) and the 1977 GSPC Core report (a document of 117 pages), whilst the IDIGS proposal was not available. Two major differences between the proposals were the inclusion of a current position concept in the GSPC Core (GKS did not have one) and the pen concept for attribute handling in GKS (GSPC Core adopted the more conventional approach of individual attribute setting) [5]. The fact that GSPC Core was a 3D system and GKS was a 2D system did not itself cause problems since GSPC Core was also capable of 2D graphics. The Editorial Board recommended changes to both proposals to bring them closer together [6]. Both DIN and GSPC discussed the Editorial Board's recommendations and a joint meeting was held in Boulder, Colorado.

By June 1979, it was recommended that the GSPC work should be passed to the formal American standards body, ANSI. The ANSI graphics working group, X3H3, had its first meeting in September 1979. At its second meeting in December of the same year, X3H3 adopted the 1979 GSPC Core as the starting point for its work.

At the following meeting of the ISO graphics working group in Budapest in October 1979, GKS 5.0, incorporating many of the Editorial Board recommendations, was presented. In addition, the input facilities had been enhanced and the ability to use multiple output devices simultaneously had been introduced. The 1979 GSPC Core was presented by ANSI including a pen concept, related to that of GKS, and enhanced text output. IDIGS was also presented.

GKS was the most technically refined of the three and the DIN members were keen that GKS should be submitted to ISO as a standard proposal. After discussions as to whether the working group could evaluate two proposals at the same time, it was eventually decided that only GKS would be put to the parent body (the programming languages subcommittee ISO/TC97/SC5) for registration as a Work Item with the aim of it becoming a Draft Proposal in a year.

1.5 THE GKS REVIEW

A technical meeting was arranged in Tiefenbach, Germany in June 1980 at which national bodies raised issues resulting from a thorough review of GKS 5.2. About 300 issues were put before the meeting of which over 200 were raised by ANSI. The issues were of varying types including clarification of the document and suggested changes to increase the functionality or reduce the complexity. The meeting was complicated by the fact that DIN presented GKS 6.0 just prior to the meeting. However, it had resolved a large number of issues particularly in the area of clarification and so it was considered the most appropriate basis for discussion. More issues were resolved during the meeting but there was no consensus on many of the main substantive issues. Some 50 issues remained unresolved. GKS 6.2, now 132 pages, was produced as a result of the meeting. It was agreed that this should be the basis of the first of two further rounds of technical discussion.

For these two rounds the issue submission and documentation procedure was formalized. Based on the ideas of GSPC and ANSI, each issue was presented as a question, followed by a description and a set of alternative answers. Arguments in favour of and against the alternatives were listed. The complete list of unresolved issues was referred to as an Active Issues List. An editorial round to improve the language and to produce the document in the correct ISO format proceeded in parallel.

The British Standards Institution (BSI) delegation made its presence felt at the technical experts' meeting in Melbourne, Florida in January 1981, where it was a major contributor. Bob Hopgood, Julian Gallop and Dale Sutcliffe were members of that delegation. The Active Issues List contained over 150 issues, divided into about ten subject areas, at the start of the meeting. There was considerable debate about input and multiple window to viewport transformations were introduced to assist in returning locator input in 'suitable' coordinates. Another area receiving much discussion was attribute handling, when the pen concept was clarified and each primitive was given a separate pen table (or bundle table as it became known) [7]. Altogether, over 100 issues were resolved including many major ones.

Each issue had new alternatives and arguments added as they were raised. Those that were resolved were transferred to the Resolved Issues List and those that were not remained on the Active Issues List. In this way, a complete discussion record was built up of the reasons for inclusion or exclusion of features in GKS.

The final technical meeting was held in Abingdon, England in October 1981. The target for the meeting was to resolve all the outstanding issues, incorporate the changes into the GKS document, and present it to the parent body (ISO/TC97/SC5) at its meeting in London the following week. Three days of intense discussion resolved most of the issues but discussion on a few difficult issues continued in parallel with the incorporation of the other changes into the GKS document. Yet again, input was a cause of great debate which resulted in a clearer, simpler input model [8]. Text also received much attention, which produced greater understanding of the aims and a clearer description of the text concepts of GKS. The segment concept was another subject of discussion; the purposes of segment operations were identified and a revised function set was defined. The division of GKS into a number of levels (for implementation purposes) was completely revised. Full agreement was reached on all the technical issues within WG2, and SC5 were recommended to accept it as a Draft Proposal (DP). SC5 did so on 8 October 1981 and circulated the Draft Proposal for comment and vote to become a Draft International Standard (DIS) [9]. David Duce led the team that produced the document that formed the DP (GKS 7.0), which was now 240 pages!

The next meeting of WG2 (the graphics working group) took place at Steensel in the Netherlands in June 1982. This meeting considered, and responded to the comments received with the letter ballot on the Draft Proposal.

Three significant additions were made to GKS. Further thought had been given since the Abingdon meeting to text alignment and a STROKE input primitive. Both were incorporated at Steensel. ANSI, whilst recognizing the importance of the bundle concept, felt strongly that there was also a need for the more conventional individual attribute setting. A combined scheme, whereby a user may define which attributes are bundled and which are set individually, was incorporated.

The revised GKS document was completed by the editors (Dale Sutcliffe, David Duce and Julian Gallop) in December 1982. This was to be registered as Draft International Standard (DIS) 7942 and circulated for comment and vote to approve it for processing to become an International Standard. However, owing to delays within ISO Central Secretariat, the six month letter ballot did not begin until the end of June 1983. This was unfortunate because the ballot was not complete when WG2 next met at Gananoque, Ontario in September 1983. Consequently, no more than provisional decisions could be taken on some early comments conveyed to the meeting by members of the working group [10].

However, much other important work took place at that meeting. Until then it had been assumed that language bindings did not need to be formal standards but could be merely ratified by the GKS Control Board, a group of experts (including Dale Sutcliffe) established by WG2 to look after GKS, as it passed through the final stages of becoming a standard. At this meeting it was agreed that language bindings should have the same status as GKS itself. A multi-part standard was envisaged with one part for each language binding. Under ISO rules, each part may be standardized separately so that one language binding will not slow down another. At this point, FORTRAN and Pascal language bindings were planned and Ada soon followed. A New Work Item (NWI) proposal was drafted with the aim that the Programming Languages subcommittee (ISO/TC97/SC5), parent of the graphics working group, should propose the NWI, as its scope potentially crossed all the working groups of SC5. SC5 agreed the following week to propose the NWI and it was accepted early in 1984. With work on GKS (a 2D system) slowing down, attention was turned towards the standardization of 3D systems. This is described in more detail in the following section.

The GKS Control Board met at the Rutherford Appleton Laboratory in February 1984 to consider the comments with the DIS letter ballot. Most of the changes were minor clarifications, resolutions of ambiguities or editorial in nature. One large change concerned the interpretation of metafiles, and the effect it had on the GKS environment. This returned GKS closer to the DP version but required many changes to make the internal workings consistent.

Another comment concerned the value ranges of certain parameters which were defined as being implementation dependent, such as linetypes and marker types beyond the standard ones. If an application area, for example cartography or astronomy, wanted to define a set of linetypes or marker types for use by that particular area, there would be a risk that the values chosen would clash with the values chosen by another such area. It was agreed that a Registration Authority should be set up to register such values so that applications could use them in the sure knowledge that if the value were available in an implementation it would always represent the same item. In GKS, for each such parameter one value range was reserved for registration and one value range was implementation dependent.

The volume of change meant that the revised document was not available until October 1984. At that time it was submitted to ISO Central Secretariat for final processing. GKS [11] was finally published on 15 August 1985.

Meanwhile work had been progressing on the language bindings. At the 1984 meeting of WG2 in Benodet, France changes to the current drafts were agreed for the FORTRAN, Pascal and Ada bindings to allow them to be registered as DPs. Work on establishing the Registration Authority was also carried out.

During this time, a reorganization within ISO/TC97, Information Processing Systems, was taking place. Graphics was moved from the Programming Languages subcommittee (SC5) to a new subcommittee, SC21 (Open Systems). At the first meeting of SC21 in Paris in February 1985, the graphics working group became WG2 of SC21.

The new WG2 held its first meeting at Timberline Lodge, Oregon in July 1985. The announcement that GKS was to be published as International Standard 7942 was greeted with acclamation. During that meeting changes were agreed to the FORTRAN and Pascal language bindings to allow them to be registered as Draft International Standard 8651 Parts 1 and 2 [12, 13]. The Ada binding had met some opposition in the DP ballot and a second DP needed to be produced [14].

1.6 FUTURE STANDARDS

At the Tiefenbach meeting of WG2 in 1980, it was agreed that the metafile definition which was part of GKS, should be moved to an annex and that the production of a metafile standard should be a separate project. In this way, GKS with a more limited scope would be standardized more quickly and the requirements for a metafile standard could be separately formulated and a standard produced on a separate timescale.

The NWI for a metafile standard was approved in early 1983 and work has proceeded steadily since. At the Timberline meeting of WG2 in 1985, changes were agreed to the Computer Graphics Metafile (CGM) for the transfer and storage of picture description information, as the document was now entitled, to enable it to be registered as Draft International Standard 8632 [15]. The CGM specifies a file and data format for the description of pictures. It enables transfer of pictures to devices, between applications and between systems as well as storage of graphical data for later use.

As technical work on GKS came to an end, attention was turned at the Gananoque meeting of WG2 in 1983 towards the standardization of 3D systems. History seemed to repeat itself, as once again there were two proposals for consideration. On the one hand, some experts wished to extend GKS to 3D in an upward compatible manner, introducing new functionality to achieve only this; the existing primitives would be planar but in 3D, specified by sets of 3D points; 3D viewing functions would be introduced; the provision of hidden line/ hidden surface removal was a point of contention. On the other hand, other experts, notably from

ANSI, wished to produce a new standard PHIGS (Programmers' Hierarchical Interactive Graphics System), a more sophisticated graphics system which provided modelling as well as viewing functions, hierarchical structuring of picture parts, modification of the picture parts, and rapid interaction without the upward compatibility from GKS. After much discussion it was decided to embark on both with the extensions to GKS (GKS-3D) starting first and taking a shorter time. Technical work progressed satisfactorily so that SC21 agreed, at its first meeting in Paris in February 1985, to register GKS-3D as a DP. Comments from the DP ballot were responded to at the Timberline meeting of WG2, but the level of change required a second DP to be produced [16] and circulated for ballot.

In the meantime the PHIGS NWI had been approved and an initial draft produced. Limited time available at the Timberline meeting meant that only minor changes were agreed to be incorporated in the first working draft [17].

GKS, GKS-3D and PHIGS are all application interface standards, produced to aid the portability of application programs. Graphical device manufacturers are more interested in lower level standards which will assist them directly in the design of future graphical devices. Another project was approved in 1985 for this area: Computer Graphics Interface (CGI) techniques for dialogues with graphical devices. The CGI document will provide a functional description together with encodings. It is closely related to the CGM. The first working draft for the CGI is currently (November 1985) being written.

As can be seen, standardization is a long process. Nevertheless, a major milestone has been reached with the adoption of GKS as an International Standard in 1985. Ten years have elapsed since the meeting in Bellinglise and over nine years since Seillac I which Richard Guedj opened by quoting:

> I have long aspired to reach for the clouds ...
> Again I come from afar
> To climb Ching Kang Shan, our old haunt
> But scenes are transformed
>   Mao Tse Tung, May 1965

1.7 REFERENCES

1.   Guedj, R.A. and Tucker, H.A. (eds), "Methodology in Computer Graphics." North-Holland, Amsterdam (1979).

2. "Status Report of the Graphic Standards Planning Committee of ACM/SIGGRAPH." *Computer Graphics* 11(3) (1977).

3. "Special Issue: Graphics Standards." *ACM Computing Surveys* 10(4) (1978).

4. "Status Report of the Graphic Standards Planning Committee." *Computer Graphics* 13(3) (1979).

5. Encarnacao, J. *et al.*, 'The workstation concept of GKS and the resulting conceptual differences to the GSPC core system.' *Computer Graphics* 14(3), 226-230 (1980).

6. ten Hagen, P.J.W. and Hopgood, F.R.A., "Towards Compatible Graphics Standards." Report 17/79, Mathematisch Centrum, Amsterdam (1979).

7. Sutcliffe, D.C., 'Attribute Handling in GKS.' In: "Eurographics 82" (Greenaway, D.S. and Warman, E.A., eds), pp 103-110. North-Holland, Amsterdam (1982).

8. Rosenthal, D.S.H. *et al.*, 'The Detailed Semantics of Graphics Input Devices.' *Computer Graphics* 16(3), 33-38 (1982).

9. Bono, P.R. *et al.*, 'GKS - The First Graphics Standard.' *IEEE Computer Graphics and Applications* 2(5), 9-23 (1982).

10. Enderle, G. *et al.*, "Computer Graphics Programming." Springer Verlag, Heidelberg (1984).

11. "ISO 7942, Information processing systems - Computer graphics - Graphical Kernel System (GKS) functional description." ISO, Geneva(1985).

12. "ISO/DIS 8651/1, Information processing systems - Computer graphics - Graphical Kernel System (GKS) language bindings - Part 1 : FORTRAN. "

13. "ISO/DIS 8651/2, Information processing systems - Computer graphics - Graphical Kernel System (GKS) language bindings - Part 2 : Pascal. "

14. "ISO/DP 8651/3, Information processing systems - Computer graphics - Graphical Kernel System (GKS) language bindings - Part 3 : Ada. "

15. "ISO/DIS 8632, Information processing systems - Computer graphics - Metafile for transfer and storage of picture description information."

16. "ISO/DP 8805, Information processing systems - Computer graphics - Graphical Kernel System (GKS) for three dimensions (GKS-3D) functional description."

17. "Information processing systems - Computer graphics - Programmer's Hierarchical Interactive Graphics System." Working draft ISO/TC97/SC21 N819 (1985).

2 Graphical Output

2.1 INTRODUCTION

The main objective of the Graphical Kernel System, GKS, is the production and manipulation of pictures (in a way that does not depend on the computer or graphical device being used). Such pictures vary from simple line graphs (to illustrate experimental results, for example), to engineering drawings, to integrated circuit layouts (using colour to differentiate between layers), to images representing medical data (from computerised tomographic (CT) scanners) or astronomical data (from telescopes) in greyscale or colour. Each of these various pictures must be described to GKS, so that they may be drawn.

In GKS, pictures are considered to be constructed from a number of basic building blocks. These basic building blocks, or *primitives* as they are called, are of a number of types each of which can be used to describe a different component of a picture. The five main primitives in GKS are:

(1) *polyline*: which draws a sequence of connected line segments.

(2) *polymarker*: which marks a sequence of points with the same symbol.

(3) *fill area*: which displays a specified area.

(4) *text*: which draws a string of characters.

(5) *cell array*: which displays an image composed of a variety of colours or grey scales.

Consideration of the cell array primitive is postponed until Chapter 12.

Associated with each primitive is a set of *parameters* which is used to define particular instances of that primitive. For example, the parameters of the text primitive are the string of characters to be drawn and the starting position of that string. Thus:

TEXT(X, Y, 'ABC')

will draw the characters ABC at the position (X,Y).

Although the parameters enable the form of the primitives to be specified, additional data are necessary to describe the actual appearance (or *aspects*) of the primitives. For example, GKS needs to know the height of a character string and the angle at which it is to be drawn. These additional data are known as *attributes*.

The attributes represent features of the primitives which vary less often than the form of the primitives. Attributes will frequently retain the same values for the description of several primitives. Once a suitable character height has been selected, for example, several character strings may be plotted using this character height (such as the labels on the axis of a graph).

In this chapter, we will look at the first four primitive types of GKS given above and their associated attributes.

In the figures, associated with the examples, the coordinate system used ranges from -5 to 34 in X and from -5 to 21 in Y.

2.2 POLYLINE

The main line drawing primitive of GKS is the polyline which is generated by calling the function:

POLYLINE(N, XPTS, YPTS)

where XPTS and YPTS are arrays giving the N points (XPTS(1), YPTS(1)) to (XPTS(N), YPTS(N)). The polyline generated consists of $N-1$ line segments joining adjacent points starting with the first point and ending with the last.

Why was the polyline chosen as the basic line drawing primitive in GKS? If we consider actual graphical devices, we can see that there are many ways of describing line segments. Incremental plotters require each individual increment of the approximated line segment to be specified. Other graphical devices rely on the concept of a current point. Only one end of each line segment need be specified and a line segment is drawn from the current point to the specified end point, which then itself becomes the current point. Yet other graphical devices expect a connected sequence of line segments to be specified.

In order to interface to all these devices, GKS uses an abstract description of a line. Unlike many graphics systems which rely on the concept of a current point with several related problems, GKS recognizes the frequency with which a set of connected line segments is drawn and, therefore, uses polyline as its basic line drawing primitive.

Suppose we wish to plot a graph of a set of data, maybe some experimental results. The data consist of a set of ordered pairs (X, Y), thus:

X	0.0	2.0	4.0	6.0	8.0	10.0	12.0	14.0	16.4	17.0	17.3
Y	8.8	7.6	7.1	7.4	8.0	8.9	9.6	9.9	9.4	9.7	12.0
X	17.8	18.5	20.0	22.0	24.0	26.0	28.0	29.0			
Y	14.0	16.1	17.0	17.0	16.0	13.9	13.1	13.2			

The graph may be drawn by joining adjacent points with straight line segments. Thus we can plot our graph by the following sequence:

```
REAL XDK(19), YDK(19)
DATA XDK/0.0,2.0,4.0,6.0,8.0,10.0,12.0,14.0,
    16.4,17.0,17.3,17.8,18.5,20.0,22.0,24.0,
    26.0,28.0,29.0/
DATA YDK/8.8,7.6,7.1,7.4,8.0,8.9,9.6,9.9,
    9.4,9.7,12.0,14.0,16.1,17.0,17.0,16.0,
    13.9,13.1,13.2/

POLYLINE(19, XDK, YDK)
```

This produces the output given in Figure 2-1. Note that in the examples in this book, only the GKS functions being illustrated, or those directly related to the example, are included. These examples on their own will not produce the output shown without the addition of introductory and terminating GKS functions, in the same way that they would not compile without the addition of a terminating FORTRAN 77 END statement. If you are interested in the appearance of a complete GKS program, one is given in Appendix C. The example used is that in Section 2.8; in Appendix C, all the introductory and terminating GKS functions are included and strict FORTRAN 77 is used.

Returning to our graph, in order to interpret it, we need to relate the graph to the coordinate data by drawing the axes. We may draw the axes with a polyline too. (In practice, a separate subroutine for drawing axes, using GKS functions, will often be available.) Without repeating the DATA statements above, we can extend our example:

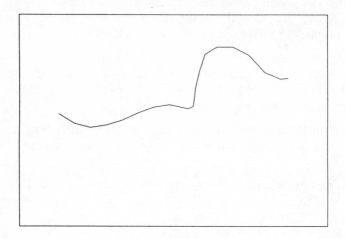

Figure 2-1

```
REAL XA(3), YA(3)

XA(1) = 29
XA(2) = 0
XA(3) = 0
YA(1) = 0
YA(2) = 0
YA(3) = 17

POLYLINE(3, XA, YA)
POLYLINE(19, XDK, YDK)
```

This will produce the output in Figure 2-2.

2.3 POLYLINE REPRESENTATION

Any complex picture will contain a number of polylines and it may be necessary to differentiate between polylines. This is done by using different *representations* for the polylines. Different representations are obtained by specifying different values for a polyline attribute associated with the polylines.

In the example above, we may wish to draw a constant Y line to enable points above the line to be identified. Even though this only requires a single line to be drawn, the polyline primitive can still be used. Note, also, that we do not need separate arrays to specify each polyline; we can reuse the arrays used to specify previous polylines. Thus, to draw the same picture with the line Y = 9.5 added, we need only add:

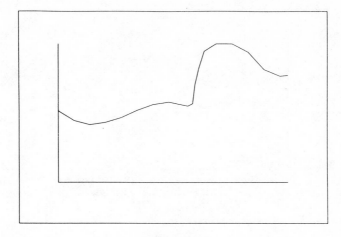

Figure 2-2

YA(1) = 9.5
YA(2) = 9.5

POLYLINE(2, XA, YA)

This will generate the graph shown in Figure 2-3. (In future, separate arrays for each polyline will be used to simplify the examples.) This does not give us an ideal result as it is not easy to distinguish between our new line and the previously drawn line representing the data. We need to draw the two lines in such a way that we can distinguish them. We will do this by specifying each polyline with a different representation.

Let us consider the facilities available on actual devices for distinguishing lines. On a pen plotter with a single pen, lines may be distinguished by using different styles of line (e.g. solid, dashed, dotted) whereas on a pen plotter with more than one pen, different thickness pens may be used to draw with different widths. On devices capable of colour, lines may be drawn in different colours. In each case there is a way of distinguishing lines. The method of distinguishing lines must be described to GKS in a device independent way. GKS does this by having a single attribute called the *polyline index*. If a user wishes to distinguish between two polylines, he does this by defining each with a different polyline index. The exact representation that the polyline will have on a specific device depends on what facilities are available. This will be described in more detail in Chapter 7. There is also a way of individually controlling the aspects that distinguish lines, that has advantages in certain applications. This is described in Chapter 13. For the moment, all that we need to know is that polylines with different polyline index values associated with

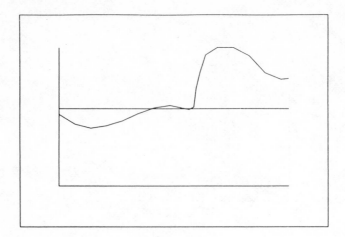

Figure 2-3

them can, and normally will, appear differently on the actual display used. The polyline index is set by the GKS function:

SET POLYLINE INDEX(N)

This sets the polyline index to the value N for all subsequent polylines until its value is reset by another call of this function.

In this chapter, we will only consider default values for the representations; later we will see how to specify our own. We will assume that polyline representation 1 is a solid line and polyline representation 2 is a dashed line. For both representations, a standard linewidth and colour are used. In the pictures drawn so far, the default value of the polyline index has been used which is, in fact, 1.

We can now draw our graph far better by distinguishing the line representing the data from the others.

First, we will define a subroutine AXES, which will be used in several places:

```
SUBROUTINE AXES(XMAX, YMAX)

REAL XA(3), YA(3)

XA(1) = XMAX
XA(2) = 0
XA(3) = 0
YA(1) = 0
YA(2) = 0
YA(3) = YMAX

POLYLINE(3, XA, YA)

RETURN
END
```

Then, we may write our example as:

```
REAL XDK(19), YDK(19), XB(2), YB(2)

XB(1) = 0
XB(2) = 29
YB(1) = 9.5
YB(2) = 9.5

SET POLYLINE INDEX(1)
AXES(29, 17)
POLYLINE(2, XB, YB)

SET POLYLINE INDEX(2)
POLYLINE(19, XDK, YDK)
```

This produces the results shown in Figure 2-4. In the example, as good practice, we set the polyline index to 1 explicitly before the first polyline (drawn by AXES), although this will not alter the polyline's appearance as the default value is 1. Note that the polyline specified by XB and YB is also drawn using a polyline index value of 1 as the polyline index has not been reset. In contrast, the line representing the data is drawn using a polyline index value of 2 to differentiate it from the axes. This method of controlling the appearance of primitives is a very powerful feature. For example, a high level graphics routine to perform contouring will need to distinguish between contours, whether to highlight contours above or below a certain height or to highlight every *nth* contour. By using a different polyline index to draw each set of contours in the high level routine, the application program which uses it may choose the representation for each index to achieve the desired contour map.

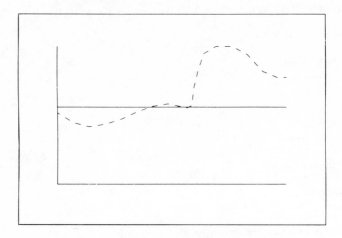

Figure 2-4

2.4 POLYMARKER

Instead of drawing lines through a set of points, we may wish just to mark the set of points. GKS provides the primitive polymarker to do just this. A polymarker is generated by the function:

POLYMARKER(N, XPTS, YPTS)

where the arguments are the same as for the polyline function, namely XPTS and YPTS are arrays giving the N points (XPTS(1), YPTS(1)) to (XPTS(N), YPTS(N)). Polymarker places a centred *marker* at each point. GKS recognizes the common use of markers to identify a set of points in addition to marking single points and so the marker function is a polymarker. We may now, as shown in Figure 2-5, plot the data points in our example rather than the line through the points. This is done by simply replacing the appropriate call to POLYLINE by a call to POLYMARKER, thus:

```
AXES(29, 17)
POLYLINE(2, XB, YB)

POLYMARKER(19, XDK, YDK)
```

Of course, we may wish both to identify the set of points and plot the lines through them, which is of course possible:

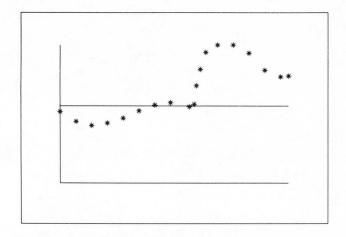

Figure 2-5

AXES(29, 17)
POLYLINE(2, XB, YB)

POLYMARKER(19, XDK, YDK)
POLYLINE(19, XDK, YDK)

This composite output is shown in Figure 2-6. In a similar manner to polyline, GKS provides a facility to distinguish different sets of points. Polymarkers may be specified with different representations. This is done by assigning different values to a polymarker attribute called the *polymarker index*.

The polymarker index is set by the GKS function:

SET POLYMARKER INDEX(N)

where N is the desired value of the polymarker index. We will assume that polymarker representation 1 is an asterisk, polymarker representation 2 is a circle and polymarker representation 3 is a plus sign, all in a standard size and colour. Let us introduce a further set of data we wish to plot on our graph relating the two variables X and Y:

X	15.7	17.0	17.7	17.3	15.3	13.0	11.0	9.0	7.0	4.7
Y	7.0	6.1	5.0	3.8	3.0	2.7	3.0	3.6	4.2	5.2

We will draw the two sets of points with different representations so that we can distinguish them:

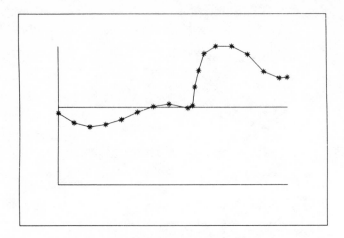

Figure 2-6

```
REAL XW(10), YW(10)
DATA XW/15.7,17.0,17.7,17.3,15.3,13.0,11.0,9.0,7.0,4.7/
DATA YW/7.0,6.1,5.0,3.8,3.0,2.7,3.0,3.6,4.2,5.2/

SET POLYLINE INDEX(1)
AXES(29, 17)

SET POLYMARKER INDEX(1)
POLYMARKER(19, XDK, YDK)
SET POLYMARKER INDEX(2)
POLYMARKER(10, XW, YW)
```

This is shown in Figure 2-7. Note that the second set of data is not single valued but this does not cause any problems.

2.5 FILL AREA

There are many applications for which line drawings are insufficient. The design of integrated circuit layouts requires the use of filled rectangles to display a layer. Animation systems need to be able to shade areas of arbitrary shape. Other applications using colour only realize their full potential when they are able to use coloured areas rather than coloured lines.

At the same time, there are now many devices which have the concept of an area which may be filled in some way. These vary from intelligent pen plotters which can cross-hatch an area to raster displays which can completely fill an area with a single colour or in some cases fill an area by

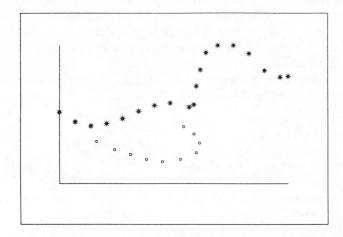

Figure 2-7

repeating a pattern.

GKS provides a fill area function to satisfy the application needs which can use the varying device capabilities. Defining an area is a fairly simple extension of defining a polyline. An array of points is specified which defines the boundary of the area. If the area is not *closed* (i.e. the first point is not the same as the last point), the boundary is the polyline defined by the points but extended to join the last point to the first point. A fill area may be generated by invoking the function:

FILL AREA(N, XPTS, YPTS)

where, as usual, XPTS and YPTS are arrays giving the N points (XPTS(1), YPTS(1)) to (XPTS(N), YPTS(N)).

Let us extend our original set of data to describe a closed area. Nineteen data points were previously defined to which we add a further 24.

X	28.8	27.2	25.0	23.0	21.5	21.1	21.5	22.8	24.1	25.1
Y	12.3	11.5	11.5	11.5	11.2	10.5	9.0	8.0	7.0	5.1
X	25.2	24.2	22.1	20.0	18.0	16.0	14.0	12.0	10.0	8.0
Y	3.6	1.9	1.1	0.9	0.7	0.8	1.0	1.0	1.2	1.8
X	6.1	4.2	3.0	1.3						
Y	2.1	2.9	4.1	6.0						

Like the other primitives we have considered, fill area has a representation accessed by a fill area attribute called the *fill area index*.

The fill area index is set by the function:

SET FILL AREA INDEX(N)

where N is the desired value of the fill area index. Filled areas may be distinguished by their filling style (called interior style in GKS) and colour. Let us assume that fill area representation 1 is interior style HOLLOW and that fill area representation 2 is interior style SOLID, each in standard colour.

We can now plot our extended set of data which represents an area. We will use fill area representation 1:

```
REAL XDK(43), YDK(43)
DATA XDK/0.0,2.0,4.0,6.0,8.0,10.0,12.0,14.0,
   16.4,17.0,17.3,17.8,18.5,20.0,22.0,24.0,
   26.0,28.0,29.0,28.8,27.2,25.0,23.0,21.5,
   21.1,21.5,22.8,24.1,25.1,25.2,24.2,22.1,
   20.0,18.0,16.0,14.0,12.0,10.0,8.0,6.1,
   4.2,3.0,1.3/
DATA YDK/8.8,7.6,7.1,7.4,8.0,8.9,9.6,9.9,
   9.4,9.7,12.0,14.0,16.1,17.0,17.0,16.0,
   13.9,13.1,13.2,12.3,11.5,11.5,11.5,11.2,
   10.5,9.0,8.0,7.0,5.1,3.6,1.9,1.1,
   0.9,0.7,0.8,1.0,1.0,1.2,1.8,2.1,
   2.9,4.1,6.0/

SET POLYLINE INDEX(1)
AXES(29, 17)

SET FILL AREA INDEX(1)
FILL AREA(43, XDK, YDK)
```

This produces the output like a *duck* given in Figure 2-8. We can see that for interior style HOLLOW, only the boundary has been drawn. It is interesting to note, however, the contrast with the result that would have been obtained if the last two statements containing fill area functions had contained the corresponding polyline functions:

```
SET POLYLINE INDEX(1)
POLYLINE(43, XDK, YDK)
```

In this case, the output would be as shown in Figure 2-9. This illustrates the fact that the fill area primitive is a true area primitive even if it is drawn by lines. The last point is joined to the first by the fill area function to complete the outline.

If the fill area example were drawn using fill area representation 2, i.e. the last two statements were:

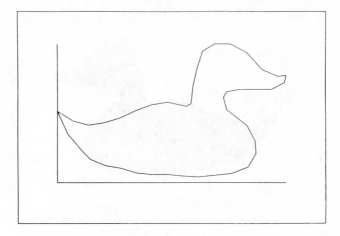

Figure 2-8

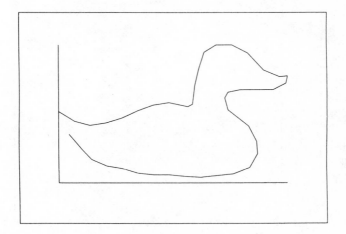

Figure 2-9

    SET FILL AREA INDEX(2)
    FILL AREA(43, XDK, YDK)

we would then get the output given in Figure 2-10. Let fill area representation 3 be interior style HATCH, using a diagonal hatch, and a standard
colour. The fill area primitive is defined to fill the area only and so does
not include drawing the boundary (apart from interior style HOLLOW
for obvious reasons!). Thus, if the last two lines of our example were:

145, 150

Figure 2-10

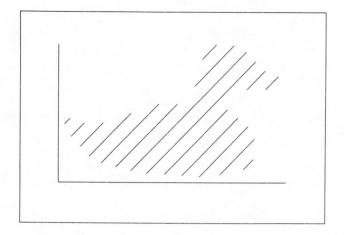

Figure 2-11

```
SET FILL AREA INDEX(3)
FILL AREA(43, XDK, YDK)
```

the picture would be as shown in Figure 2-11. If we wish to include the boundary, we may additionally draw a polyline around the area. Here we must be careful. As we saw earlier, the fill area function will join the last point to the first (if they are not the same) to define the area but the polyline function, of course, will not. Therefore, if we wish to draw the boundary by means of a polyline, we must ensure that the last point of the set is the same as the first to achieve the desired result. In our example set of data, this means that we must add a 44th point which is the same as the first:

```
XDK(44)=XDK(1)
YDK(44)=YDK(1)
```

Then we can again replace our last two lines by:

```
SET FILL AREA INDEX(3)
FILL AREA(43, XDK, YDK)
POLYLINE(44, XDK, YDK)
```

to give the hatched duck shown in Figure 2-12. So far we have only considered filling simple shapes. Suppose we add even more data to our example set. Let us concatenate our other set of data (XW,YW), introduced to illustrate the polymarker index in Section 2.4, by making the 44th point of our data the first point of that set, the 45th point the second, and so on:

```
      DO 100 I=1,10
      XDK(I+43)=XW(I)
100   YDK(I+43)=YW(I)
```

This gives us 53 points. If we draw it with fill area representation 1, which uses interior style HOLLOW, the output would be as shown in Figure 2-13. Our area is now complex. If we were to fill it with fill area

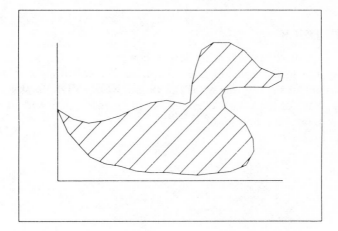

Figure 2-12

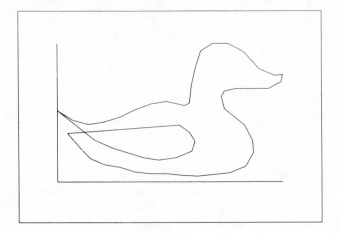

Figure 2-13

representation 2, which uses interior style SOLID, which areas would be filled? What is the inside of the area? GKS is not the first system to face this problem. The rule used to decide is that if a line drawn from any point to infinity crosses the boundary an even number of times (including zero), the point is outside but if the line crosses the boundary an odd number of times, the point is inside. We can now confidently plot our data with fill area representation 2, giving the output shown in Figure 2-14.

2.6 THE DUCK

At this point, it is convenient to write a complete subroutine to draw our duck, for use in examples in later chapters. We will draw our duck as two polylines defined by the arrays of points XDK, YDK for the outline and XW, YW for the wing. We have already seen the data and so we can write our subroutine thus:

Figure 2-14

SUBROUTINE DUCK

```
REAL XDK(44), YDK(44), XW(10), YW(10)
DATA XDK/0.0,2.0,4.0,6.0,8.0,10.0,12.0,14.0,
    16.4,17.0,17.3,17.8,18.5,20.0,22.0,24.0,
    26.0,28.0,29.0,28.8,27.2,25.0,23.0,21.5,
    21.1,21.5,22.8,24.1,25.1,25.2,24.2,22.1,
    20.0,18.0,16.0,14.0,12.0,10.0,8.0,6.1,
    4.2,3.0,1.3,0.0/
DATA YDK/8.8,7.6,7.1,7.4,8.0,8.9,9.6,9.9,
    9.4,9.7,12.0,14.0,16.1,17.0,17.0,16.0,
    13.9,13.1,13.2,12.3,11.5,11.5,11.5,11.2,
    10.5,9.0,8.0,7.0,5.1,3.6,1.9,1.1,
    0.9,0.7,0.8,1.0,1.0,1.2,1.8,2.1,
    2.9,4.1,6.0,8.8/
DATA XW/15.7,17.0,17.7,17.3,15.3,13.0,11.0,9.0,7.0,4.7/
DATA YW/7.0,6.1,5.0,3.8,3.0,2.7,3.0,3.6,4.2,5.2/

POLYLINE(44, XDK, YDK)
POLYLINE(10, XW, YW)

RETURN
END
```

Note that we have not included the axes in the subroutine as we do not always wish the axes to be drawn and, in any case, we already have a subroutine to draw them. To draw the duck with a set of axes we may write:

AXES(29, 17)
DUCK

The output is illustrated in Figure 2-15.

2.7 TEXT

So far we have not attempted to put a title on our pictures. To do this, GKS has a text primitive which is used to title pictures or place labels on them as appropriate. A text string may be generated by invoking the function:

TEXT(X, Y, STRING)

where (X, Y) is the *text position* and STRING is a string of characters.

However, text is more complicated than the other primitives that we have examined. Everybody is used to good quality text in books whether it is the printed text of the book itself or text within the context of diagrams. Text is printed at different sizes, in different fonts, at different orientations and at different spacings. Graphics devices, on the other hand, are often not good at text; indeed some are not capable of text at all. Those that do often only have a restricted number of sizes, one or perhaps two orientations, and a single font.

What are the requirements of graphics applications? If a picture is produced as one of a (possibly rapidly changing) sequence on the screen of an interactive graphics device, it is most likely that quickly produced

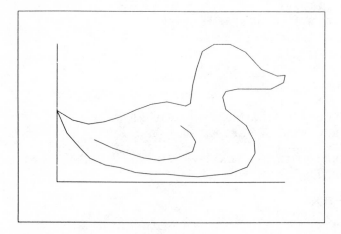

Figure 2-15

text is required without placing constraints on quality. On the other hand, if a high quality hardcopy picture is being produced it is likely that text of a similar high quality would be required. If such a picture were being previewed on an interactive device before final hardcopy was produced, a reasonable approximation to the high quality text would be needed.

GKS attempts to match these requirements with its text primitive. Each of the other primitives that we have examined has had a single attribute which controls the aspects of its appearance (via a representation). Since text is more complex, its appearance is affected by a larger number of aspects. Some of these are too important to be controlled by a representation. At the same time, they do not vary with every text string that is output. (Those that usually do are supplied as parameters to the text primitive: the text position and the character string itself.) These important aspects are the *character height, character up vector, text path,* and *text alignment.*

In GKS, they are each attributes of text which may be individually assigned values. Of course, text also has a representation, accessed by the *text index,* which will be described later (in Section 2.7.2).

An example of the text primitive is:

    TEXT(6, 3, 'A Character String')

which produces the output shown in Figure 2-16.

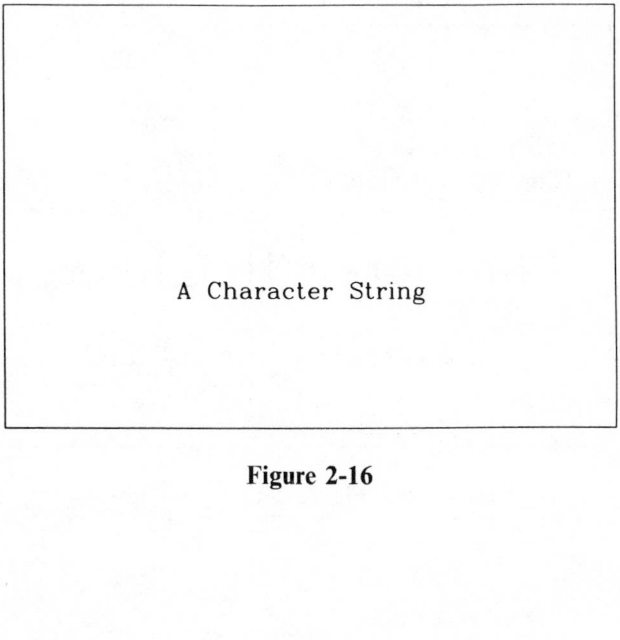

A Character String

Figure 2-16

2.7.1 Text Attributes

The character height attribute determines the height of the characters in the string. Since a character in a font will have a designed aspect ratio, the character height also determines the character width. The character height is set by the function:

SET CHARACTER HEIGHT(H)

where H is the character height. For example, Figure 2-17 would result if the following were executed:

```
SET CHARACTER HEIGHT(1)
TEXT(-2, 11, 'Character Height 1')
SET CHARACTER HEIGHT(2)
TEXT(-2, 5, 'Character Height 2')
```

The character up vector is perhaps the most important text attribute. Its main purpose is to determine the orientation of the characters. However, it also sets a reference direction which is used in the determination of text path and text alignment. The character up vector specifies the up direction of the individual characters. It also specifies the orientation of the character string in that, by default, the characters are placed along the line perpendicular to the character up vector. The function:

SET CHARACTER UP VECTOR(X, Y)

is used for setting the character up vector. X and Y are the offsets from

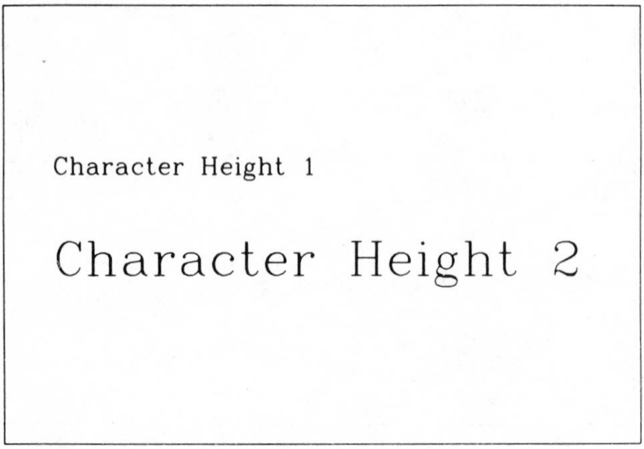

Character Height 1

Character Height 2

Figure 2-17

the text position of the up direction of the characters. Specifying a vector is just a way of specifying an angle. The magnitude of the vector is not used. Thus:

SET CHARACTER UP VECTOR(-1, 1)

has the same effect as:

SET CHARACTER UP VECTOR(-15, 15)

Both cause subsequent character strings to be plotted at 45 degrees to the horizontal (for the default value of text path, see below). Thus:

SET CHARACTER UP VECTOR(-1, 1)
TEXT(6, 3, 'A Character String')

would generate the text string shown in Figure 2-18. Not all character sets are left to right character sets, nor do we always require the character path to be at right angles to the character up vector. For example, a y axis is sometimes labelled using a 'hotel sign', that is, where letters are placed one underneath the other. GKS provides a text path attribute to solve both these problems. It is set by the function:

SET TEXT PATH(PATH)

where PATH has one of the four values: RIGHT, LEFT, UP, and DOWN. These are all relative to the direction defined by the character up vector (see Figure 2-19). RIGHT (the default) causes the characters to

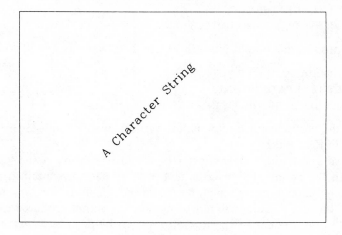

Figure 2-18

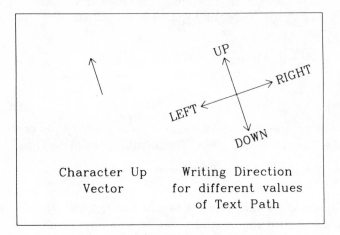

Character Up   Writing Direction
    Vector   for different values
                         of Text Path

Figure 2-19

be placed one after another along the line perpendicular (in a clockwise direction) to the character up vector. LEFT causes characters to be placed in the opposite direction and so is suitable for right to left character sets. DOWN causes characters to be placed one underneath the other and UP causes them to be placed one on top of the other. For example, using the default vertical character up vector, the sequence:

```
SET CHARACTER UP VECTOR(0, 1)
SET TEXT PATH(DOWN)
TEXT(10, 17, 'GRAND HOTEL')
```

would produce the output given in Figure 2-20, whereas:

```
SET CHARACTER UP VECTOR(1, 6)
SET TEXT PATH(DOWN)
TEXT(12, 16, 'HOTEL PISA')
```

where the character up vector is not vertical, would produce the output shown in Figure 2-21.

As we know, the first parameter of the text primitive is the text position. In the examples above, the text position has been specified but has not been marked on the pictures produced. This is for two reasons. Firstly, the text position will not be marked on output produced by GKS. Secondly, on account of the text attribute to be described next, the text position does not always occupy the same position in relation to the plotted character string.

This text attribute is text alignment. It allows the complete character string to be aligned in different ways with respect to the text position.

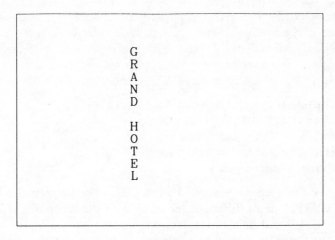

Figure 2-20

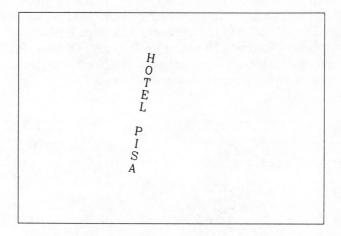

Figure 2-21

Text may be aligned separately along horizontal and vertical axes. (Note that these are relative to the character up vector and not necessarily horizontal and vertical. The vertical axis is orientated in the direction of the character up vector and the horizontal axis is perpendicular to it.) Text alignment is set by the function:

SET TEXT ALIGNMENT(HORIZ, VERT)

where HORIZ and VERT are the horizontal and vertical alignments.

Along the horizontal axis, text may be aligned to the LEFT, CEN-
TRE, or RIGHT. If the text is aligned to the LEFT, it means that the
character string is aligned with the left hand side through the text position. RIGHT is similarly defined, with the right hand side through the
text position. For example, if we mark the text position with an asterisk
(and ignore the vertical component of alignment), then:

```
SET CHARACTER HEIGHT(1.25)
SET TEXT ALIGNMENT(LEFT, BASE)
TEXT(15, 11, 'Left Aligned')
SET TEXT ALIGNMENT(RIGHT, BASE)
TEXT(15, 5, 'Right Aligned')
```

would give the output shown in Figure 2-22. The horizontal alignment
value CENTRE aligns the character string with the text position half way
between the left and right extremes of the string.

Text may also be aligned in a number of ways along the vertical axis:
TOP, CAP, HALF, BASE, and BOTTOM. The values TOP and BOT-
TOM align the appropriate extremes of the character string along the
vertical axis in a similar manner to LEFT and RIGHT along the horizontal axis. The values CAP, HALF, and BASE align internal font lines of
the characters in the string along the vertical axis. Of these, BASE is the
most important being an alignment with the baseline of the characters,
that is the line on which upper case characters sit.

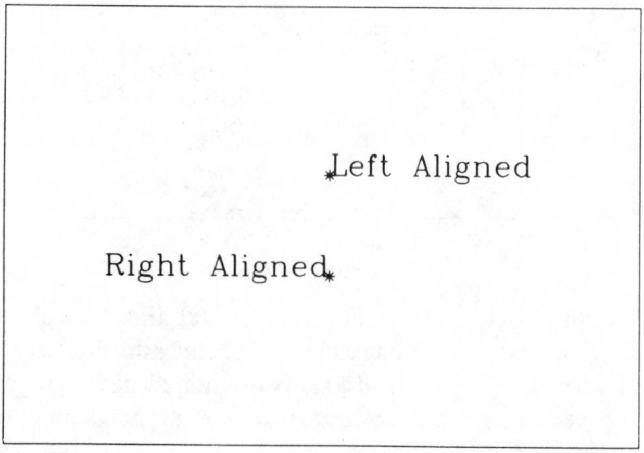

Figure 2-22

These values have been described generally in terms of the horizontal text paths. The definitions only need extending slightly to have reasonable interpretations for all text paths, as is illustrated by the following example (where BOX is a subroutine to draw a box described by the limits in x followed by the limits in y):

```
BOX(-1, 30, 14, 17.25)
SET CHARACTER HEIGHT(2.25)
SET TEXT ALIGNMENT(LEFT, BASE)
SET TEXT PATH(RIGHT)
TEXT(0, 14.5, 'A. B. JONES')
SET CHARACTER HEIGHT(0.9)
SET TEXT ALIGNMENT(RIGHT, CAP)
TEXT(29, 16.75, 'TOYS')
SET TEXT ALIGNMENT(RIGHT, BASE)
TEXT(29, 14.5, 'SWEETS')

SET CHARACTER HEIGHT(1)
SET TEXT ALIGNMENT(CENTRE, TOP)
SET TEXT PATH(DOWN)
TEXT(3, 9, 'HOTEL')

SET TEXT PATH(RIGHT)
TEXT(23.5, 7, 'PLEASE')
TEXT(23.5, 5, 'PAY')
TEXT(23.5, 3, 'HERE')

SET TEXT ALIGNMENT(LEFT, BOTTOM)
SET TEXT PATH(DOWN)
TEXT(11, -1, 'SAVINGS')
TEXT(13, -1, 'BANK')
```

This would produce the output shown in Figure 2-23. In the earlier example (see Figure 2-22), we used the default value of text path (RIGHT). If we had used the value LEFT for text path by inserting:

```
SET TEXT PATH(LEFT)
```

at the start of the example, we would have obtained the results shown in Figure 2-24. The character strings have been reversed because of the opposite text path, but they each occupy the same space as before. The effect of text alignment has not been affected by the value of text path.

However, the *normal* text alignments are dependent upon text path. For a text path of RIGHT, the normal horizontal text alignment is LEFT but for a text path of LEFT (usually used in connection with a right to left character set) the normal horizontal text alignment is RIGHT. In order that the expected text alignment is achieved for each text path,

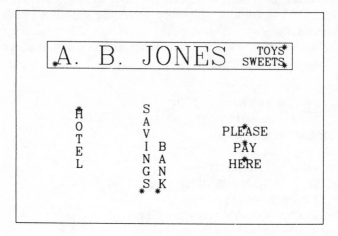

Figure 2-23

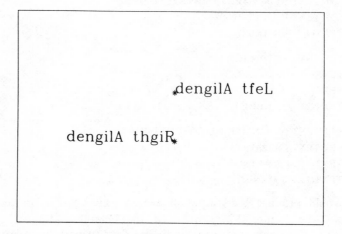

Figure 2-24

when text alignment has not been explicitly set, a value of NORMAL for each of the horizontal and vertical components exists. When a text alignment component has the value NORMAL (which is the default), the normal text alignment for the text path is used. If a text alignment component has another value, that value is used irrespective of text path. The following example illustrates the NORMAL alignments for each text path:

```
SET CHARACTER HEIGHT(1.75)
SET TEXT ALIGNMENT(NORMAL, NORMAL)
SET TEXT PATH(RIGHT)
TEXT(16, 11, 'Right')
SET TEXT PATH(LEFT)
TEXT(12, 11, 'Left')
SET TEXT PATH(DOWN)
TEXT(14, 9, 'Down')
SET TEXT PATH(UP)
TEXT(14, 13, 'Up')
```

which gives the output shown in Figure 2-25.

2.7.2 Text Representation

As mentioned earlier, text also has a representation accessed via the text index. The text index is set by the function:

SET TEXT INDEX(N)

where N is the desired value of the text index. Let text representation 1 be a roman font at STROKE precision (the highest quality), using a unit character expansion factor, zero spacing and a standard colour. Let text representation 2 be the same except that it uses CHAR precision (medium quality), and let text representation 3 be the same except that it uses STRING precision (the lowest quality). Then the following example:

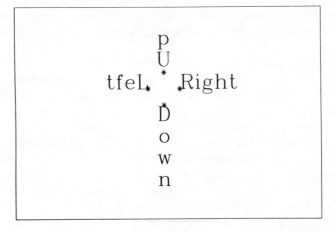

Figure 2-25

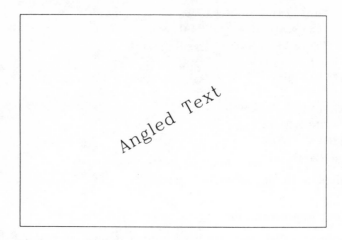

Figure 2-26

```
SET CHARACTER UP VECTOR(-1, 1.732)
SET TEXT PATH(RIGHT)
SET TEXT ALIGNMENT(LEFT, BASE)
SET TEXT INDEX(1)
TEXT(8, 4, 'Angled Text')
```

would give the output shown in Figure 2-26, which is an accurate representation of the requested text. However, if we use text index 3, we get the output shown in Figure 2-27. This is because the STRING precision text does not need to use all the text attributes. It is the text that will often be used on interactive devices where it needs to be produced quickly.

The highest precision text is that which would be used for the high quality output referred to earlier. To preview this high precision text we can use the medium precision text; using text index 2 gives the output shown in Figure 2-28. Here the position of the characters is precise but the orientation of the individual characters is upright. This gives a reasonable representation of the text suitable for preview but does not take the time required to produce the final copy.

Suppose text representation 4 is the same as text representation 1 but uses an italic font. Then using text index 4 in the above example will give the output shown in Figure 2-29.

These examples show both the flexibility of the text primitive of GKS and how text in GKS answers the application requirements referred to earlier.

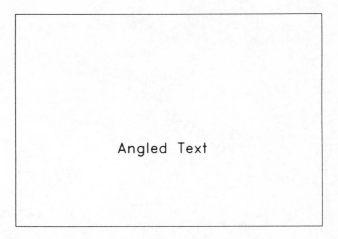

Figure 2-27

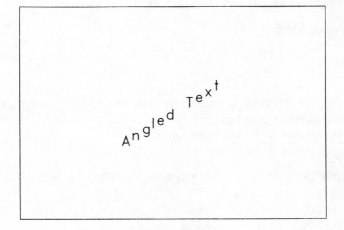

Figure 2-28

2.8 PRIMITIVES AND ATTRIBUTES

In this chapter we have examined the four primitives polyline, poly-marker, fill area, and text. One attribute has been described for each primitive except text for which five have been described. By suitable combinations of primitives and values of primitive attributes, quite complex pictures may be described to GKS with suitable annotations and titles, as

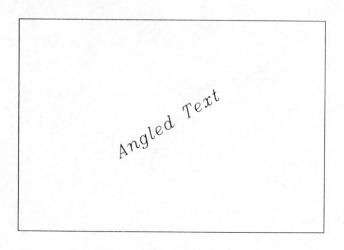

Figure 2-29

is shown in the following example:

```
REAL XNEWDK(44), YNEWDK(44), XNEWW(10), YNEWW(10)

PI = 4*ATAN(1)
XC = 45
YC = 45
R = 30

MOVE DUCK(XC, YC, R, 5*PI/6, XNEWDK, YNEWDK, XNEWW, YNEWW)
SET POLYLINE INDEX(1)
POLYLINE(44, XNEWDK, YNEWDK)
POLYLINE(10, XNEWW, YNEWW)

MOVE DUCK(XC, YC, R, PI/2, XNEWDK, YNEWDK, XNEWW, YNEWW)
SET POLYLINE INDEX(2)
POLYLINE(44, XNEWDK, YNEWDK)
POLYLINE(10, XNEWW, YNEWW)

MOVE DUCK(XC, YC, R, PI/6, XNEWDK, YNEWDK, XNEWW, YNEWW)
SET POLYMARKER INDEX(1)
POLYMARKER(44, XNEWDK, YNEWDK)
SET POLYMARKER INDEX(3)
POLYMARKER(10, XNEWW, YNEWW)
```

```
MOVE DUCK(XC, YC, R, -PI/6, XNEWDK, YNEWDK, XNEWW, YNEWW)
SET FILL AREA INDEX(2)
FILL AREA(44, XNEWDK, YNEWDK)

MOVE DUCK(XC, YC, R, -PI/2, XNEWDK, YNEWDK, XNEWW, YNEWW)
SET FILL AREA INDEX(3)
FILL AREA(44, XNEWDK, YNEWDK)
SET POLYLINE INDEX(1)
POLYLINE(44, XNEWDK, YNEWDK)

MOVE DUCK(XC, YC, R, -5*PI/6, XNEWDK, YNEWDK, XNEWW, YNEWW)
FILL AREA(44, XNEWDK, YNEWDK)
SET POLYLINE INDEX(2)
POLYLINE(44, XNEWDK, YNEWDK)

SET TEXT INDEX(1)
SET CHARACTER HEIGHT(7.5)
SET TEXT ALIGNMENT(RIGHT, HALF)
TEXT(23.5, 45, 'G')
SET CHARACTER HEIGHT(3)
SET TEXT ALIGNMENT(LEFT, HALF)
TEXT(23.5, 45, 'RAPHICAL')
SET TEXT ALIGNMENT(RIGHT, HALF)
TEXT(59, 45, 'DUC')
SET CHARACTER HEIGHT(7.5)
SET TEXT ALIGNMENT(LEFT, HALF)
TEXT(59, 45, 'KS')
```

where MOVE DUCK calculates the coordinates of the duck and wing, when the centre of the duck is placed at a point on a circle with centre (XC,YC) and radius R at an angle THETA from the horizontal radius. The new coordinates of the duck are returned in the arrays XNWDK and YNWDK and those of the wing are returned in the arrays XNWW and YNWW, thus:

```
SUBROUTINE MOVE DUCK(XC, YC, R, THETA,
    XNWDK, YNWDK, XNWW, YNWW)

REAL XNWDK(44), YNWDK(44), XNWW(10), YNWW(10)
REAL XDK(44), YDK(44), XW(10), YW(10)

DATA initialise XDK, YDK, XW, YW as earlier
```

```
        XPOS = XC + R*COS(THETA)
        YPOS = YC + R*SIN(THETA)
        DO 100 I = 1,44
        XNWDK(I) = XDK(I)-14.5 + XPOS
100     YNWDK(I) = YDK(I)-8.85 + YPOS
        DO 200 I = 1,10
        XNWW(I) = XW(I)-14.5 + XPOS
200     YNWW(I) = YW(I)-8.85 + YPOS
        RETURN
        END
```

The output is shown in Figure 2-30. A complete GKS program based on this example is given in Appendix C.

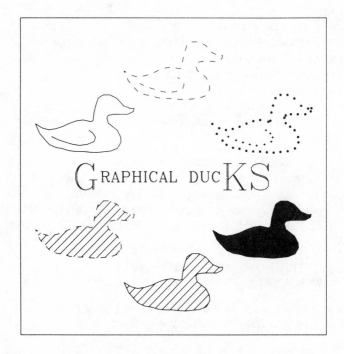

Figure 2-30

3 Coordinate Systems

3.1 INTRODUCTION

In Chapter 2, the main output primitives of GKS have been described without giving any indication of the *coordinate system* being used to define positions. For example, a polyline joining five points can be defined as:

```
      DO 100 I = 1, 5
      X(I) = I
      Y(I) = 0.1*I**2
100   CONTINUE

      POLYLINE(5, X, Y)
```

The polyline could be visualized as shown in Figure 3-1. Here, the coordinate systems on the two axes have been chosen so that the unit length on the two axes is the same. If the unit length was different, a quite different picture of the polyline would have been produced. For example, see Figure 3-2. The user needs to be able to specify the form that the polyline will take on a specific device. He needs the ability to define differential scaling on the two axes if that is appropriate to his problem.

3.2 USER AND WORLD COORDINATES

For any problem, the user will have a preferred coordinate system in which he would like to work. The term *user coordinates* is used for this coordinate system. Most frequently, this coordinate system will be a cartesian coordinate system. However, it is possible that the user coordinate system might be logarithmically scaled or polar coordinates. The

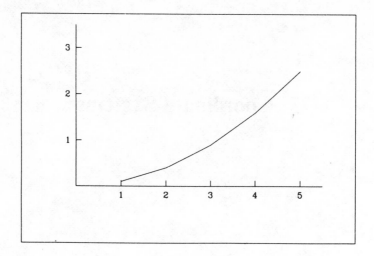

Figure 3-1

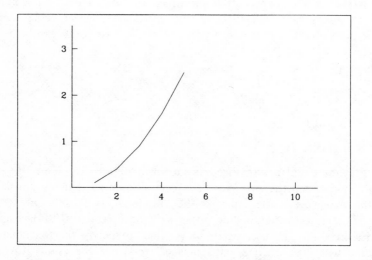

Figure 3-2

only coordinate systems understood by GKS are cartesian coordinate systems. Consequently, if the user coordinate system is not cartesian, the user himself must map his coordinate system onto a cartesian system. On the other hand, if the user coordinate system is cartesian, this can be the coordinate system in which output is described to GKS. To differentiate between the preferred user coordinates and the ones presented to GKS, the term *world coordinates* (WC) is used to define a coordinate system used to present graphical output to GKS. The difference between the two coordinate systems is illustrated in Figure 3-3.

3.3 NORMALIZED DEVICE COORDINATES

Let us consider a typical example of graphical output and how it would be dealt with in GKS. The table below indicates some characteristics of New York City temperatures that are to be displayed in a graphical form on some output device.

Month	Over 100 years		1965	
	Max	Min	Max	Min
Jan	72	-6	55	9
Feb	75	-15	61	13
Mar	86	3	61	21
Apr	92	12	80	29
May	99	32	94	46
Jun	101	44	95	52
Jul	106	52	93	58
Aug	104	50	91	50
Sep	102	39	92	44
Oct	94	28	81	32
Nov	84	5	71	31
Dec	70	-13	63	18

New York City Temperatures

We may be interested in displaying the range of temperatures experienced by New York over a 100 year period or how 1965 compares with the extremes of temperature reached in the city during that period. In this example, the user coordinate system and world coordinate system can be made identical if temperature is used as the Y coordinate and the X coordinates go from 1 to 12 indicating the 12 months of the year.

The above data could be input to the computer and stored in four real arrays MAXPR (maximum over the 100 year period), MINPR, MAX65, and MIN65 with the elements 1 to 12 giving the temperature each month. A separate real array MONTH where MONTH(I) is set to I will also be required. To produce a display on some output device, it is necessary to convert the world coordinates by some transformation to the coordinates relevant to the specific device. This requires the following to be done:

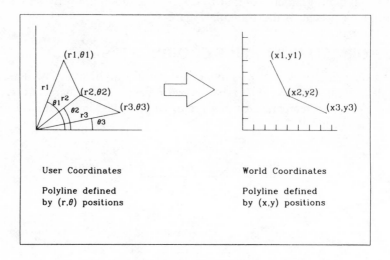

Figure 3-3

(1)   The world coordinate origin has to be positioned on the display screen.

(2)   A unit in world coordinate space has to be defined as a number of device coordinate units in each of the X and Y directions.

Looking at specific devices, the device coordinates vary significantly from one device to another. For example, the Tektronix 4010 storage tube has a screen with coordinates 0 to 1023 in the X direction and 0 to 779 in the Y direction. Other devices have different ranges of device coordinates and some position the origin not at the lower left corner.

To provide a more concrete example of how GKS allows users to define their output in world coordinates and have them transformed to device coordinates, a virtual or normalized device is defined which has a display surface visible in the range 0 to 1 in both the X and Y directions. The coordinates of this device will be called *normalized device coordinates* (NDC). This is shown in Figure 3-4. To produce visible output, the world coordinates defining the output must be mapped into coordinate positions within the NDC unit square from 0 to 1 in both the X and Y directions.

3.4 WINDOW TO VIEWPORT TRANSFORMATION

As mentioned in the previous section, the transformation from world coordinates to NDC must specify the position in NDC space equivalent to a fixed position in the world coordinate space and the extent in the X and Y directions in NDC space of a single unit in world coordinate space.

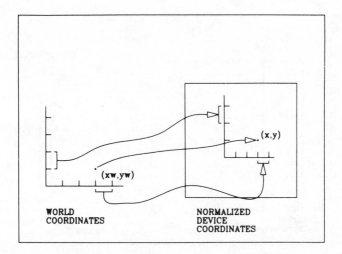

Figure 3-4

This enables the user to define the position and extent that his graphical output will occupy on the normalized device. He may wish the output to take up the whole visible area in NDC space. Alternatively, he may wish it to extend over a small part of the complete space.

A convenient method for doing this, and one that has been used extensively in the past, is to define a rectangular area in world coordinate space (called the *window*) and define where this area will appear on the normalized device (called the *viewport*). GKS uses this method of specifying how world coordinates are transformed to NDC. This is shown in Figure 3-5. In the world coordinate space, the window is defined by giving the limits of the window in the X direction (XWMIN to XWMAX) and the Y direction (YWMIN to YWMAX). This is transformed into the viewport in NDC space such that the range of X coordinates in NDC space go from XVMIN to XVMAX and the Y coordinates from YVMIN to YVMAX.

The mapping in GKS is defined such that the point (XWMIN,YWMIN) is transformed to the position (XVMIN,YVMIN) and, similarly, (XWMAX,YWMAX) is transformed to (XVMAX,YVMAX). Any position such as (XW,YW) in the world coordinate plane is mapped to a position (XV,YV) in the NDC space in such a way as to preserve its relative position in the rectangle. Thus the ratio of the distance of the point from one of the X boundaries to the length of the X range in world coordinates is equal to the same ratio in NDC. This also applies to the Y axis. Note that both the window and viewport are rectangles, but that there is no constraint that the *aspect ratio* of the

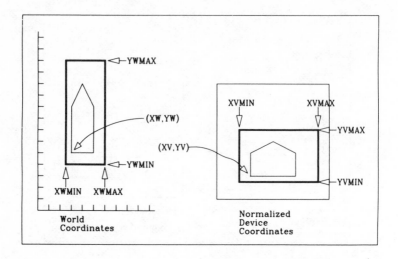

Figure 3-5

viewport is the same as the aspect ratio of the window. Consequently, a tall thin house (in the diagram) can be mapped into a short fat house on the device.

GKS uses two functions to define a window and viewport as given below:

SET WINDOW(N, XWMIN, XWMAX, YWMIN, YWMAX)
SET VIEWPORT(N, XVMIN, XVMAX, YVMIN, YVMAX)

The first parameter N will be ignored for the moment. The other four parameters in each function define the limits of the window and viewport.

Thus, to produce a graph of the New York City maximum temperatures for 1965 which fills the whole of NDC visible space would require window and viewport definitions as follows:

    SET WINDOW(N, 0, 12, 0, 100)
    SET VIEWPORT(N, 0, 1, 0, 1)

    POLYLINE(12, MONTH, MAX65)

This is shown in Figure 3-6. If output is generated before either SET WINDOW or SET VIEWPORT is called, default values for these are used, equal to the unit square. Thus, calling the POLYLINE above before defining the window or viewport is equivalent to:

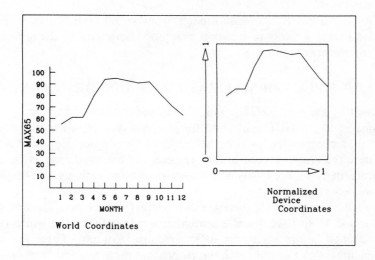

Figure 3-6

```
SET WINDOW(N, 0, 1, 0, 1)
SET VIEWPORT(N, 0, 1, 0, 1)

POLYLINE(12, MONTH, MAX65)
```

It is good practice not to accept the defaults but define the windows and viewports explicitly.

The main purpose of the window and viewport definitions is to define the transformation from world coordinates to NDC. It is possible for several window and viewport combinations to give the same mapping of coordinates from world to NDC. For example:

```
SET WINDOW(N, 0, 12, 0, 100)
SET VIEWPORT(N, 0.25, 0.75, 0.25, 0.75)
```

gives the same mapping as:

```
SET WINDOW(N, -6, 18, -50, 150)
SET VIEWPORT(N, 0, 1, 0, 1)
```

Both define the position (0,0) in world coordinates as being mapped onto the NDC position (0.25,0.25). Both define the scaling in the X direction such that 1 unit in world coordinates is equivalent to 1/24 of a unit in NDC space. The scaling in the Y direction in both cases is such that 1 unit in the world coordinate space is equivalent to 1/200 in the NDC space. Later, we shall see that the viewport boundary is used for other purposes as well. Consequently, a specific viewport may have to be used in some cases.

The transformation of coordinates from world coordinates to NDC defined by the window to viewport mapping is often called the *normalization transformation* in GKS.

3.5 MULTIPLE NORMALIZATION TRANSFORMATIONS

Frequently, the user of GKS will wish to generate quite complex graphical images in the NDC space and the image may have different appropriate world coordinates for different parts of the picture. For example, to annotate the graph defined in the previous section, units such as the temperature in New York City are inappropriate for defining the height of the characters in the text.

To solve this problem, there are two distinct approaches. The first solution would be to have a single normalization transformation which could be redefined before each part of the picture is output. There are some disadvantages to this approach which become more important when locator input and interaction are used. The second solution, and the one adopted in GKS, is to allow the user to define a number of window to viewport mappings. In the previous section, the parameter N in the definitions of the functions SET WINDOW and SET VIEWPORT is used to differentiate between the different normalization transformations. Values of N range from 0 (which has a special significance and will be described later) to some installation defined maximum which will be of the order of 20 or more. Thus:

SET WINDOW(N, XWMIN, XWMAX, XYMIN, XYMAX)

defines the N*th* window and similarly for SET VIEWPORT.

It is good programming practice to define the windows and viewports used in a particular application at the head of the program. They can be thought of as a declaration defining the overall structure of the output.

To define which window to viewport mapping is to be used with a particular output primitive, a function is provided which selects a particular transformation as being in force until another is selected. The function:

SELECT NORMALIZATION TRANSFORMATION(N)

specifies that normalization transformation N should be selected. The default transformation is number 0. Consequently, the examples in the previous section were not strictly accurate and should have been:

```
SET WINDOW(N, 0, 12, 0, 100)
SET VIEWPORT(N, 0, 1, 0, 1)

SELECT NORMALIZATION TRANSFORMATION(N)
POLYLINE(12, MONTH, MAX65)
```

An example showing how multiple normalization transformations might be used is given below. The aim is to produce four graphs with axes giving the maximum and minimum temperatures over the 100 year period and for the year 1965. We make use of a subroutine AXES which was defined in Section 2.3. It outputs axes from the origin to maximum values in the X and Y directions. Producing the four graphs requires:

```
SET WINDOW(1, 0, 12, -15, 110)
SET VIEWPORT(1, 0.1, 0.4, 0.6, 0.9)

SET WINDOW(2, 0, 12, -15, 110)
SET VIEWPORT(2, 0.6, 0.9, 0.6, 0.9)

SET WINDOW(3, 0, 12, -15, 110)
SET VIEWPORT(3, 0.1, 0.4, 0.1, 0.4)

SET WINDOW(4, 0, 12, -15, 110)
SET VIEWPORT(4, 0.6, 0.9, 0.1, 0.4)

      DO 100 I = 1, 4
      SELECT NORMALIZATION TRANSFORMATION(I)
      AXES(12, 110)
100   CONTINUE

SELECT NORMALIZATION TRANSFORMATION(1)
POLYLINE(12, MONTH, MAX65)

SELECT NORMALIZATION TRANSFORMATION(2)
POLYLINE(12, MONTH, MIN65)

SELECT NORMALIZATION TRANSFORMATION(3)
POLYLINE(12, MONTH, MAXPR)

SELECT NORMALIZATION TRANSFORMATION(4)
POLYLINE(12, MONTH, MINPR)
```

The output is given in Figure 3-7.

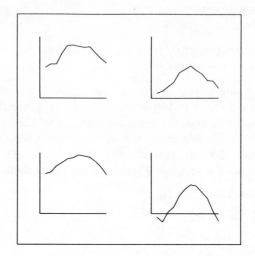

Figure 3-7

3.6 GRAPHICAL ANNOTATION

As another example of how to use several window to viewport transformations to compose a picture, consider the problem of annotating the graph of maximum New York temperatures. As stated before, a coordinate system with temperature in one direction and months of the year in the other is not the most ideal for defining the size and position of textual annotations to the graph.

The graphical output falls into three distinct classes:

(1)   the graphical information

(2)   annotation on the Y axis

(3)   annotation on the X axis

and these three windows need to be mapped onto viewports as shown in Figure 3-8. A possible set of window to viewport mappings would be:

```
SET WINDOW(1, 0, 12, 0, 120)
SET VIEWPORT(1, 0.2, 0.8, 0.15, 0.75)

SET WINDOW(2, 0, 4, 0, 16)
SET VIEWPORT(2, 0.0, 0.2, 0.15, 0.95)

SET WINDOW(3, 0, 15, 0, 3)
SET VIEWPORT(3, 0.2, 0.95, 0.0, 0.15)
```

Note that the second and third normalization transformations preserve the aspect ratio. Space has also been left to allow the Y axis text to

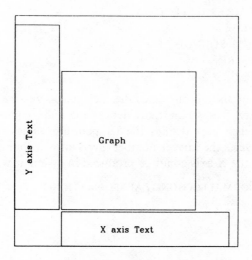

Figure 3-8

extend above the height of the graph and the X axis text to extend past the right hand end of the graph. The graph can be drawn as before by:

```
SELECT NORMALIZATION TRANSFORMATION(1)
AXES(12, 120)
POLYLINE(12, MONTH, MAXPR)
```

To draw the text on the Y axis would require:

```
SELECT NORMALIZATION TRANSFORMATION(2)

      DO 100 I = 1, 12
      X(I) = 4
      Y(I) = I
100   CONTINUE
      SET POLYMARKER INDEX(3)
      POLYMARKER(12, X, Y)

      SET CHARACTER HEIGHT(0.5)
      SET CHARACTER UP VECTOR(-1, 0)
      TEXT(1.5, 2.5, 'MAX NEW YORK TEMP')
```

```
        SET CHARACTER UP VECTOR(0, 1)
        DO 200 I = 1, 12
        CONVTX(I*10, STRING)
        TEXT(2, I, STRING)
200     CONTINUE
```

The first part of the output generates tick marks on the axes using the plus sign marker. The second part defines the main annotation on the Y axis while the last part defines the temperature values. The subroutine CONVTX converts the integer number given into its character form.

The text on the X axis could be produced in a similar way:

```
        SELECT NORMALIZATION TRANSFORMATION(3)

        DO 300 I = 1, 12
        X(I) = I
        Y(I) = 3
300     CONTINUE

        POLYMARKER(12, X, Y)

        SET CHARACTER HEIGHT(0.25)
        SET CHARACTER UP VECTOR(0, 1)
        SET TEXT INDEX(N)
        TEXT(0.625, 2, 'JAN FEB MAR APR MAY JUN JUL AUG SEP OCT NOV DEC')
```

where text representation N is assumed to be a font with the width of each character being the same (i.e. mono spaced) and equal to the height. The output would be as shown in Figure 3-9.

3.7 CLIPPING

A problem that comes to light if we attempt to generate a graph of the minimum temperature rather than the maximum can be seen if we substitute:

```
        POLYLINE(12, MONTH, MINPR)
```

for the call to POLYLINE in the above example. Does this give the output shown in Figure 3-10? Because the Y coordinates of the minimum temperature go negative, the polyline is drawn outside the boundary of the viewport defined by the first normalization transformation. If the complete polyline is drawn, the effect is as in Figure 3-10. The graph overwrites the titling causing a rather poor representation.

GKS, in fact, allows two possibilities if the user attempts to draw outside the boundary of the viewport. In one mode, drawing is allowed as shown in Figure 3-10 and, in the other, drawing is *clipped* at the

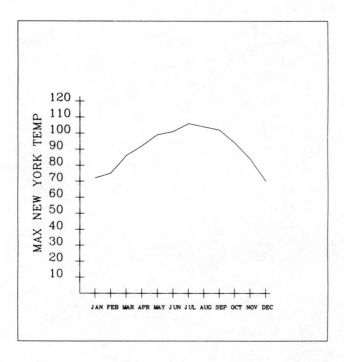

Figure 3-9

boundary of the viewport, so that only those parts of the polyline primitive inside the viewport are actually drawn. Both possibilities have their uses and it is up to the user to define which he requires. In fact, the default in GKS is to clip the output to the viewport boundary so that the output shown above would not have been generated. In GKS, it is possible to choose whether or not to clip to the viewport boundary by calling the function:

SET CLIPPING INDICATOR(IND)

where IND can take the values CLIP and NOCLIP as appropriate. Thus the graph in Figure 3-10 would be produced by:

```
SELECT NORMALIZATION TRANSFORMATION(1)
SET CLIPPING INDICATOR(NOCLIP)
AXES(12, 120)
POLYLINE(12, MONTH, MINPR)
```

To produce the clipped output shown in Figure 3-11, the program would be:

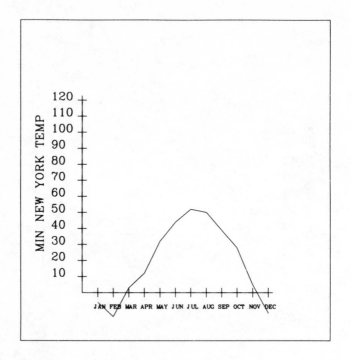

Figure 3-10

SELECT NORMALIZATION TRANSFORMATION(1)
SET CLIPPING INDICATOR(CLIP)
AXES(12, 120)
POLYLINE(12, MONTH, MINPR)

Alternatively, if the clipping indicator has not been reset previously, it will retain the original default value of CLIP so that the call to SET CLIPPING INDICATOR can be omitted.

Note that the clipping indicator is associated with the currently selected normalization transformation. There is not a separate clipping switch for each normalization transformation.

If the clipping indicator is set to CLIP, polylines will always be clipped at the boundary of the viewport. However, the situation as far as other output primitives is concerned is not always as straightforward. In the case of polymarkers, the individual markers will only be output if the centre of the marker is within the viewport. This does mean that a marker which is just inside the viewport may have some part of its form outside the boundary if the centre is within. The clipping of TEXT depends on the precision of the text being output. The lowest (STRING) precision

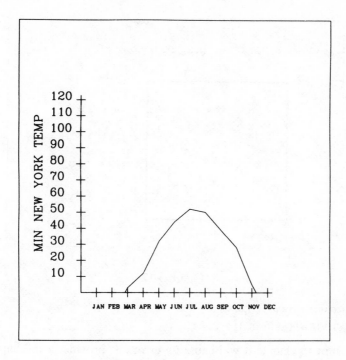

Figure 3-11

text may be completely removed if the position of the start of the text is outside the viewport. For CHAR precision text, clipping is done on a per character basis with the character only being output if the complete character box is within the viewport. For STROKE precision text, clipping is performed at the boundary of the viewport. The difference between CHAR and STROKE clipping is shown in Figure 3-12; the dashed lines indicate those parts that would be removed by clipping.

3.8 NORMALIZATION TRANSFORMATION 0

In general, normalization transformations can be redefined at any time by either redefining the window or viewport. It is usual to define all the normalization transformations required in a picture prior to outputting it. However, although this is regarded as good practice, it is not mandatory. In some circumstances, it may even be necessary to redefine the normalization transformation during the output.

Normalization transformation 0 is rather special in that it cannot be redefined ever. Its value is equivalent to:

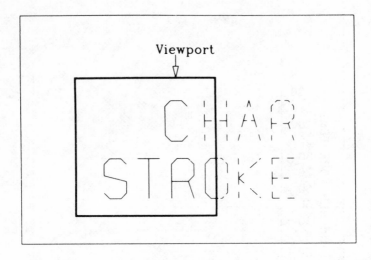

Figure 3-12

SET WINDOW(0, 0, 1, 0, 1)
SET VIEWPORT(0, 0, 1, 0, 1)

An attempt to change it will cause an error. It provides a mechanism so that a user can define his output directly in NDC rather than using world coordinates. Occasions may arise when this is preferable.

4 Segments and their Attributes

4.1 INTRODUCTION

The earlier chapters in this book have described how to construct a picture and position it on a virtual device in a natural way. In many application areas, there is a need to display the same or similar graphical information many times possibly at different positions on the device. This leads to the need for some storage mechanism whereby pictures or subpictures can be saved for later use during a program's execution. GKS has the concept of a *segment* for this purpose. Graphical output can be stored in segments during the execution of a program and later reused. Segments have a number of *segment attributes* associated with them which allow the user to modify the appearance of the whole segment in a significant way when it is reused.

To take a simple example not using segments, consider a crude animation system in which the user constructs a scenic background and then displays an object moving across the scene on successive frames; the initial frame might be something like Figure 4-1. Suppose it is the duck we want to move across the pond on successive frames; the position of the duck can be input by the operator on a keyboard and read by the program using a FORTRAN READ statement. A sequence of frames with the duck in positions such as shown in Figure 4-2 might be generated. The outline of a program to do this might be:

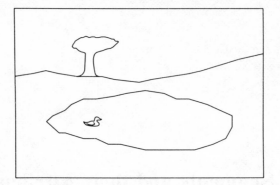

Figure 4-1

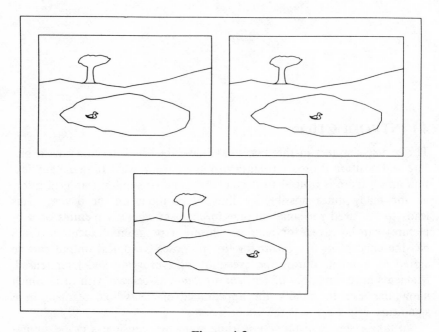

Figure 4-2

```
100    CONTINUE
       READ(5, '(2F6.2)') X, Y
       NEW FRAME
       DRAW BACKGROUND
       DRAW DUCK AT(X, Y)
       GOTO 100
```

where the subroutine DRAW BACKGROUND draws the outline of the tree, pond and landscape and the subroutine DRAW DUCK AT draws the duck at the position (X,Y). Note that NEW FRAME clears the display but is not a GKS function. Control of the display surface and how it is cleared will be described in Chapter 7.

This is, however, a very inefficient program, because unnecessary work has to be performed. For example, the normalization transformation has to be applied afresh to the background scene for each frame despite the fact that the background does not change from frame to frame. An obvious solution to this problem would be for GKS to store the background after the normalization transformation has been applied so that on each new frame it is only necessary to perform the minimum of computation to redraw the background on the display. That is a good solution if the display is, say, a storage tube or pen plotter. However, there are more sophisticated displays, such as vector refresh displays and raster displays which allow the user to selectively erase parts of the picture or move parts of a picture. Using such a display, the most efficient implementation of this example program would be to draw the background and the duck in its initial position, then erase the duck (if necessary) and move it to the new position specified. As another example, consider the left hand picture in Figure 4-3. The picture contains one tree, one pond, one landscape and three ducks. A program to draw such a picture might well be structured as four subroutines, each corresponding to one of the graphical objects (tree, pond, landscape and duck), where the subroutine to draw the duck would be parameterized on the position of the duck:

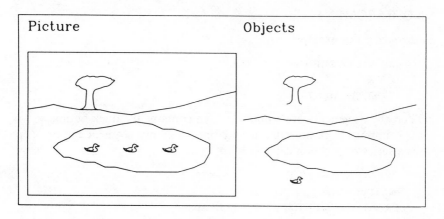

Figure 4-3

```
     TREE
     LANDSCAPE
     POND
     DO 100 I = 1, 3
100   DRAW DUCK AT(X(I), Y(I))
```

Figure 4-3 illustrates the correspondence between graphical objects and the picture. In particular, note that one object can have more than one instance in the picture. The order in which the output primitives are presented to GKS then reflects the structure of the picture, but we have as yet seen no way in which this structure can be recorded and made use of in GKS.

In GKS, as mentioned above, output primitives may be grouped together into segments, which are then associated with the output device. They can be manipulated in several ways as will be described later in this chapter. Further segment manipulations are described in Chapter 10.

4.2 CREATING AND DELETING SEGMENTS

A segment is created by the function:

CREATE SEGMENT(ID)

where ID is the name by which the segment is to be known. This segment is then the *open segment*. Subsequent calls to output primitive functions will result in those primitives being inserted into this open segment, as well as being output, until such time as the function:

CLOSE SEGMENT

is invoked. For example:

```
     CREATE SEGMENT(1)
     DUCK
     CLOSE SEGMENT
```

will create a segment with name '1' which contains the duck outline.

It is important to note that at any time, only one segment can be open, thus a series of function calls such as:

```
     CREATE SEGMENT(1)
     output primitives
     CREATE SEGMENT(2)          ILLEGAL!!
     output primitives
     CLOSE SEGMENT
     CLOSE SEGMENT
```

is not permitted and will generate an error. It is also important to realize that once a segment has been closed, further output primitives cannot be added to it.

Once created, there are a number of operations which can be performed on segments. The simplest of these is deletion! A segment is deleted by calling the function:

DELETE SEGMENT(ID)

where ID is the name of the segment to be deleted. After a segment has been deleted, the segment's name can be reused.

4.3 SEGMENT ATTRIBUTES

4.3.1 Segment Transformations

In the introduction to this chapter we discussed the need to move objects, or parts of objects, around on a display in response either to some computation or to some operator direction. *Segment transformations* provide the way to do this efficiently. The segment transformation is a transformation operating on all the coordinates in the segment definition. When a segment is created, the segment transformation is set to the null, or *identity,* transformation. The segment transformation can be subsequently changed by invoking the function:

SET SEGMENT TRANSFORMATION(ID, MATRIX)

where ID is the name of the segment whose transformation is to be changed. Note that this name can be the name of the open segment; this is very useful as examples later will show. The parameter MATRIX is a 2×3 *transformation matrix.*

Constructing transformation matrices can be a tricky task and so GKS provides two utility functions, EVALUATE TRANSFORMATION MATRIX and ACCUMULATE TRANSFORMATION MATRIX to help the application programmer. The first function:

EVALUATE TRANSFORMATION MATRIX(FX, FY, TX, TY, R,
SX, SY, SWITCH, MATRIX)

calculates a transformation matrix which may be fed straight into SET SEGMENT TRANSFORMATION. FX and FY specify a *fixed point;* TX and TY specify a translation or *shift vector;* R is an *angle of rotation* in radians and SX and SY are *scale factors.* The transformation matrix computed is returned in the parameter MATRIX. Scale and rotation are relative to the specified fixed point. The *coordinate switch,* SWITCH, can take the value WC or NDC. In the former case, the values specified for the fixed point and shift vector are taken as world coordinates, in the latter case as normalized device coordinates (Chapter 3 explains the

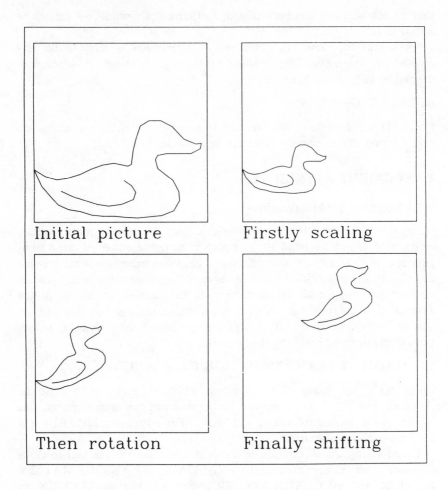

Initial picture   Firstly scaling

Then rotation   Finally shifting

Figure 4-4

distinction). If SWITCH takes the value WC, then the fixed point (FX,FY) and the shift vector (TX,TY) are transformed to normalized device coordinates by the current normalization transformation.

The elements of the resulting transformation matrix, which represent the shift component of the transformation, are expressed in normalized device coordinates. The transformation matrix is computed so that the order in which the transformations are applied to coordinate data is scale, rotate and shift. The sequence of diagrams in Figure 4-4 illustrates this.

We will now see some examples of the use of EVALUATE TRANSFORMATION MATRIX. The duck used in the earlier examples in this chapter is defined by a polyline beginning at the point (0,8.8) as shown in Figure 4-5. Suppose we want to move the duck so that it starts at the point (5,13.8), in world coordinates. First we need to construct a transformation matrix, which expresses the fact that we want to move the point (0,8.8) to the point (5,13.8). The point (0,8.8) has to be shifted by (5,5) to produce the point (5,13.8); no rotation or scaling (other than by 1) is required. Thus we have determined the following parameters to EVALUATE TRANSFORMATION MATRIX:

TX = 5
TY = 5
R = 0
SX = 1
SY = 1
SWITCH = WC

What values do we assign to FX and FY? It is clear that a fixed point does not need to be specified for a shift operation, since the effect of a shift is the same on all points in the picture. However, since EVALU-ATE TRANSFORMATION MATRIX computes the combined effects of a scale, rotation and shift, and a fixed point does need to be specified for the first two, a fixed point must be given. Any point could be chosen in this instance, since the scaling and rotation operations (by unity and zero) do not affect the appearance of the picture. Typically the origin (0,0)

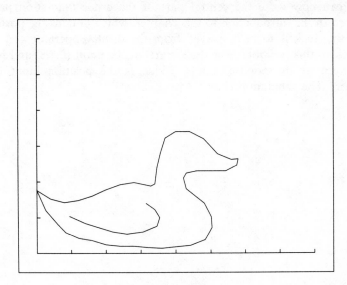

Figure 4-5

would be specified as the fixed point, although if a particular point is used to calculate the shift vector, it may be clearer to take that point as the fixed point. We will use (0,8.8) as the fixed point.

Thus, the complete program to create a segment containing the duck, display it at position (0,8.8), and then move it to position (5,13.8) would be:

```
CREATE SEGMENT(1)
DUCK
CLOSE SEGMENT
FX = 0
FY = 8.8
TX = 5
TY = 5
R = 0
SX = 1
SY = 1
SWITCH = WC
EVALUATE TRANSFORMATION MATRIX(FX, FY, TX, TY, R, SX, SY,
    SWITCH, MAT)
SET SEGMENT TRANSFORMATION(1, MAT)
```

The final effect of this program is shown in Figure 4-6.

We can now write the central part of the crude animation program described in the introduction to this chapter, which obtains the position at which the duck is to be displayed from the display operator and moves the duck to this position. The duck starts at the point (0,8.8) and is to be redisplayed at the point (XL,YL) which is the position input by the operator. The program is thus:

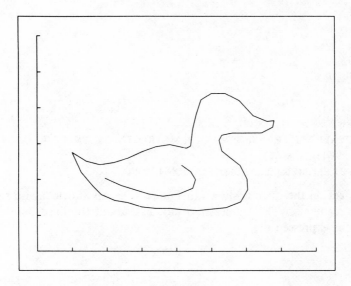

Figure 4-6

```
CREATE SEGMENT(1)
DUCK
CLOSE SEGMENT
FX = 0
FY = 8.8
R = 0
SX = 1
SY = 1
SWITCH = WC
```

100   CONTINUE

```
READ(5, '(2F6.2)') XL, YL
TX = XL
TY = YL-8.8
EVALUATE TRANSFORMATION MATRIX(FX, FY, TX, TY, R, SX, SY,
   SWITCH, MAT)
SET SEGMENT TRANSFORMATION(1, MAT)
```

GOTO 100

The size, at which a segment is displayed, is controlled by the scaling factors. To decrease the size uniformly by a factor of 2, relative to the start point (0,8.8), the transformation matrix is constructed as follows:

```
FX = 0
FY = 8.8
TX = 0
TY = 0
R = 0
SX = 0.5
SY = 0.5
SWITCH = WC
EVALUATE TRANSFORMATION MATRIX(FX, FY, TX, TY, R, SX, SY,
   SWITCH, MAT)
SET SEGMENT TRANSFORMATION(1, MAT)
```

The effect on the duck is shown in Figure 4-7. An anticlockwise rotation of the segment by 30 degrees ($\pi/6$ radians), about the fixed point (0,8.8) would be expressed by:

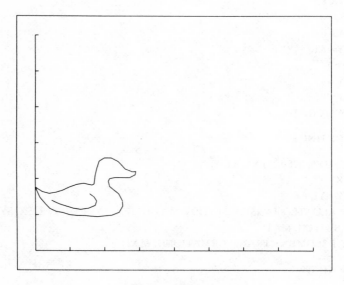

Figure 4-7

```
FX = 0
FY = 8.8
TX = 0
TY = 0
R = PI/6
SX = 1
SY = 1
SWITCH = WC
EVALUATE TRANSFORMATION MATRIX(FX, FY, TX, TY, R, SX, SY,
   SWITCH, MAT)
SET SEGMENT TRANSFORMATION(1, MAT)
```

and the effect produced is shown in Figure 4-8.

It is important to remember that the order in which transformations are computed by EVALUATE TRANSFORMATION MATRIX is scale, rotate, shift. It is important because if rotation is applied before scaling different effects may be produced, for example in the case where scaling is not uniform (i.e. X scale factor differs from Y scale factor).

The function ACCUMULATE TRANSFORMATION MATRIX allows more general transformation matrices to be composed:

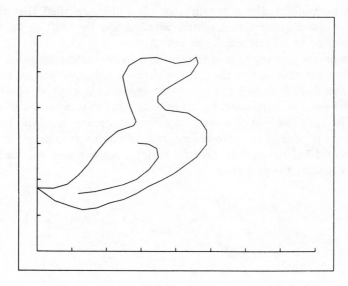

Figure 4-8

ACCUMULATE TRANSFORMATION MATRIX(MATIN, FX, FY,
  TX, TY, R, SX, SY, SWITCH, MATOUT)

The parameters FX, FY, TX, TY, R, SX, SY and SWITCH have the
same meanings as in EVALUATE TRANSFORMATION MATRIX.
The transformation specified by these parameters is concatenated with the
transformation specified by the matrix, MATIN, and the resulting
transformation matrix is returned in MATOUT. The order in which the
transformations are applied is input matrix, scale, rotate and shift.

One likely use of this function is to change the order in which scale,
rotate and shift are applied, by specifying each elementary transformation
separately and using a call to EVALUATE TRANSFORMATION
MATRIX followed by two calls to ACCUMULATE TRANSFORMA-
TION MATRIX to build up the required matrix.

4.3.2 Segment Transformation and Clipping

To explain the effects of clipping on transformed segments, something has
to be said about when segment transformation takes place. The segment
transformation is actually applied *after* the normalization transformation
(which, it will be recalled, maps world coordinates into normalized device
coordinates) but *before* any clipping. Coordinates stored in segments are
in fact normalized device coordinates. It will be recalled that the elements of the transformation matrix which define the shift to be applied
are expressed in normalized device coordinates.

A primitive in a segment is transformed by the normalization and segment transformations and then, if the clipping indicator was set to CLIP
when the primitive was put into the segment, is clipped against the
viewport (of the normalization transformation) that was active at that
time. In each segment is stored, in effect, a clipping rectangle for each
primitive it contains. However, the clipping rectangles are *not*
transformed by the segment transformation. An example will make this
clear. Consider the program:

SET WINDOW(1, 0, 30, 0, 30)
SET VIEWPORT(1, 0, 0.5, 0, 0.5)

SELECT NORMALIZATION TRANSFORMATION(1)
SET CLIPPING INDICATOR(NOCLIP)
CREATE SEGMENT(1)
DUCK
CLOSE SEGMENT

EVALUATE TRANSFORMATION MATRIX(0, 0, 0.25, 0.25, 0, 1, 1, NDC, MAT)
SET SEGMENT TRANSFORMATION(1, MAT)

If the clipping indicator is NOCLIP when a primitive is put into a segment, the clipping rectangle $[0,1] \times [0,1]$ in normalized device coordinates
is stored with the primitive. Thus, in this example, the clipping rectangle
$[0,1] \times [0,1]$ is stored with the polyline primitives describing the duck. The
effect of this program is to generate a picture in the lower left hand qua-
drant of NDC space as shown in the left hand picture in Figure 4-9. This
is then shifted by (0.25, 0.25) in NDC space, as shown in the right hand
picture. (Note the use of the coordinate switch NDC in EVALUATE
TRANSFORMATION MATRIX.) Now if the clipping indicator is set to
CLIP before CREATE SEGMENT is invoked, the clipping rectangle
stored with the polyline primitives is the viewport of normalization
transformation 1 $([0,0.5] \times [0,0.5])$. The polyline primitives will be clipped
against this rectangle as shown in Figure 4-10.

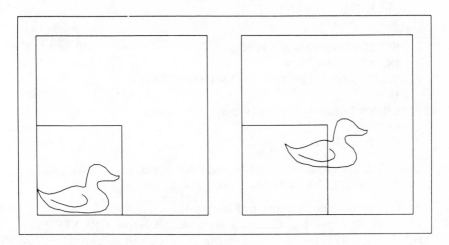

Figure 4-9

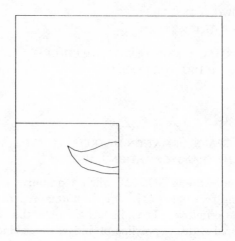

Figure 4-10

Note that the clipping rectangle was *not* transformed by the segment transformation.

Now we will consider a more complicated example in which more than one normalization transformation is used in the definition of a segment:

```
SET WINDOW(1, 0, 30, 0, 30)
SET VIEWPORT(1, 0, 0.5, 0, 0.5)

SET WINDOW(2, 0, 70, 0, 70)
SET VIEWPORT(2, 0, 0.5, 0.5, 1)

SET CLIPPING INDICATOR(NOCLIP)
CREATE SEGMENT(1)
SELECT NORMALIZATION TRANSFORMATION(1)
DUCK
SELECT NORMALIZATION TRANSFORMATION(2)
TREE
CLOSE SEGMENT

EVALUATE TRANSFORMATION MATRIX(0, 0, 0.25, 0, 0, 1, 1, NDC, MAT)
SET SEGMENT TRANSFORMATION(1, MAT)
```

The picture produced is shown in Figure 4-11.

Now if the clipping indicator is set to CLIP before CREATE SEGMENT is invoked, the polyline defining the duck will be clipped against the NDC space rectangle $[0,0.5] \times [0,0.5]$ and the tree will be clipped against the rectangle $[0,0.5] \times [0.5,1]$, as shown in Figure 4-12.

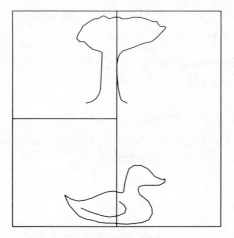

Figure 4-11

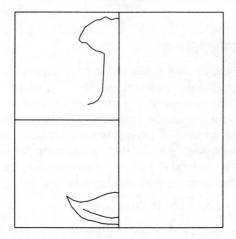

Figure 4-12

4.3.3 Segment Visibility

The segment *visibility* attribute determines whether a segment will be displayed or not. By default when a segment is created it is visible; thus:

    CREATE SEGMENT(1)
    DUCK
    CLOSE SEGMENT

will result in the duck picture being displayed. Normally the operator will see the picture being built up on the display as each line is drawn. The visibility attribute may be changed by the function:

SET VISIBILITY(ID, VIS)

where VIS specifies the visibility of segment ID. VIS may take the values VISIBLE and INVISIBLE. Hence, if the program is modified by the insertion of:

SET VISIBILITY(1, INVISIBLE)

after the call to CREATE SEGMENT, the duck will not be displayed on the screen. A subsequent invocation of:

SET VISIBILITY(1, VISIBLE)

will cause the duck to be made visible.

The visibility attribute is particularly useful for controlling the display of messages and menus (though there are other ways to deal with menus in GKS). Typically each message will be put into a separate segment, initially invisible. As a message is required, the segment containing it is made visible.

4.3.4 Segment Highlighting

Most vector refresh display hardware has the capability of *highlighting* a segment, for example by causing it to blink. The principal use of this facility is in drawing the operator's attention to some facet of the display. For example, in the animation program described in this chapter, when the operator has selected a new position at which the duck is to be displayed, we might highlight the duck segment in this new position and ask the operator to confirm that this is the position he really intends.

The highlighting attribute is set by the function:

SET HIGHLIGHTING(ID, HIGH)

where HIGH specifies the highlighting for segment ID. HIGH may take the values HIGHLIGHTED and NORMAL. When a segment is created, the highlighting attribute is NORMAL. It is set to HIGHLIGHTED by:

SET HIGHLIGHTING(SEGNAME, HIGHLIGHTED)

For a segment to appear highlighted, not only must the highlighting attribute have the value HIGHLIGHTED, but also the visibility attribute must have the value VISIBLE. If a segment needs to be highlighted as it is being created, the CREATE SEGMENT function should be followed by the SET HIGHLIGHTING function. The precise manner in which highlighting is implemented will depend on the particular display hardware that is being used. For some hardware, there will be no visible distinction between HIGHLIGHTED and NORMAL segments.

4.3.5 Segment Priority

Suppose that the scene at the start of this chapter is to be displayed on a raster scan display; then it might be done as follows. Firstly cover the entire display surface with a blue background. This could be done using a fill area primitive with a rectangular area whose boundary corresponds with that of the display surface. We now have a blue sky over the entire display! Now paint-in the rolling green pastures. This could be done using a fill area primitive. Painting-in means changing the current colour value of every picture element (or pixel), in the portion of the frame buffer over which the filled area lies, to the colour associated with the fill area primitive. Similarly the tree, pond and duck can be added to produce the scene shown in Figure 4-1.

Now it is clear that the appearance of the final picture depends on the order in which the fill area primitives are written into the frame buffer; for example, if the duck is created before the pond, then since the area defining the duck lies wholly within the pond, the pixels corresponding to the duck will be overwritten with the colour of the pond and the duck will disappear.

Suppose now we add the sun and wish, over a series of frames to observe a sunset! We could define the sun as a segment, and let the operator define successive positions of the sun. This works very well until the sun meets the green landscape, because the sun will then overwrite pixels corresponding to the landscape and will not be observed to set. If the landscape had a higher priority than the sun, in the sense that pixels corresponding to the landscape were not overwritten by the setting sun, the desired effect would be achieved.

GKS provides a mechanism for doing this, *segment priority,* which can be set by the function:

SET SEGMENT PRIORITY(ID, PRIORITY)

where PRIORITY is a value in the range 0 to 1, which specifies the priority of segment ID.

In this example, the sun would be put in a segment with priority higher than the sky, but lower than that of the tree, landscape, pond and duck; the pond and tree need priority higher than the landscape and the duck needs priority higher than the tree and pond. Suitable priorities would be:

Segment	Priority
sky	0
sun	0.25
landscape	0.5
pond	0.75
tree	0.75
duck	1.0

Segment priority controls the order in which segments are redrawn when the picture is changed.

There are a number of points which need to be stressed about segment priority, because it is not as universally useful as it might at first sight seem. The first point is that segment priority only works for devices which have the *appropriate hardware capability*. It cannot be used to force software checking of interference between segments for displays which do not have the appropriate hardware capability. In practice this is likely to mean that segment priority will only be available for colour raster scan displays. Secondly, the description of the SET SEGMENT PRIORITY routine given above conveys the impression that it is possible to distinguish between an infinite number of segment priorities. In practice the particular display being used is likely to have a finite range of priorities available, in which case the priority value specified is mapped onto this range. This means that segments specified to GKS as having different priorities can end up having the same priority because the hardware cannot distinguish sufficient levels.

A final point to note is that if two segments of the same priority overlap, or if primitives within a given segment overlap, then the effects will be defined, but may vary from one implementation of GKS to another.

4.4 RENAMING SEGMENTS

Segments can also be renamed, by invoking the function:

RENAME SEGMENT(OLD, NEW)

where OLD and NEW are the old and new segment names respectively. Thus, if segment 1 contains the duck outline and we invoke:

    RENAME SEGMENT(1, 2)

the duck outline will now be segment 2 and the segment name 1 can be reused for some other purpose. There are two points to note about this function. Firstly, there must be no segment called NEW in existence when the function is called. If there is, an error message will be generated. Secondly, it is perfectly permissible to do the following:

```
CREATE SEGMENT(1)
output primitives
RENAME SEGMENT(1, 2)
output primitives
CLOSE SEGMENT
```

that is, rename the open segment.

A typical usage of RENAME SEGMENT is the following. In the animation program at the start of this chapter, the operator wishes to determine a new position for the duck. Sometimes the placement is facilitated if the duck in the initial position is still displayed whilst the new position is selected. However, the application program wishes to use a particular segment name for the duck, say 1. The duck would be created in segment 1 and a second duck in some other segment, say 2. When the new position has been determined by positioning segment 2, segment 1 is deleted and segment 2 is renamed segment 1. In some applications, a common technique is to use a set of segment names cyclically to hold a segment in intermediate positions, renaming the latest segment when the position is correct and deleting the others.

5 Graphical Input Devices

5.1 INTRODUCTION

So far, this book has been primarily concerned with the output of graphical images. To a large extent, it has not been important to ask whether anyone is looking at the result at the time the image is being generated. (If you wish to consider GKS as a graphical output system only, you should continue reading at Chapter 7.)

This chapter concentrates on the person who sees an image and reacts by rotating, moving, pressing or switching some piece of hardware in order to change the behaviour of an application program. This person's actions may simply be transferring data values to the program or may affect its flow of control in a more radical and interactive way. We refer to this person as *the operator,* to distinguish him from the other user - the programmer.

Not until Chapter 4 was some interactive programming done and, there, the FORTRAN READ statement was used to input values to the program to control the graphical information being displayed. An example was given in Section 4.1 where an (X, Y) value was read and used to place the duck at the next required position on the pond.

Most displays will have hardware which allows graphical information to be entered directly to the system rather than always using the keyboard. For example, a storage tube will often have a pair of crosshairs to indicate positions on the display screen and these provide an alternative to the keyboard for inputting positional information. However, the variety of input hardware is very great and input data is supplied in many different forms. These different forms of data must be organized in a uniform way, that does not depend on particular physical devices, to match the needs of application programs.

In GKS, the data that can be input to the program by the operator are divided into six different types and six classes of *logical input device* are defined corresponding to these data types. Just as, when output was described, we did not talk about physical output devices and their characteristics so here we will not discuss physical input devices in detail but we will concentrate on the logical input devices. We will show how physical input devices are mapped onto these logical devices in Chapter 7.

The six classes of logical input device in GKS are:

(1)   *locator*: which inputs a position - an (X, Y) value.

(2)   *pick*: which identifies a displayed object.

(3)   *choice*: which selects from a set of alternatives.

(4)   *valuator*: which inputs a value.

(5)   *string*: which inputs a string of characters.

(6)   *stroke*: which inputs a sequence of (X, Y) positions.

Locator and pick supply input data directly related to some feature of the display. In contrast, the other input devices supply quite simple data not directly related to the display. However, they are frequently generated by physical devices associated with graphics displays and can be conveniently echoed on these graphics displays. In addition these data are commonly required by interactive programs.

Note that these are logical input devices associated with the normalized device having the NDC unit square as its display area. Physical devices will map into one or more of these logical devices. In the positioning of the duck in Section 4.1, the READ statement has input an (X, Y) value and effectively acts as a kind of locator device. However, it does not correspond precisely with the logical locator device described below. Typical physical devices that are often used to map onto these logical devices are:

(1)   *locator*: crosshairs and thumbwheels on a storage tube.

(2)   *pick*: lightpen hitting an object displayed on the screen.

(3)   *choice*: button box or menu selection using a lightpen.

(4)   *valuator*: potentiometers or inputting a value from a keyboard.

(5)   *string*: keyboard input of a line of text.

(6)   *stroke*: tablet input.

The precise description of the logical input devices will be given later in this chapter. First, we must describe how they operate.

5.2 REQUEST MODE

As well as the type of input, we also need to specify when it takes place and under whose control. Discussion of styles of interaction will be deferred until Chapter 6. In this chapter, we will just use the type of input called *REQUEST mode* which corresponds almost identically to the type of input used in FORTRAN.

In a FORTRAN program, when a READ statement is executed, the FORTRAN program is suspended and waits for the input system to provide the values that have been requested. Execution of the FORTRAN program continues when the input system delivers the values to the FORTRAN program. Effectively, either the FORTRAN program or the input system is active but not both together. This corresponds directly to REQUEST mode in GKS. A program will REQUEST an input from a logical input device and will then wait while the logical input device takes over. Once the logical input device has obtained the required data, it returns it to the GKS program and effectively goes back to sleep. Either the GKS program is executing or the logical input device is active but never both together (in REQUEST mode).

One constraint this imposes is, of course, that never more than one logical input device can be active at a time. We shall see in Chapter 6 how the GKS program can be executed in modes whereby both it and the logical input devices are active at the same time and how GKS allows several logical input devices to be active together. However, while we are mainly concerned with the characteristics of the logical input devices themselves, we will restrict ourselves to describing these as they would be used in REQUEST mode. It is sufficient to say at this point that all logical input devices can be used in the other more versatile modes.

The form of the GKS function for REQUEST input is:

REQUEST XXX(WS, DV, ST, ...)

The XXX part of the function name defines the class of logical input device (LOCATOR, PICK etc) and the first two parameters specify the specific device of that class from which input is requested; WS specifies the workstation (see Chapter 7) on which the device is located and DV specifies which of the devices of the class it is. (It is possible to have more than one logical input device of a particular type.) The third parameter, ST, is a status indicator which returns information concerning how successful the logical device was in providing the requested values. It will be described in Chapter 6. In the next few sections, we will concentrate on the parameters specific to each logical input device.

5.3 LOCATOR

The LOCATOR logical input device returns a single position to the application program. The program can initiate this in REQUEST mode by calling the GKS function:

REQUEST LOCATOR(WS, DV, ST, NORMTR, XPOS, YPOS)

The REQUEST LOCATOR function returns a position (XPOS, YPOS) in world coordinates and a normalization transformation NORMTR which was used to map back from normalized device coordinates to world coordinates.

The LOCATOR logical input device obtains a position in NDC space from the physical device. It is possible that the picture being displayed has been constructed using a number of different window to viewport transformations. The logical input device identifies which viewport the position in NDC space lies within and uses this to transform the position back to world coordinates.

The example in Section 4.1, which repositioned the duck on the pond, could now use a LOCATOR device to define the position as follows:

```
         SET WINDOW(1, XWMIN, XWMAX, YWMIN, YWMAX)
         SET VIEWPORT(1, XVMIN, XVMAX, YVMIN, YVMAX)
         SELECT NORMALIZATION TRANSFORMATION(1)

100      CONTINUE
         REQUEST LOCATOR(WS, DV, ST, NT, X, Y)
         NEW FRAME
         DRAW BACKGROUND
         DRAW DUCK AT(X, Y)
         GOTO 100
```

It is assumed that the operator has specified a position within the viewport used to define the picture so that the value of NT returned is 1. Figure 5-1 shows what the operator might see. The position of the duck is defined by the top of its tail. In the left hand part of the figure, the new position is identified by the crosshairs. In the right part of the figure, the duck is redrawn at the new position specified. This same example could have been redefined using segments as was done in Chapter 4.

5.3.1 Several Viewports

Commonly, several normalization transformations are used by the program. For example, Figure 5-2 shows a picture where the duck is drawn in viewport 1 and the word QUIT is displayed in viewport 2. In this case, we would like the operator to be able to input a locator value in either viewport. If the locator input is in the upper viewport, the duck is drawn

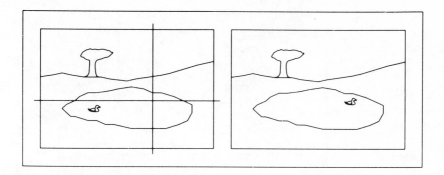

Figure 5-1

at the position defined by the locator whereas, if the locator input is in the lower viewport, this part of the program is completed and control is returned. Assuming window to viewport transformations have already been defined, where normalization transformation 1 is the upper and normalization transformation 2 is the lower, the program would be:

```
100    CONTINUE
       REQUEST LOCATOR(WS, DV, ST, NT, X, Y)
       IF(NT .EQ. 2) RETURN
       DRAW DUCK AT(X, Y)
       GOTO 100
```

5.3.2 Overlapping Viewports

So far, all the locator input examples assumed that the viewports did not overlap. However, there is no reason why viewports should not overlap. In fact, this always occurs as normalization transformation 0 is defined to map the unit square in world coordinates to the whole of the NDC space unit square (see Section 3.8). This ensures that there is always one viewport which a locator input lies within. In the case where two viewports overlap, we need to define which normalization transformation is used to determine the mapping from NDC back to world coordinates.

Consider an example (see Figure 5-3) in which viewport 1 is the area where the main picture is to be drawn. Viewport 2 is an area where a detail of the main picture is being drawn. Viewport 3 defines a set of options which can be identified by their Y coordinates. For example, the MOVE operation could be defined by specifying a position in either the detailed picture or the main one. As the detailed picture has a viewport which is also part of the main picture's viewport, it is unclear which viewport would be used for the transformation back to world coordinates.

Figure 5-2

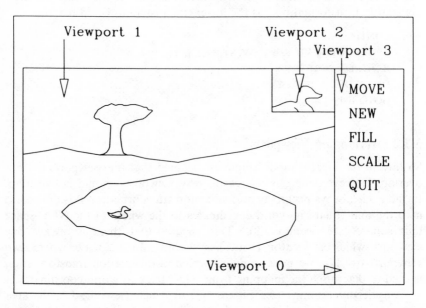

Figure 5-3

In GKS, this is decided by associating a *viewport input priority* with each transformation. If the input locator position lies within more than one viewport, the viewport with the *highest* viewport input priority is selected to perform the transformation back to world coordinates.

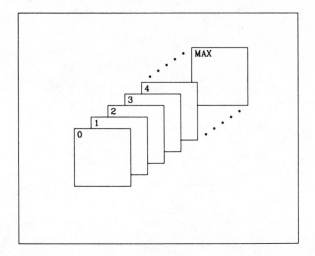

Figure 5-4

The viewport input priorities are initially set up as in Figure 5-4, where MAX is the maximum transformation number. As can be seen, normalization transformation 0 has the highest viewport input priority initially so that all locator inputs are returned in NDC coordinates until the viewport input priority is changed (thus our examples so far have not been strictly correct). To change the viewport input priorities, the following GKS function is provided:

SET VIEWPORT INPUT PRIORITY(TR1, TR2, HILO)

This defines the viewport input priority of transformation TR1 to be higher or lower than TR2 depending on the value of the parameter HILO. For example:

SET VIEWPORT INPUT PRIORITY(T1, T2, HIGHER)

moves transformation T1 to have a priority immediately above T2 (see Figure 5-5).
Similarly:

SET VIEWPORT INPUT PRIORITY(T1, T2, LOWER)

moves transformation T1 to have a priority immediately below T2 (see Figure 5-6). This method of associating viewport input priorities ensures that no two transformations have the same viewport input priority.

In our original example in Section 5.3, to ensure that the coordinate position giving the new position of the duck is returned in the coordinates of normalization transformation 1 rather than 0, we should have called:

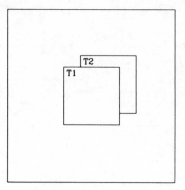

Figure 5-5

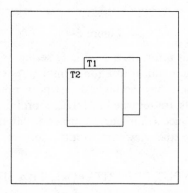

Figure 5-6

SET VIEWPORT INPUT PRIORITY(1, 0, HIGHER)

before entering the loop to input (X, Y) coordinate values. In the example in Figure 5-3, if the MOVE operation requires the (X, Y) position in the detailed drawing (normalization transformation 2) to take precedence over the main picture (normalization transformation 1), we would need to call:

SET VIEWPORT INPUT PRIORITY(2, 1, HIGHER)

Before either of these normalization transformations (or normalization transformation 3 for the menu) could be used, we would need to move all three viewports in front of viewport 0. This could be done by calling:

SET VIEWPORT INPUT PRIORITY(0, 3, LOWER)

This would leave the priority ordering as in Figure 5-7.

Figure 5-8, illustrates for this example, the different normalization transformations used to return locator values depending on which viewport the input is in and on the viewport input priorities derived above. In the first situation, the locator position would be returned in the world coordinates associated with normalization transformation 1 (the main picture) whereas, in the second situation, the position would be returned in the world coordinates associated with normalization transformation 2 (the detailed drawing). In the third situation, a position in the world coordinates associated with normalization transformation 3 would be returned. The lower right hand corner does not have a user specified normalization transformation associated with it and so, in the fourth situation, the locator position would be returned in world coordinates equivalent to normalized device coordinates (normalization transformation 0).

5.4 PICK

The PICK logical input device returns the name of a segment to the application program identifying the object that has been indicated by the pick device. The program can initiate this in REQUEST mode by calling

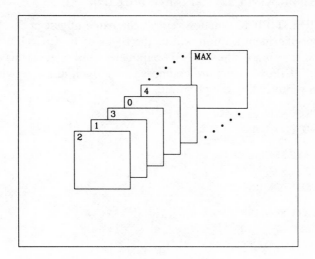

Figure 5-7

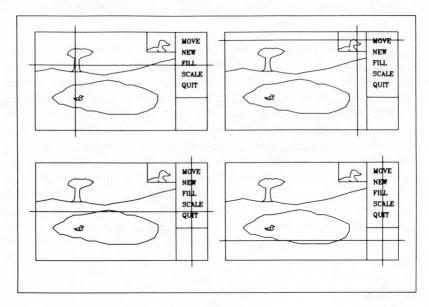

Figure 5-8

the GKS function:

REQUEST PICK(WS, DV, ST, SEG, PICKID)

The REQUEST PICK function returns the name of a segment, SEG, and a more specific identification within the segment by PICKID. We shall leave the discussion of the PICKID parameter until later in this section.

Figure 5-9 shows a picture composed of a duck and tree which could have been produced by the program:

```
LANDSCAPE
POND

CREATE SEGMENT(1)
TREE
CLOSE SEGMENT

CREATE SEGMENT(2)
DUCK
CLOSE SEGMENT
```

Consider the case where an operator wishes to perform an operation on one or other of the two objects in the picture. The program invites the operator to select which object by:

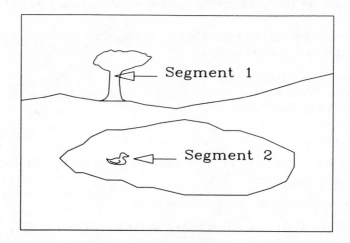

Figure 5-9

REQUEST PICK(WS, DV, ST, SEG, PICKID)

If SEG was set to 1 by the REQUEST PICK function, the tree has been
picked by the operator and, if set to 2, the duck has been picked. To
move either the duck or tree to a new position in NDC space, we could
define the program:

```
100    CONTINUE
       REQUEST PICK(WS, DV1, ST1, SEG, PICKID)
       REQUEST LOCATOR(WS, DV2, ST2, NT, X, Y)
       EVALUATE TRANSFORMATION MATRIX(0, 0, X, Y, 0, 1, 1, NDC, MAT)
       SET SEGMENT TRANSFORMATION(SEG, MAT)
       GOTO 100
```

The PICK input defines which object is to be moved. The REQUEST
LOCATOR function returns a position in NDC coordinates as the
viewport input priority has not been reset. The EVALUATE
TRANSFORMATION MATRIX function defines the move to be applied
to the segment by the SET SEGMENT TRANSFORMATION function.
Note that it is the point (0,0) in NDC of each segment in the initial situation that is moved to the new position.

5.4.1 Pick Identifier

The PICKID parameter returned by REQUEST PICK identifies the
operator's action more closely within the segment.

Suppose we have a diagram of a circuit board on the screen (see Figure 5-10).

To allow a particular connection to be identified, we could store each connection in a separate segment:

```
        DO 100 J = 1, JMAX
        CREATE SEGMENT(J)
        DRAW CONNECTION(J)
        CLOSE SEGMENT
100     CONTINUE
```

where **DRAW CONNECTION** is a subroutine to draw the *Jth* connection. Then, by calling:

        REQUEST PICK(WS, DV, ST, SEG, PICKID)

the number of the connection picked would be returned in SEG. However, for a typical circuit board, this would be a lot of segments and our local GKS may have only limited space for storing segments. An alternative is to use the *pick identifier* to give us a second level of naming. The pick identifier is specified by the function:

SET PICK IDENTIFIER(N)

Subsequent output primitives will have a pick identifier value of N associated with them until another call of SET PICK IDENTIFIER. For

Figure 5-10

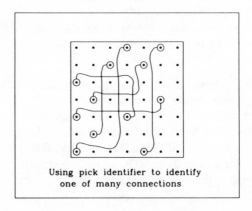

Using pick identifier to identify
one of many connections

Figure 5-10

example:

```
     CREATE SEGMENT(1)
     DO 100 J = 1, JMAX
     SET PICK IDENTIFIER(J)
     DRAW CONNECTION(J)
100  CONTINUE
     CLOSE SEGMENT
```

Each connection has a different pick identifier associated with it, so that if we call:

```
REQUEST PICK(WS, DV, ST, SEG, PICKID)
```

on return, SEG would contain a value of 1 indicating that one of the connecting wires, in segment 1, had been hit and the value of PICKID would indicate which one.

5.4.2 Segment Detectability

In Section 4.3, some segment attributes were described which affect the appearance of segments. There is a further segment attribute, *segment detectability*, which affects which segment is returned as a pick value. Segment detectability is set by the function:

SET DETECTABILITY(ID, DET)

where DET is the desired detectability and may take the values DETECTABLE and UNDETECTABLE. A segment may only be picked if it is detectable (that is, its detectability attribute has the value DETECTABLE). Since the default value is UNDETECTABLE, our examples so far have not been strictly correct as the detectability attribute for each segment should have been set to DETECTABLE. Thus, our example in Section 5.4, where we were moving the duck or tree, should have been preceded by:

```
SET DETECTABILITY(1, DETECTABLE)
SET DETECTABILITY(2, DETECTABLE)
```

to allow the duck and tree to be picked. If, subsequently, the call:

```
SET DETECTABILITY(2, UNDETECTABLE)
```

was obeyed, then segment 2 containing the duck would be made undetectable, in which case only the tree could be picked and moved. The duck could be made detectable again by resetting its detectability to DETECTABLE. Making a segment undetectable has no effect on its appearance.

However, if a segment is invisible, it is also impossible to pick it. This reflects the behaviour of a physical device like a lightpen which can only 'see' images that are visible. It is also reasonable that the only objects that can be picked, should be those that the operator can see.

5.5 CHOICE

The CHOICE logical input device returns an integer to the application program defining which of a number of possibilities has been chosen. The program can initiate this in REQUEST mode by calling the GKS function:

REQUEST CHOICE(WS, DV, ST, CH)

where CH returns the integer representing the choice. Figures 5-3 and 5-8 show examples where one of a set of actions has been chosen by displaying a set of words in a column and using a locator input to specify which of the words has been chosen to define the next operation. Although we have used locator input so far for this purpose, it would be more usual for this to be done using a CHOICE logical input device, particularly if the display in use had a lightpen associated with it. The actual realization of the CHOICE device on a physical device can vary quite significantly, from a menu hit by a lightpen, to a set of buttons to be pushed, to a name to be typed at a keyboard.

The example in Section 5.3.2 (Figure 5-3) could have consisted of two viewports 1 and 2 containing the main picture and the detailed view. A CHOICE device could have been defined which displayed the options on the right side of the screen. To decide the next action would require:

```
50    CONTINUE
      REQUEST CHOICE(WS, DV, ST, CH)
      GOTO(100, 200, 300, 400, 500), CH

100   MOVE OBJECT
      GOTO 50

200   DEFINE NEW OBJECT
      GOTO 50

300   FILL OBJECT
      GOTO 50

400   SCALE OBJECT
      GOTO 50

500   STOP
```

The exact method of specifying the options will be described fully in Chapter 9. Here, the subroutines, such as MOVE OBJECT, specify the action to be performed in each case.

5.6 VALUATOR

The VALUATOR logical input device returns a real value to the application program. The program can initiate this in REQUEST mode by calling the GKS function:

REQUEST VALUATOR(WS, DV, ST, VAL)

where VAL returns the real number that was input.

Clearly a single number could be input digit by digit from a keyboard without using a graphics system. However, if an interactive graphics system is in use, the operator can review the effect of a given input value without delay. If the operator does not know in advance what the best value is, then several values must be input, with the operator reviewing each in turn until the best value is obtained. If each successive value has to be input from a keyboard, the interactive dialogue is less likely to achieve an optimum value.

By contrast, REQUEST VALUATOR reads from whatever physical input hardware has been provided by a particular installation. Devices like dials can continuously provide values and graphical echoes can therefore always be up to date.

As an illustration of valuator input, we return to our flat footed friend and attempt to vary his size by valuator input. The program calls REQUEST VALUATOR, which in this instance displays a scale; the scale has marks for a minimum and a maximum and a movable current value. The movable current value is the echo for the operator input and provides an up to date indication of the current valuator value. Whenever the operator completes the input (possibly by pressing a button with the dial), the valuator value is used by our program to update the size of the duck. This continues repeatedly.

The program is as follows:

```
100    CONTINUE
       REQUEST VALUATOR(WS, DV, ST, SIZE)
       EVALUATE TRANSFORMATION MATRIX(FX, FY, 0, 0, 0, SIZE, SIZE,
          WC, MAT)
       SET SEGMENT TRANSFORMATION(DUCK, MAT)
       GOTO 100
```

It is assumed that scaling is about a fixed point (FX, FY) and DUCK is the name of the segment containing the drawing of the duck. A possible interaction sequence resulting from this program is shown in Figure 5-11. The movement of the scale is as continuous as the underlying computing system and graphics hardware allows. The duck only changes size when the operator terminates each request. In Figure 5-11, there are six

Figure 5-11

snapshots. In the first, the program has drawn the duck at a standard size. In the second, REQUEST VALUATOR is called which displays as an echo the scale on the right of the screen with the initial value marked. In the third snapshot, the operator changes the valuator to a new position (lower) on the scale. Note that the duck has not changed yet because REQUEST VALUATOR has not terminated yet. In the fourth snapshot, the operator terminates the request, the program regains control and the duck now changes size. The last two snapshots show another call to REQUEST VALUATOR, with a larger value being selected in the first and the resulting change in the size of the duck, once the REQUEST

VALUATOR has been completed, in the second.

The interaction could be improved if the duck was able to change size without the operator needing to press a button repeatedly. This can be achieved with SAMPLE input which is described in Chapter 6.

5.7 STRING

The STRING logical input device returns a character string to the application program. In most cases the string is echoed character by character somewhere on the display. Later (in Chapter 9), a means of controlling the position of the echo will be described. The program can initiate string input in REQUEST mode by calling the GKS function:

REQUEST STRING(WS, DV, ST, NCHARS, STR)

where STR returns the character string that was input and NCHARS returns the number of characters it contains.

String input is most often used for unknown text strings like choosing a filename or inputting a title. Selecting from a small number of strings already known to the application program, for example by using a menu, is actually closer to choice input and this usage is described later in Section 9.3.4.

5.8 STROKE

The last logical input device to be described, STROKE, returns a sequence of points to the application program, rather like a multiple locator. The program can initiate this in REQUEST mode by calling the GKS function:

REQUEST STROKE(WS, DV, PTSMAX, ST, NT, NPTS, X, Y)

An additional input parameter to the function is PTSMAX which specifies the maximum number of points that can be input by the STROKE device and effectively defines the storage available in the arrays X and Y. The STROKE input returns a sequence of positions in the arrays X and Y, from position 1 to position NPTS, and the normalization transformation NT used to transform the points back to world coordinates.

All points are transformed back using the same normalization transformation and lie within the window of that transformation. Viewport input priority is used to arbitrate between overlapping viewports in a way similar to locator input.

In Figure 5-12, if A, B, and C are three strokes input by the operator, stroke A (the pond) would be returned in viewport 1; stroke B (an enlarged view of the duck's beak) in viewport 2; and stroke C in viewport

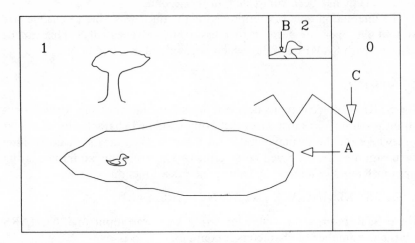

Figure 5-12

0. (Only viewport 0 contains the whole of stroke C and so it is used to transform the stroke back to world coordinates.)

If echoing is on, GKS echoes the individual points of the stroke as they are input. The echo, like the echoes of other logical input values, is intended to be ephemeral, disappearing when the input is complete, where possible on the selected hardware.

When the input is over, the points delivered by REQUEST STROKE can be redisplayed using POLYLINE:

```
REQUEST STROKE(WS, DV, PTSMAX, ST, NT, NPTS, X, Y)
SELECT NORMALIZATION TRANSFORMATION(NT)
POLYLINE(NPTS, X, Y)
```

The particular implementation of STROKE input may provide a means of sieving out unwanted points. For instance, a particular implementation of STROKE may only select points occurring at selected time intervals. The idea in this case is to capture the data describing the motion of the operator's input, not just the points passed through. This is useful in animation and signature recognition, but is impossible to achieve if the individual points are input with REQUEST LOCATOR.

5.9 A FULLER EXAMPLE OF REQUEST INPUT

This section consists of a single example which illustrates most of the logical input devices described in the chapter. It is part of an interactive program which allows the operator to control the drawing of a curve. Initially the operator inputs the points using a STROKE device. When that is done, the operator has the choice of changing the tension (tightness of fit) in the curve, selecting and moving the points, or finishing. Changing the tension is controlled by the real value returned by a VALUATOR device. In this case, it is not necessary to draw the points again, only the curve. To change the position of one of the points, it is necessary to pick one of them and then use the LOCATOR device to move it. In this case both the points and the curve are redrawn.

```
        TENSION = INITVALUE

        REQUEST STROKE(WS, DVS, PTSMAX, ST, NT, NP, X, Y)

10      CREATE SEGMENT(1)
        SET DETECTABILITY(1, DETECTABLE)
        DO 20 KEY = 1, NP
        SET PICK IDENTIFIER(KEY)
        POLYMARKER(1, X(KEY), Y(KEY))
20      CONTINUE
        CLOSE SEGMENT

30      CREATE SEGMENT(2)
        CURVE(TENSION, NP, X, Y)
        CLOSE SEGMENT

        REQUEST CHOICE(WS, DVC, ST, NCH)
        GOTO(100, 200, 300), NCH

100     REQUEST VALUATOR(WS, DVV, ST, TENSION)
        DELETE SEGMENT(2)
        GOTO 30

200     REQUEST PICK(WS, DVP, ST, SEG, PKID)
        REQUEST LOCATOR(WS, DVL, ST, NT, X(PKID), Y(PKID))
        DELETE SEGMENT(1)
        DELETE SEGMENT(2)
        GOTO 10

300     CONTINUE
```

6 Styles of Interaction

6.1 INTERACTION MODES

In Chapter 5, the different logical input devices were described using the REQUEST mode of input as an example. In this chapter, we will concentrate on the different modes of input available in GKS and show how they allow different styles of interaction to take place.

The interaction process, involving a logical input device, can be considered as taking place between two processes. One is the application program and the other is the input process, which looks after the input device and delivers data from this device to the application program. The relationship between these two processes can vary and, in so doing, will produce different styles of interaction which will affect the way that the operator sees the system. For example, a program may wish to read the operator's actions at any time or only at certain significant moments controlled by the operator.

The three operating modes of logical input devices specify who (the operator or the application program) has the initiative: SAMPLE input is acquired directly by the application program; REQUEST input is produced by the operator in direct response to the application program; EVENT input is generated asynchronously by the operator.

These three modes of interaction work as follows:

(1) *REQUEST mode*: the application program and input process work alternately. First the application program requests an input and then waits for a response. The input process is started up by the request, delivers the input data to the application program and returns to a wait state. One or other process is active but not both together.

(2) *SAMPLE mode*: the application program and input process are both active together. The application program is the dominant partner. The input process works in the background providing the latest input data from the device which may or may not be used by the application program. On the other hand, the application program continues executing, taking and using the current input data from a device when it requires it.

(3) *EVENT mode*: the application program and input process are again active together but the dominant partner is the input process. It delivers input data to the application program and expects the program to act, depending on the data received. The operator controls when input data is available and, effectively, drives the interaction.

As was stated in Chapter 5, all logical input devices can operate in each of the three modes. Of those in REQUEST mode, at most one can actually be responding to a request at one time. However, any number can be active in SAMPLE mode at the same time, while others can be active in EVENT mode. This provides a rich environment for interaction within GKS.

6.2 MODE SETTING

Each device can be in only one mode of operation at a time. The mode is selected by calling a function of the type:

SET LOCATOR MODE(WS, DV, MODE, EC)

As was mentioned in Section 5.2, the first two parameters define the specific device of that type from which input is required. The third parameter defines the mode of operation and can take one of the three values REQUEST, SAMPLE and EVENT. The last parameter EC can have one of two values, ECHO and NOECHO. If ECHO is selected, the operator will get some indication of the input data that is being entered to the program. For example, a string device might echo the keys hit on a keyboard, by allowing the characters that have been hit to be displayed on the screen at some position.

The default mode of operating for all devices is REQUEST mode. For this reason, the examples in the previous chapter did not need to have mode setting functions included in them. Also, the default situation is to have devices in the ECHO state.

6.3 REQUEST MODE

REQUEST mode was introduced in Section 5.2 and is described more precisely here. A program can only issue REQUESTs to a device when it is in the REQUEST operating mode. The exact form of the REQUEST function for each type of logical input device was given in Chapter 5. A typical example is:

REQUEST LOCATOR(WS, DV, STATUS, NORMTR, XPOS, YPOS)

The first three parameters are required for each device. As before, the first two define the specific device from which data is required while the third, STATUS, returns information concerning how successful the logical input device was in providing the requested data.

The call of REQUEST LOCATOR will cause the starting echo to appear on the screen, if echoing is selected. It will normally be apparent to the operator which physical device is to be used. The operator moves the physical device (rotates a trackerball, moves a tablet stylus) which adjusts the screen echo. When satisfied with the position of the echo, the operator can activate a trigger to signal that the input is complete. (The physical trigger may be a button or a key or even the tipswitch of a tablet stylus, depending upon the particular logical input device.) This is the normal way in which REQUEST LOCATOR terminates. Figure 6-1 shows one physical realization of what the operator sees. In the first of the five snapshots, no input is taking place. The picture of the duck is on the screen. An *unlit* button to the right of the screen shows that no button press is expected or required.

If the program now calls REQUEST LOCATOR, a pair of crosshairs appears as in the second snapshot to show that the locator input device is available. This is the *prompt*. The position of the crosshairs gives the initial value. The button is lit to show the operator that once he has moved the locator to the required position, he should press it to input the locator value.

The third snapshot shows how the operator has moved the physical device (possibly thumbwheels) to a new position and the crosshairs have moved *echoing* the operator's action.

If the operator presses the button, the locator position will be input. The cursor disappears and the button light goes out as in the fourth snapshot. This provides *acknowledgement* of the button press. REQUEST LOCATOR is now complete and the application program continues, reacting to the data input.

In the final snapshot, the program provides *feedback* to the operator by shifting the duck to the specified position. This will happen as fast as the system can allow. It is possible that the fourth snapshot picture is so transitory that it is not seen.

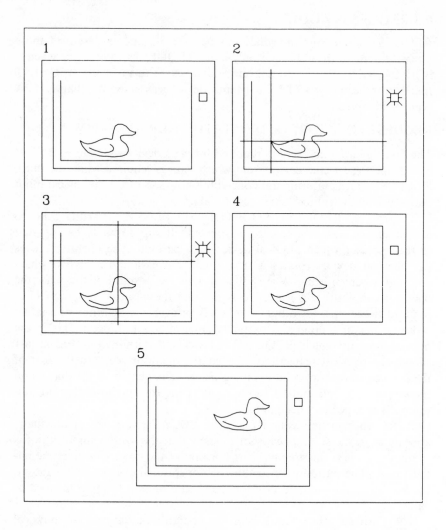

Figure 6-1

6.4 STATUS

The STATUS parameter is returned by each REQUEST function to indicate success or failure. STATUS can return with a value OK or NONE. The value OK means that the operator completed the input in the normal way, by activating a trigger and that the input data (transformation number and position in the case of locator) are valid.

If STATUS returns with the value NONE, the input data are invalid because the operator indicated a *break*. A break could be interpreted by the program as the end of a series of input values.

How the operator indicates a break depends on the input device. If the operator selects an invalid locator position, that could be interpreted as a break. Another way the operator can signal a break is to hit an alternative button. The device could have 2 buttons: one to signal normal completion, the other to signal a break.

An analogy in a non-graphics context is when an operator makes use of a facility on some operating systems to indicate an end-of-file on a terminal. If the operator does this, the contents of the input string are usually undefined.

In the animation example in Section 5.3 where REQUEST LOCATOR was illustrated, there was no way of terminating the loop. The status parameter provides a means of doing that. Instead of the loop shown in Section 5.3, we can write:

```
100   CONTINUE
      REQUEST LOCATOR(WS, DV, STATUS, NT, X, Y)
      IF(STATUS .EQ. NONE) GOTO 200
      NEW FRAME
      DRAW BACKGROUND
      DRAW DUCK AT(X, Y)
      GOTO 100

200   CONTINUE
```

The function REQUEST PICK can return a status reply other than OK and NONE. The operator could cause a pick input (by activating a trigger) when he is not pointing at a segment at all. In this case, the STATUS parameter returns with the value NOPICK.

Similarly, the function REQUEST CHOICE can also return a status reply NOCHOICE as well as OK or NONE. The logical input device provides a method by which the operator can cause this to be returned.

6.5 SAMPLE MODE

We have seen how making a REQUEST for input from an input device causes our program to be suspended until the operator chooses to make the input available. By contrast, *sampling* returns a value immediately without waiting for a trigger. Sampling works for any of the logical input devices, but first we illustrate it for LOCATOR. The device is first put into SAMPLE mode by calling the function:

SET LOCATOR MODE(WS, DV, SAMPLE, EC)

Unlike REQUEST mode, echoing begins immediately as the mode setting function starts up the input process to deliver values from the device.

To sample from the device requires the following function to be called:

SAMPLE LOCATOR(WS, DV, NT, X, Y)

Note that SAMPLE functions do not need to return a NONE status. Therefore only SAMPLE CHOICE and SAMPLE PICK have a status parameter, which can take the values OK or NOCHOICE and OK or NOPICK respectively. The SAMPLE function returns the current value of the locator device provided by the input process.

Rewriting the example in Section 5.3 but using SAMPLE mode, we would have:

```
    SET LOCATOR MODE(WS, DV, SAMPLE, ECHO)

100 CONTINUE
    SAMPLE LOCATOR(WS, DV, NT, X, Y)
    NEW FRAME
    DRAW BACKGROUND
    DRAW DUCK AT(X, Y)
    GOTO 100
```

Note that the style of interaction is rather different. As the operator moves the position of the locator, its value is sampled and the duck redrawn at that position. Consequently, the duck moves around as the locator position is changed, assuming that the redrawing speed is fast enough.

This differs significantly from the REQUEST mode where the operator moves the locator to a new position and activates the trigger before the picture is redrawn. The SAMPLE mode of interaction is much freer with the ability to respond in a more dynamic way to input from the operator.

One problem with the SAMPLE mode of input is that it does not have the status parameter to indicate that the input value is unavailable. As SAMPLE is a continuous process, there is always a last read value which is available. This means that it is not possible to break out of the loop in the above example by the operator indicating a break. One possibility would be to use the number of the normalization transformation to achieve the break. As the operator moves the locator within the viewport, the duck is redrawn. As soon as he moves outside the viewport, the interaction terminates:

```
       SET WINDOW(1, XMIN, XMAX, YMIN, YMAX)
       SET VIEWPORT(1, XVMIN, XVMAX, YVMIN, YVMAX)
       SELECT NORMALIZATION TRANSFORMATION(1)
       SET VIEWPORT INPUT PRIORITY(1, 0, HIGHER)

       SET LOCATOR MODE(WS, DV, SAMPLE, ECHO)

100    CONTINUE
       SAMPLE LOCATOR(WS, DV, NT, X, Y)
       IF(NT .EQ. 0) GOTO 200
       NEW FRAME
       DRAW BACKGROUND
       DRAW DUCK AT(X, Y)
       GOTO 100

200    CONTINUE
```

This is not a very good way to terminate the interaction as it is difficult to indicate a final position. A better way of doing this will be given after EVENT mode has been described (see Section 6.7).

SAMPLE mode has been demonstrated with a locator device, but a device of any input class can operate in SAMPLE mode. Let us consider the example in Section 5.6 (see Figure 5-11) where REQUEST input was used to change the size of the duck and redisplay it. The operator could not see the effect of any input until the trigger had been pressed to input the next value. Only at this time would the program redisplay the duck at the new size. SAMPLE removes this difficulty, in the same way as we have already achieved for locator. Also, we can sample more than one device at the same time. This is not possible with any REQUEST function, because, in that case, the program is suspended until the input is terminated.

In the following example, one valuator device controls the size of the duck and one its orientation.

```
       SET VALUATOR MODE(WS, DV1, SAMPLE, NOECHO)
       SET VALUATOR MODE(WS, DV2, SAMPLE, NOECHO)

100    CONTINUE
       SAMPLE VALUATOR(WS, DV1, SIZE)
       SAMPLE VALUATOR(WS, DV2, ROT)
       EVALUATE TRANSFORMATION MATRIX(FX, FY, 0, 0, ROT, SIZE, SIZE,
          WC, MAT)
       SET SEGMENT TRANSFORMATION(DUCK, MAT)
       GOTO 100
```

6.6 EVENT MODE

If an input device is put into EVENT mode, any input values are placed in the *input queue* for the application program to read. The application program reads each input value in order and deals with it before handling the next.

As the application program and input process are both active together, it is possible for the application program to look at the queue when no new inputs have been made. Alternatively, it is possible for the input device to fill the queue completely up before the application program examines it. The condition of input queue overflow is examined in more detail in Chapter 9.

Consequently, GKS needs functions to check the queue for events and to remove items from the queue.

It should be remembered that there is a single input queue for all devices. It is possible to have several devices active in EVENT mode at the same time. Input data from each device are added to the queue as they are generated, together with information indicating which device produced the input. The GKS function to check the queue is:

AWAIT EVENT(TIMEOUT, WS, DVCLASS, DV)

The queue is examined to see if it is empty. If it is, the application program is suspended until an event is generated or a maximum of TIMEOUT seconds have elapsed. In the latter case, DVCLASS returns the value NONE. TIMEOUT can be zero, in which case AWAIT EVENT always returns without suspending the application program.

If the queue is not empty, either when AWAIT EVENT is called or before the TIMEOUT occurs, information concerning the first event in the queue is returned. WS and DV specify the input device while DVCLASS specifies its input class (LOCATOR, PICK, etc). The input data are removed from the queue and transferred to the *current event report*.

Once it is known that an event has occurred from a particular class of device, the appropriate GET function is called to read the input data from the current event report. To read locator input data, the function:

GET LOCATOR(NT, X, Y)

is used, where NT is the transformation number and (X, Y) is the position. Note that it is only necessary to return the data values specific to the device. The class of device from which the data originated is known from the information returned by the call to AWAIT EVENT.

Let us consider a simple example where an operator uses a single locator device to input a set of positions defining a polyline. Each locator position that is input is indicated by a marker. The operator indicates that he has completed the polyline by inputting a position in a small top region of the screen. At this stage, the polyline will be drawn through the sequence of marked points that have been input (see Figure 6-2). The program might be:

```
SET WINDOW(1, XMIN, XMAX, YMIN, YMAX)
SET VIEWPORT(1, 0, 1, 0, 0.8)
SET WINDOW(2, X2MIN, X2MAX, Y2MIN, Y2MAX)
SET VIEWPORT(2, 0, 1, 0.8, 1)
SET VIEWPORT INPUT PRIORITY(0, 2, LOWER)
SELECT NORMALIZATION TRANSFORMATION(1)
SET LOCATOR MODE(WS, DV, EVENT, ECHO)
NPTS = 0
```

```
100   CONTINUE
      AWAIT EVENT(6000, WST, CLASS, DEV)
      GET LOCATOR(NT, X(1), Y(1))
      IF(NT .EQ. 2) GOTO 200
      NPTS = NPTS + 1
      XLIST(NPTS) = X(1)
      YLIST(NPTS) = Y(1)
      POLYMARKER(1, X, Y)
      GOTO 100
```

```
200   IF(NPTS .GE. 2) POLYLINE(NPTS, XLIST, YLIST)
```

As there is only a single device active, any input data must be from the

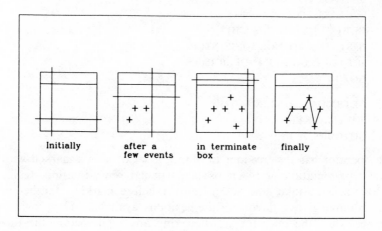

Figure 6-2

locator specified by WS and DV. Consequently, it has been assumed that the values of WST and DEV returned have these values. Similarly, it is assumed that CLASS has the value LOCATOR when an input is received. The only other possibility is NONE but we have set the TIMEOUT value very high so that the operator is bound to have input a value before the timeout occurs. Of course, a more precise program would do all the necessary checks.

This simple example does not really show the power of EVENT mode over REQUEST mode. The particular strength of EVENT mode is if the operator has a number of devices under his control or if the application program has other things to do between accepting events (like controlling a power station).

An example showing how more than one device can be used in EVENT mode illustrates the power of this type of input. Suppose we wish to input a number of points to be marked on the screen by one of several different representations. The particular representation can be selected using a CHOICE device. The representation selected will be used for all subsequent points input until another representation is selected:

```
      SET POLYMARKER INDEX(1)

      SET LOCATOR MODE(WS, DV1, EVENT, ECHO)
      SET CHOICE MODE(WS, DV2, EVENT, ECHO)

100   CONTINUE
      AWAIT EVENT(600, WST, CLASS, DEV)
      IF(CLASS .EQ. NONE) STOP
      IF(CLASS .EQ. LOCATOR) GOTO 200
      GET CHOICE(STATUS, CH)
      IF(STATUS .EQ. NOCHOICE) STOP
      SET POLYMARKER INDEX(CH)
      GOTO 100

200   GET LOCATOR(NT, X(1), Y(1))
      POLYMARKER(1, X, Y)
      GOTO 100
```

The operator has the freedom to output a set of points marked with the same representation or to choose a particular representation, realize he had made a mistake, and select another before marking another point. This example gives a flavour of the flexibility available. The program terminates when the operator stops making any input before the timeout expires, or makes no selection with the CHOICE device.

A third GKS function exists to provide a housekeeping function on the queue. It is feasible for the operator to input more than one value from a device when only one was required by the program. In GKS, the following function exists to remove all unwanted input from the queue:

FLUSH DEVICE EVENTS(WS, DVCLASS, DV)

When called, it removes all inputs in the queue from the device whose class is DVCLASS and which is specified by WS and DV.

6.7 MIXED MODES

In Section 6.5, we saw how to achieve a much smoother interaction using SAMPLE mode rather than REQUEST mode. In the example, the duck moved around as the locator position was changed rather than waiting for the operator to indicate that the duck should be redrawn at a particular new position as happens with REQUEST mode. We also saw, however, that it was rather clumsy to terminate this style of interaction as it was impossible to indicate that an input value was unavailable. The solution suggested was to use a different normalization transformation but this necessitated moving the duck outside the viewport of the normalization transformation being used. This is not a natural termination and, in any case, makes it difficult to indicate a final position for the duck.

We can provide a much more elegant solution to the problem if we use a second input device in EVENT mode to indicate the end of the interaction. A button could be pressed or a key could be hit. In either case, this could be done using a choice device having a single choice, but any choice device would suffice. Thus:

```
        SET LOCATOR MODE(WS, DV1, SAMPLE, ECHO)
        SET CHOICE MODE(WS, DV2, EVENT, NOECHO)

100     CONTINUE
        SAMPLE LOCATOR(WS, DV1, NT, X, Y)
        NEW FRAME
        DRAW BACKGROUND
        DRAW DUCK AT(X, Y)
        AWAIT EVENT(0, WST, CLASS, DEV)
        IF(CLASS .NE. CHOICE) GOTO 100

        FLUSH DEVICE EVENTS(WS, CHOICE, DV2)
```

Now, the duck will move around as the locator position is changed, assuming that the redrawing speed is fast enough, and when the desired position is achieved the operator may press the appropriate button or key to stop the process.

In this example, any choice value will suffice so that an event occurring will be taken as the terminating condition. To make sure that the sampling is not held up, we have used a timeout value of zero so that the application program continues to sample the locator immediately without waiting. Until the button is pressed, the CLASS value returned will be NONE.

We have used FLUSH DEVICE EVENTS just in case the operator pressed the button twice by accident and, therefore, left an extra event in the queue.

We may use a mixture of input devices in different modes for a more complex example. Suppose we wish the operator to define an area by use of a locator device and we wish to provide him with an up to date echo of the currently defined area. GKS does not provide such an echo and so we must provide the echo from the application program (this is called feedback). In the example, the operator moves a point around using a locator device, and the application program displays the current area, as feedback. When the operator is satisfied with that point he presses the key corresponding to the first choice. In a similar manner, he then uses the locator to decide on the next point pressing the key when he is satisfied. When he is satisfied with the complete area he presses the key corresponding to the second choice. If the operator indicates NOCHOICE, that is ignored. Thus:

```
      SET LOCATOR MODE(WS, DV1, REQUEST, ECHO)
      REQUEST LOCATOR(WS, DV1, ST, NT, XAR(1), YAR(1))
      NP = 1

      SET LOCATOR MODE(WS, DV1, SAMPLE, ECHO)
      SET CHOICE MODE(WS, DV2, EVENT, NOECHO)
      CREATE SEGMENT(AREA)
      CLOSE SEGMENT

100   CONTINUE
      NP = NP + 1
      XAR(NP + 1) = XAR(1)
      YAR(NP + 1) = YAR(1)

200   CONTINUE
      SAMPLE LOCATOR(WS, DV1, NT, XAR(NP), YAR(NP))
      DELETE SEGMENT(AREA)
      CREATE SEGMENT(AREA)
      FILL AREA(NP + 1, XAR, YAR)
      CLOSE SEGMENT
      AWAIT EVENT(0, WST, CLASS, DEVICE)
      IF(CLASS .NE. CHOICE) GOTO 200
```

```
GET CHOICE(STATUS, CH)
IF(STATUS .EQ. NOCHOICE) GOTO 200
IF(CH .EQ. 1) GOTO 100

FLUSH DEVICE EVENTS(WS, CHOICE, DV2)
```

Figure 6-3 illustrates the situation when the operator is choosing the fifth point of the area. As we wish to display the current area, we have put the fill area in a segment. This allows us to delete the old area each time round the sampling loop.

Once again, we have used FLUSH DEVICE EVENTS to remove any extra unwanted events remaining in the queue.

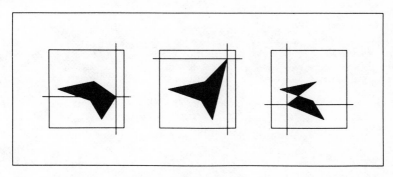

Figure 6-3

7 Workstations

7.1 INTRODUCTION

It is time for us to consider the problems that arise when we start to think about output appearing on real devices. So far the description has considered virtual devices. The application program has been able to specify output in terms of world coordinate systems which have been mapped on to a hypothetical or normalized device having a display surface with a range 0 to 1 in both the X and Y directions. For output primitives of the same type, it is possible to differentiate between primitives by associating different primitive indices with specific primitives. The realization of how these primitives are differentiated on real devices has not been discussed.

This splitting of the description of GKS into two parts in this book - a virtual part followed by a description of how this relates to real devices - closely parallels the philosophy of GKS itself. In GKS, there is a clear distinction between the part of the program which defines a graphical application in a virtual or device independent way and the part which describes how the program will be interfaced to the devices available for an operator at a particular installation.

Let us consider an example to illustrate the picture composition on normalized device coordinate space so far. The scene to be generated consists of a house, tree and duck each of which is defined with its own coordinate system. We will use the array of data points defined in Chapter 2 to describe the duck. An array for describing the tree would be:

```
REAL XT(58), YT(58)
DATA XT/14,18,21,23,24,25,25,23,19,16,13,10,8,9,11,12,15,18,20,
   22,24,26,28,30,33,37,38,42,46,50,54,57,59,62,63,64,67,68,67,
   65,63,61,58,53,50,48,45,42,39,37,36,35,35,36,37,38,40,42/
DATA YT/10,11,13,16,19,40,43,44,45,47,50,50,52,55,58,60,62,64,65,
   65,66,67,66,65,66,66,65,65,66,66,65,64,63,63,61,60,60,59,58,
   56,54,52,50,49,48,47,46,45,44,42,40,35,30,20,15,12,11,10/
```

A house with a window and a door could be defined by:

```
REAL XHS(6), YHS(6), XWN(5), YWN(5), XDR(5), YDR(5)
DATA XHS/1,1,5,9,9,1/
DATA YHS/0,6,9,6,0,0/
DATA XWN/3,3,7,7,3/
DATA YWN/4,6,6,4,4/
DATA XDR/4,4,6,6,4/
DATA YDR/0,3,3,0,0/
```

Composing the picture in NDC space can be done by:

```
SET WINDOW(1, 0, 30, 0, 20)
SET VIEWPORT(1, 0.25, 0.55, 0.05, 0.25)
SET WINDOW (2, 0, 70, 0, 70)
SET VIEWPORT (2, 0.05, 0.4, 0.05, 0.4)
SET WINDOW(3, 0, 10, 0, 10)
SET VIEWPORT(3, 0.55, 0.9, 0.05, 0.75)

SELECT NORMALIZATION TRANSFORMATION(1)
SET POLYLINE INDEX(1)
DUCK

SELECT NORMALIZATION TRANSFORMATION(2)
SET POLYLINE INDEX(2)
POLYLINE(58, XT, YT)

SELECT NORMALIZATION TRANSFORMATION(3)
SET POLYLINE INDEX(1)
POLYLINE(6, XHS, YHS)
SET POLYLINE INDEX(2)
POLYLINE(5, XWN, YWN)
SET POLYLINE INDEX(3)
POLYLINE(5, XDR, YDR)
```

The polyline index settings are such that the duck and house outline are drawn with polyline index 1, the tree and house window with polyline index 2, and the house door with polyline index 3. Schematically, the picture is composed as shown in Figure 7-1.

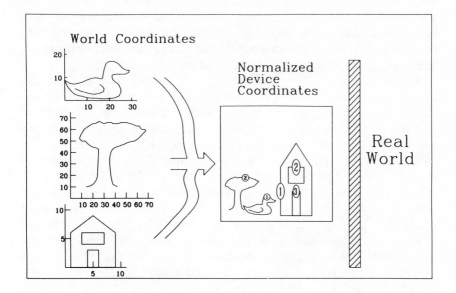

Figure 7-1

Labels have been added to the polylines to indicate the polyline index associated with each one. We must now consider how the picture that has been composed can be viewed or output to a real device and what will be the appearance of the various polylines on the display or plotter.

On the input side, the application program receives logical input values of one of the types LOCATOR, STROKE, VALUATOR, CHOICE, PICK and STRING, which are associated with the picture composed in NDC space and, thence, the parts of the picture specified in world coordinates. Again, nothing has been said so far as to how these logical input values are derived from devices in the real world.

7.2 WORKSTATIONS

GKS has been defined so that it is equally applicable as a graphic system in a wide range of different environments. In graphics today, there is a wide range of devices on the market for input and output. Depending on whether the application environment is simple or complex, an operator may be working on a single device or using a number of devices. For example, GKS might be used to off-line graphical output to a remote plotter or it might be used in a very simple interactive mode at a storage tube, with text commands at the keyboard causing pictures to be displayed on the screen. At the other end of the spectrum, an operator may have a refresh display with lightpen, tablet, keyboard and button box together with a small plotter and large digitizer to provide a sophisticated workbench for a CAD application. The aim in GKS is that all these environments should be catered for in a similar way while still allowing the application program to make best use of both the total environment available and the specific characteristics of each device.

Rather than consider individual input or output devices, GKS has introduced the concept of a *workstation,* which in simple environments closely approximates to the display and associated input peripherals attached to a single line to the computer. Considering first a workstation capable of input and output, its main characteristic is that it can only have a single *display surface* for graphical output. However, it may have a number of real input devices associated with it. Thus, for example, a storage tube with keyboard and thumbwheels would be regarded as a workstation in GKS. It is not necessary, however, for a workstation to be capable of both output and input. Consequently, both digitizers and plotters can be regarded as workstations in their own right. They are called INPUT and OUTPUT workstations respectively. Workstations capable of doing both output and input are called OUTIN workstations. OUTPUT, INPUT and OUTIN are referred to as workstation *categories.*

If an operator has a complex workbench involving a pair of displays or a display and plotter, this environment cannot be described to GKS as a single workstation. Instead it is described as several workstations clustered together under the control of one operator and one application program. It is therefore necessary in GKS to allow several workstations to be used together.

The definition of GKS workstations will depend to a large extent on the devices available at a particular installation. It is envisaged that each site will have an installation manager who will provide a handbook indicating the *types* of workstation available, the category that they belong to, and their location. It is possible that the same device may be configured as part of more than one workstation type. It is up to the local installation to provide GKS with the necessary information concerning the devices available. Normally, the user will not need to worry about this but he will need to know the workstation types (and their categories) and devices available. A typical installation might have a variety of devices available in which case a possible entry in the *installation handbook* is given in Table 7-1.

It should be noticed that the storage tube can be used in three different modes. In the simplest mode, the thumbwheels would not be used and it is practically an output only workstation except that keyboard input can be used to control the program. In the second mode, it can be used effectively with the thumbwheels being used for locator input etc. In the third mode, a tablet is attached which allows more flexibility in the way a

WS Type	WS Category	WS Description	Location	Device Coordinates	Logical Devices Supported
1	OUTIN	Storage Tube or raster look alike with use of keyboard input only	Many located around site	1024 × 780	All
2	OUTIN	Storage Tube with full use of keyboard and thumbwheels	Many located around site	4096 × 3120	All
3	OUTIN	Storage Tube with tablet attached	Two systems in X Terminal Pool	4096 × 3120	All
4	OUTIN	Vector Refresh Displays	Available at A, B, C Locations	1024 × 1024	All
5	OUTPUT	Central Plotter	Computer Room	1000 × 5000	None
6	OUTPUT	Portable Pen Plotters	On loan from Pool	2000 × 2000	None
7	INPUT	Digitizers	Available at locations A and B	16384 × 16384	LOCATOR CHOICE STROKE
8	OUTIN	Colour Raster Display	In location A only	512 × 512	All
9	OUTIN	Vector Refresh Displays	Available at A and B (used with digitizer)	1024 × 1024	PICK VALUATOR STRING

Table 7-1

logical device such as a STROKE device can be implemented.

7.3 WORKSTATION SELECTION

Each program must identify the workstation that it is going to use, indicate the type of each one, describe how it is connected to the computer and identify when it is in use. If several workstations are used together, they will most likely be connected to the computer over different lines. Similarly, a single workstation is likely to have a single connection to the computer. The channel to be used by the computer will normally be defined by some operating system command and there is likely to be some convention concerning channels that can be used for input and output.

The function used for specifying that a particular workstation is to be used is:

OPEN WORKSTATION(WS, CONNECTID, WSTYP)

The first parameter, WS, is the workstation identifier, which specifies the number to be used by the program to identify the workstation. CONNECTID specifies the channel that the operating system will use for communication to the workstation. WSTYP defines the workstation type of this particular workstation. For example:

OPEN WORKSTATION(1, 6, 3)

This defines the workstation to be the one identified as 1 by the program. It is connected to channel 6 and has a workstation type of 3 indicating (in our example installation) that it is a storage tube with a tablet attached.

As the operator may be provided with several workstations to complete the task, the OPEN WORKSTATION function may be called several times with different WS values. For example, adding:

OPEN WORKSTATION(2, 5, 6)

indicates that a second device is available to the operator which is a portable pen plotter connected to channel 5 via a separate line.

So far, the workstations to be used have been defined but neither has been activated. Consequently, if some output primitives were created, GKS would exit with an error indicating that no workstations are active. To activate a workstation so that it receives output, the function:

ACTIVATE WORKSTATION(WS)

is called. From the time that a workstation is activated, all output is sent to the device for display. It is possible for several workstations to be active together in which case they will all receive the graphical output. As the program executes, workstations may be activated and deactivated so that only some fraction of the complete output appears on each workstation. The function to deactivate a workstation is:

DEACTIVATE WORKSTATION(WS)

Before creating output, it is necessary to define a function which moves to the next frame on film or to the next sheet in the plotter or clears the screen of a display. Such a function might always perform this action or might only perform it when necessary. For example, on film it is often necessary to know precisely how many frames are generated or to include a precise number of blank frames. Conversely, it is sensible to move to the next sheet on the plotter only if the previous sheet has been used. GKS provides both these alternatives with the function:

CLEAR WORKSTATION(WS, FLAG)

where FLAG may take the values CONDITIONALLY and ALWAYS. If FLAG has the value CONDITIONALLY, the film is advanced or the screen cleared only if something has been drawn. If FLAG has the value ALWAYS, the film is always advanced or the screen is always cleared even if nothing has been drawn.

It should be noted that this function has side effects if segments have been stored on the workstation (see Section 7.10).

As an example of the functions described in this section, the program below outputs a set of frames to the first workstation while only outputting every 10th frame to the second workstation.

```
OPEN WORKSTATION(1, 6, 3)
OPEN WORKSTATION(2, 5, 6)

ACTIVATE WORKSTATION(1)

DO 100 I = 1, 200
J = MOD(I, 10)
READ COORDS(X, Y)
IF(J .EQ. 0) ACTIVATE WORKSTATION(2)
POLYLINE(15, X, Y)
CLEAR WORKSTATION(1, ALWAYS)
IF(J .EQ. 0) CLEAR WORKSTATION(2, CONDITIONALLY)
IF(J .EQ. 0) DEACTIVATE WORKSTATION(2)
100    CONTINUE
```

READ COORDS reads in a set of X,Y coordinates. At the end of the program, any workstation still active should be deactivated and all the workstations should be closed down. The function to close a workstation is:

CLOSE WORKSTATION(WS)

Thus the above program should be terminated by:

```
DEACTIVATE WORKSTATION(1)
CLOSE WORKSTATION(1)
CLOSE WORKSTATION(2)
```

This will ensure that all output has been transferred to the device and that a hygenic disconnection is made from the channels in use.

7.4 WORKSTATION TRANSFORMATIONS

The section above defines when output may be sent to a workstation and, therefore, to its associated display screen. As has been described in the introduction to this chapter, a picture has been composed in NDC space and it must be output to the active workstations. The simplest approach would have been to insist that all devices viewed the whole of the NDC space within the unit square. This is what happens by default. However, there are distinct advantages if some control is allowed over what part of NDC space is to be seen on a particular device.

A good method of visualizing what is going on is to use the analogy of a camera focussed on the normalized device coordinate space. Each workstation can focus on a specific part of the complete square and can zoom in or out. Consequently, only a part of the output to NDC space may appear on a display screen.

This is shown schematically in Figure 7-2. In this example, the first workstation is focussed on the trunk of the tree while the second is focussed on the house. The method of defining which part of NDC space is to appear on the workstation is very similar to the way positioning of output on NDC space is achieved. A *workstation window to viewport mapping* defines which part of NDC space will be seen at the workstation and

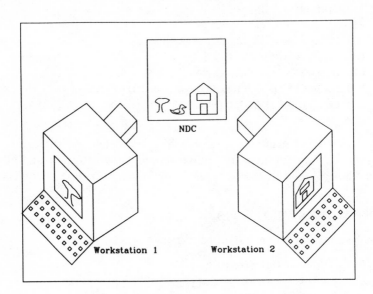

Figure 7-2

where it will appear on the display screen. The two functions used are:

SET WORKSTATION WINDOW(WS, XNMIN, XNMAX,
    YNMIN, YNMAX)
SET WORKSTATION VIEWPORT(WS, XDMIN, XDMAX,
    YDMIN, YDMAX)

The SET WORKSTATION WINDOW function specifies that area of the NDC space in the range 0 to 1 which will be output to workstation WS. The window is specified in NDC coordinates.

The SET WORKSTATION VIEWPORT function defines where on the display screen the view of NDC space will appear. The viewport is specified in the appropriate device coordinates.

However, unlike normalization transformations, there is only one workstation transformation (per workstation) which is used for the whole picture. If the workstation transformation is changed, the whole picture is displayed with the new transformation. This may have side effects as explained in Section 7.11.

There is a major difference between the normalization transformations used to compose the picture in NDC space and the workstation transformation defined above to view the picture on the display. Whereas the normalization transformation allows differential scaling, this is not the case for the workstation transformation. In our example (see Figure 7-1), the house is elongated in the Y direction as it is defined in NDC space by the normalization transformation. Such possibilities are not available at the workstation level where the aspect ratio of the display in NDC space must be the same as how it appears on the device screen.

This raises the question of what happens if the aspect ratio of the workstation window and viewport are defined differently. In this case, the complete window is displayed on the device in the correct aspect ratio using a rectangle with its bottom left corner equal to the bottom left corner of the viewport specified and as large as possible. Some examples in Figure 7-3 show viewports used when the window and viewport have different aspect ratios. To avoid confusion, it is good practice to always specify the workstation window and viewport with the same aspect ratio.

Default settings are available for each workstation and, if not changed, these will map the whole unit square of NDC space on to the largest square on the device with the lower left hand corner of NDC space at the lower left hand corner of the display screen. Specific default settings, for different display aspect ratios are shown in Figure 7-4.

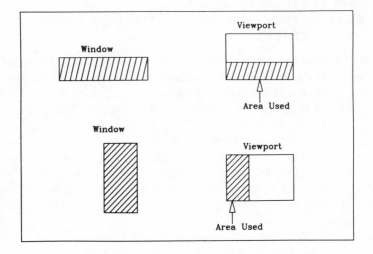

Figure 7-3

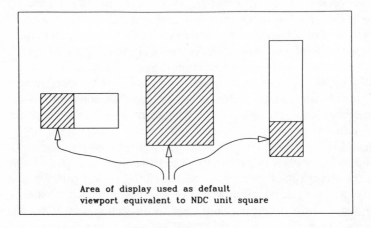

Figure 7-4

7.5 POLYLINE REPRESENTATION

The example in Section 7.1 shows polyline primitives used to compose a picture in NDC space and indicates the polyline index for each primitive. Polylines with different index values associated with them should be displayed in differentiable ways on the actual devices of workstations.

This section describes how this is done.

For polylines, GKS identifies three aspects that a workstation could use to differentiate between polylines - linetype, linewidth and colour. A particular workstation may use one of these aspects or a combination to ensure that polylines with different index values are differentiated on its display. As not all these possibilities may exist on a particular workstation, it is up to the application program to define the mapping unless the defaults provided by the local installation are accepted.

For each polyline index value, its representation on a particular workstation is defined by the function:

SET POLYLINE REPRESENTATION(WS, PLI, LT, LW, PLCI)

The WS parameter specifies the workstation in question and PLI specifies which polyline index is being defined. The three other parameters specify the representation associated with the polyline index PLI:

LT specifies the *linetype,* for which the standardized values are:

1 solid line
2 dashed line
3 dotted line
4 dashed - dotted line

Other values of the parameter may also be used to select other linetypes allowed on this type of workstation. Values higher than 4 are the subject of registration. These values do not appear in the GKS standard, but will be allocated by the ISO Registration Authority. Any of the registered values can be supported by a workstation, but must have the meaning that has been registered. Negative values of the parameter may be defined by the local installation to give other linetypes allowed on this type of workstation. Later in this book, there will be other instances of parameter values being the subject of registration.

LW specifies the *linewidth scale factor:* this is a real number giving the width of the line relative to the width of a standard line on this device. Values less than 1 specify lines thinner than the standard line. For example, a value of 0.5 defines a line half the thickness of a standard line on the device while a value of 2 defines a line with twice the thickness of a standard line. The workstation will use the closest available linewidth to the specified one.

PLCI specifies the *polyline colour index:* this does not define a colour directly but instead points to a colour table for the workstation where the colours are actually specified as RGB intensity values. For pen plotters, it will be usual for the colour table to be set up for the workstation by the installation manager. For example:

COLOUR INDEX	COLOUR PEN
0	White
1	Black
2	Red
3	Blue
4	Green
5	Yellow
6	Orange
7	Brown
8	Grey

For colour displays, it is possible for the entries in the table to be changed as will be seen later.

If workstations 1 and 2 were active and specified to be of types 3 (storage tube) and 6 (portable plotter with several pen colours) respectively, the picture in NDC space could have its form on the workstation controlled by:

    SET POLYLINE REPRESENTATION(1, 1, 1, 1, 1)
    SET POLYLINE REPRESENTATION(1, 2, 3, 1, 1)
    SET POLYLINE REPRESENTATION(1, 3, 2, 1, 1)
    SET POLYLINE REPRESENTATION(2, 1, 1, 1, 2)
    SET POLYLINE REPRESENTATION(2, 2, 1, 1, 4)
    SET POLYLINE REPRESENTATION(2, 3, 1, 1, 3)

If colour is unavailable on a device, it is usual for colour index 1 to indicate the natural colour for the display.

In the example, the three different polyline representations will be output on the storage tube as solid, dotted and dashed lines, respectively, while their appearance on the pen plotter will be as red, green and blue lines. GKS has the aim of differentiating the different polyline index values on all devices thus providing true device independence. If necessary, the user can define the representations corresponding to the index values so that they appear as nearly the same as possible on all devices being used. However, this is only one of the possibilities open to the user. GKS gives the user the opportunity to define the mapping, unlike many systems where the mapping is made within the system.

An expert user defining a system to run with several workstations in use at a time may need to take quite a bit of time specifying the appearance of primitives on each workstation. However, it can be seen that the description of the graphics program in terms of the virtual world defines one part of the system and this can be kept quite independent of the other part defining the realization of the system on particular devices available at an installation.

7.6 COLOUR TABLE

For a colour display, it is possible to redefine the entries in the *colour look up table* pointed at by the *colour index*. Each entry in the table consists of:

COLOUR	RED	GREEN	BLUE
INDEX	INTENSITY	INTENSITY	INTENSITY

The intensity values are specified in the range 0 to 1. Particular entries in the table can be redefined by:

SET COLOUR REPRESENTATION(WS, CI, RED, GREEN, BLUE)

where CI is the colour index and RED, GREEN and BLUE specify the respective intensities. For a raster display with an internal colour table, this command would alter its colour table. For a pen plotter, it would cause the pen with the nearest colour to this value to be used when the colour index was specified.

On a raster display, it is also possible to alter the background colour, that is the colour of the display surface before anything is drawn. For a pen plotter, it may be possible to specify the colour of the paper to be used. Entry 0 in the colour table (that is, the entry corresponding to a colour index value of 0) defines the colour of the background. On those devices, where the background colour cannot be changed, attempting to redefine the representation of colour index 0 will have no effect.

To set the first five entries of the colour table for WS2 to black (background colour), white, yellow, green and blue would require:

        SET COLOUR REPRESENTATION(WS2, 0, 0, 0, 0)
        SET COLOUR REPRESENTATION(WS2, 1, 1, 1, 1)
        SET COLOUR REPRESENTATION(WS2, 2, 1, 1, 0)
        SET COLOUR REPRESENTATION(WS2, 3, 0, 1, 0)
        SET COLOUR REPRESENTATION(WS2, 4, 0, 0, 1)

It should be noted when other primitives are described that there is a single colour table for each workstation. If polyline index values and text index values use the same colour index in their representation, the same colour will be used as they both point to the same colour table.

7.7 POLYMARKER REPRESENTATION

The aspects of the polymarker primitive controlled by the workstation via the polymarker index are defined by the function:

SET POLYMARKER REPRESENTATION(WS, PMI, MT, MS, PMCI)

In a similar way to polyline, WS specifies the particular workstation and PMI specifies which polymarker index is being defined. PMCI is the *polymarker colour index*, which is treated in the same way as the polyline colour index.

MT specifies the *marker type*, which defines the form of the marker to be displayed. The standard marker types are:

Marker Type	Marker Form
1	.
2	+
3	*
4	0
5	×

The first marker type defines the smallest displayable point while the other markers have a size that is workstation dependent. Marker types greater than 5 may be allocated marker shapes by the ISO Registration Authority in a similar way to linetypes. Negative values may access non-standard and non-registered marker shapes.

MS specifies the *marker size scale factor*, which is a real number giving the size of the marker relative to the workstation standard marker size. A value of 2 will specify a marker twice as large while 0.5 will specify one half the normal size. The workstation will output markers as close to this size as possible.

7.8 FILL AREA REPRESENTATION

The aspects of the fill area primitive controlled by the workstation via the fill area index are defined by the function:

SET FILL AREA REPRESENTATION(WS, FAI, IS, SI, FACI)

where, as usual, WS specifies the workstation and FAI and FACI specify the fill area index and fill area colour index. IS and SI specify the fill area interior style and the fill area style index.

Chapter 2 has described FILL AREA. A set of coordinates define the outline of the area to be filled. The method of filling the area is defined in NDC space by the fill area index. Individual workstations will attempt to differentiate between fill area primitives with different index values by giving them different representations.

The possible values for the *fill area interior style* are HOLLOW, SOLID, PATTERN and HATCH. The *fill area style index* only has meaning for the interior styles PATTERN and HATCH.

HOLLOW will cause the boundary to be drawn in a colour defined by the colour index. SOLID will cause the interior to be completely covered using the colour selected via the colour index specified.

PATTERN will shade the area by repeating a pattern, using the size and positioning defined in a workstation independent way by the pattern size and pattern reference point attributes. These attributes are set by the respective functions:

SET PATTERN SIZE(SX, SY)
SET PATTERN REFERENCE POINT(PX, PY)

where SX and SY are the size of each instance of the pattern in the X and Y directions and PX and PY are the coordinates of the pattern reference point. Note that for this interior style the colour index is not used. Thus, for example:

```
REAL XAR(4), YAR(4)
DATA XAR/2, 2, 10, 10/
DATA YAR/2, 10, 10, 2/

SET FILL AREA REPRESENTATION(WS, 1, PATTERN, 1, 0)
SET FILL AREA INDEX(1)
SET PATTERN SIZE(2, 2)
SET PATTERN REFERENCE POINT(1, 1)
FILL AREA(4, XAR, YAR)
```

produces the fill area shown in Figure 7-5. The actual shading applied to the individual squares is defined by the style index given to fill area index 1. The fill area style index points to a separate pattern table where individual patterns are defined. As an example using just two colours, black and white, in the pattern definitions, the fill area index defines patterns as in Figure 7-6.

Entries in the pattern table may be already preset by the installation or they may be set by the user using:

SET PATTERN REPRESENTATION(WS, PI, DIMX, DIMY,
    SX, SY, DX, DY, NA)

where PI specifies the pattern index associated with the entry to be defined. DX and DY specify the number of cells of the pattern in the X and Y directions while the NA array, which is DIMX by DIMY, specifies the colour table index for each cell. SX and SY specify the starting indices of the pattern in the array. In the example above, the second pattern entry would be defined by:

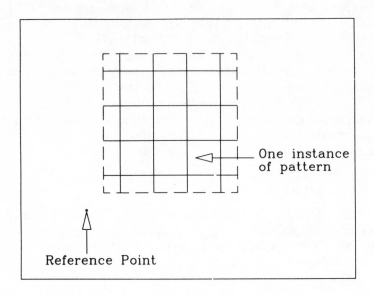

Figure 7-5

SET PATTERN REPRESENTATION(WS, 2, 3, 3, 1, 1, 3, 3, NA)

where the array NA contains the values 3 and 4 in the elements corresponding to the black and white squares, respectively, in the pattern.

Note that the colour index of the fill area representation is not used for the PATTERN interior style but only for SOLID, HOLLOW and HATCH (see below) interior styles. The colours in the pattern are derived from the elements of the pattern array.

The fourth method of shading the fill area is by interior style HATCH. In this case, the style index defines the different styles of hatching available on the workstation. Positive hatch style values will be registered and negative values may be defined for a particular workstation or installation. The difference from linetypes and marker types, which may also be registered, is that there are no standard hatch style values.

Not all workstations provide all interior styles and it will be necessary for the user to consult the local installation manual to decide what is available. Only style HOLLOW has always to be provided.

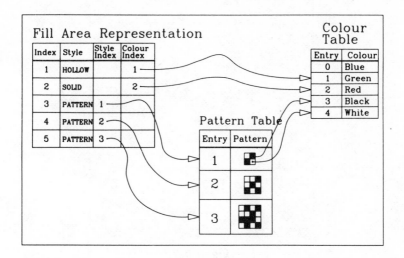

Figure 7-6

7.9 TEXT REPRESENTATION

Text is the most complex of the GKS primitives and certainly the one with the most attributes. In Chapter 2, it was shown how the text position, height, writing direction, alignment and orientation could be defined in a device independent way. Thus the appearance of a text string in terms of its overall size and shape is defined in NDC space.

For example:

```
SET WINDOW(1, 0, 100, 0, 100)
SET VIEWPORT(1, 0, 1, 0, 1)
SELECT NORMALIZATION TRANSFORMATION(1)

SET CHARACTER HEIGHT(5)
SET CHARACTER UP VECTOR(-1, 1)
SET CHARACTER PATH(RIGHT)
SET TEXT ALIGNMENT(LEFT, BASE)
SET TEXT INDEX(1)

TEXT(50, 50, 'Example')
```

This defines output on NDC space approximately of the form given in Figure 7-7. However, a number of characteristics associated with the text string have not been set globally but are controlled by the text index in the same way that linetype, linewidth and colour are controlled by the polyline index in the workstation. The text aspects controlled by the

Figure 7-7

workstation independent text index are:

> Text font and precision
> Character expansion factor
> Character spacing
> Text colour index

Text font and precision: a workstation may have access to a number of different fonts. GKS lays down rules for font designers indicating that character height is the major attribute. Fonts may be defined as mono or proportionally spaced with sufficient space around the characters that they fit together without usually needing additional spacing. The height to width ratio of characters is a property of the font. The text font and precision aspect defines the characteristics of the font type being used in two parts: font and precision. The font part defines the number of the font to be used while the precision part specifies how well the font type can describe the output in NDC space. The three possible precision values are:

(1) STRING: of the global attributes only character height need be used. The minimum requirement is that the text string will be drawn horizontally left to right from the position specified at a height as close to the one specified as possible. A workstation can use its hardware character set and if this can only be output in one size, that is acceptable.

(2) CHAR: the global attributes are used to define the position of the character boxes accurately. The appearance of the individual characters within the box may not take account of all the attributes. For example, characters may still be horizontal.

(3) STROKE: the font will display the text string precisely using all attributes.

Character expansion factor: the assumed width of the characters relative to the height can be increased or decreased by redefining the character expansion factor. For example, a value of 2 will produce characters twice as wide as they would otherwise be.

Character spacing: the assumed space between character bodies is zero although the font will be defined so that space is provided around the character in the character body. Character spacing can be used to increase or decrease the space between characters. It is defined in terms of the character height. For example, a value of 0.5 would insert space equal to half the character height between each of the character bodies.

Text colour index: as for the other primitive colour indices, this is a pointer to an entry in the colour table defining the colour to be used.

The function which defines the workstation characteristics of each text primitive is:

SET TEXT REPRESENTATION(WS, TI, TF, TP, CEF, CS, TCI)

where TF and TP together specify the text font and precision, CEF and CS specify the character expansion factor and character spacing and TCI specifies the text colour index, all to be associated with the text index TI. If two workstations 1 and 2 are active with text index 1 specified by:

SET TEXT REPRESENTATION(1, 1, 2, STROKE, 2, 0.5, 1)
SET TEXT REPRESENTATION(2, 1, 1, STRING, 1, 0, 1)

the output on the two workstations may be as shown in Figure 7-8. Thus, unlike polyline, the workstation is likely to output text in significantly different ways depending on the hardware facilities supported.

7.10 SEGMENT STORAGE ON WORKSTATION

Chapter 4 described how segments are created and manipulated. However, it did not give any indication where storage for these segments takes place. Conceptually, segments are stored on the workstations active when the segment is created. A particular implementation of GKS could store segments centrally but, for intelligent workstations with local storage, the aim would be to store the segments on the workstation to improve the performance seen by the user in terms of segment manipulation. Even if

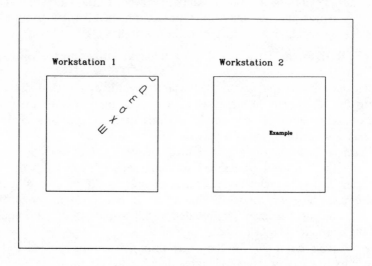

Figure 7-8

stored centrally, the implementation must be such that the user can imagine that segments are stored on the workstation. For example:

OPEN WORKSTATION(1, 6, 3)
OPEN WORKSTATION(2, 7, 4)
ACTIVATE WORKSTATION(1)

CREATE SEGMENT(8)
POND
CLOSE SEGMENT

ACTIVATE WORKSTATION(2)
CREATE SEGMENT(9)
DUCK
CLOSE SEGMENT

DEACTIVATE WORKSTATION(1)

CREATE SEGMENT(10)
TREE
CLOSE SEGMENT

DELETE SEGMENT(9)

DEACTIVATE WORKSTATION(2)

The pond (segment 8) would be stored on Workstation 1, while the duck (segment 9) would be stored on Workstations 1 and 2. The tree (segment 10) is only stored on Workstation 2 as Workstation 1 has been deactivated by the time segment 10 is defined. Deleting a segment removes all knowledge of it from the system so deleting segment 9 will delete the duck from both Workstation 1 and 2 even though the deletion takes place when Workstation 1 is inactive.

The functions for manipulating a segment, by assigning a value to a segment attribute (see Section 4.3), affect all copies of the specified segment stored in GKS.

It is possible to delete a segment from a single workstation by calling:

DELETE SEGMENT FROM WORKSTATION(WS, ID)

The effect is as if the workstation WS had not been active when the segment ID had been created.

The function CLEAR WORKSTATION deletes all the segments stored on the specified workstation. The function REDRAW ALL SEGMENTS ON WORKSTATION (see Section 7.11) can be used to clear the display surface without deleting segments.

Simple uses of GKS are likely to have nearly the same set of segments defined on each workstation. Some skill is required to define segments on a specified subset of the workstations that are open. It would normally only be used in a complex program.

Closing down a workstation deletes from that workstation all the segments currently defined on it. If it is reopened, it will be initialised with an empty segment storage.

If a segment is deleted from each workstation, on which it is stored, (either by using DELETE SEGMENT FROM WORKSTATION or by closing the workstation) then the segment itself is deleted (as if DELETE SEGMENT had been called).

7.11 DEFERRING PICTURE CHANGES

If an intelligent refresh display is being used as a workstation, the operator would expect that picture changes would take place immediately. For example, if a polyline is output by the program, the operator would expect to see the polyline image on the display screen immediately. However, if a less powerful system is being used or if there are inefficiencies in the link between the host computer running GKS and the display, this may not be possible and may, in some cases, not be desirable due to the high overhead it places on the system.

Two examples where it may be undesirable to update the picture immediately are an off-line plotter and a storage tube connected to the host via a network. In the first case, output for the plotter may be accumulated as records on a magnetic tape. Rather than output a record for each primitive output, it would be more efficient to buffer the output into reasonable size blocks before sending to the magnetic tape. In the second case, sending small packets of output across the network is inefficient and it would be more efficient to save them up if the application allowed.

There are occasions, however, particularly in an interactive mode of working, where, if the display is not up to date, it may be difficult for the operator to continue. An example might be where the operator is defining locator positions to be joined by lines. If the last locator position does not have the associated line drawn, it is difficult for the operator to know where the starting point of the next line is.

GKS allows the user to specify the mode in which he wishes a particular workstation to perform (the *deferral mode*). Normally, he will choose the mode which is most efficient. The possible deferral modes are:

ASAP: the effect of the visual change must be achieved As Soon As Possible.

BNIG: the effect of the visual change must be achieved Before the Next Interaction Globally - that is on any workstation currently open. Thus, the display screen may not always be up to date but it is always made current as soon as input is requested from any workstation.

BNIL: the effect of the visual change must be achieved Before the Next Interaction Locally - that is on this workstation. Thus, the display screen may not always be up to date but it is always made current as soon as input is requested from this workstation.

ASTI: the effect of the visual change must be At Some TIme but there is no guarantee when this will be.

Another source of inefficiency on some displays is that certain functions cause an *implicit regeneration* of all the displayed information. For example, changing the polyline representation on a workstation, for a particular polyline index already used in the picture, should cause all polylines with that index as attribute to take on the new representation. On a storage tube, this could only be done if the whole picture on the screen was redrawn. Similarly, a pen plotter would need to redraw the complete picture. On the other hand, a refresh display could probably perform this change immediately.

The following functions may cause an implicit regeneration:

SET POLYLINE REPRESENTATION
SET POLYMARKER REPRESENTATION
SET TEXT REPRESENTATION
SET FILL AREA REPRESENTATION
SET PATTERN REPRESENTATION
SET COLOUR REPRESENTATION

SET WORKSTATION WINDOW
SET WORKSTATION VIEWPORT
SET SEGMENT TRANSFORMATION
SET VISIBILITY
SET HIGHLIGHTING
SET SEGMENT PRIORITY
DELETE SEGMENT
DELETE SEGMENT FROM WORKSTATION
ASSOCIATE SEGMENT WITH WORKSTATION (see Section 10.3)
INSERT SEGMENT (see Section 10.3)
INTERPRET ITEM (see Section 11.3)

The output functions may also cause an implicit regeneration if a primitive is added to a segment which overlaps a segment of higher priority.

For any of the situations listed above, it is possible to ascertain for each workstation whether an implicit regeneration is required, by use of inquiry functions (see Section 8.4).

GKS recognizes that implicit regeneration may be inefficient on some workstations and allows the user to delay such picture changes if it is not a problem for the application program. GKS allows a workstation to perform in one of two modes:

SUPPRESSED: implicit regenerations of the picture are suppressed.
ALLOWED: implicit regenerations of the picture are allowed.

An implicit regeneration consists of clearing the display surface and redrawing all the segments stored on the workstation. This may result in a loss of information if parts of the picture are not stored in segments.

The user specifies the setting of the deferral and implicit regeneration modes by:

SET DEFERRAL STATE(WS, DM, IGM)

where DM and IGM are the desired deferral mode and implicit regeneration mode for the workstation WS. If the deferral mode has a value other than ASAP or the implicit regeneration mode has the value SUPPRESSED, it must be possible to force the display to be current and that is achieved by the function:

UPDATE WORKSTATION(WS, RF)

where RF is the regeneration flag which may take the values PERFORM or POSTPONE. The function performs all the deferred actions, but only does an implicit regeneration if one is necessary and the regeneration flag is specified as PERFORM. In contrast, the function:

REDRAW ALL SEGMENTS ON WORKSTATION(WS)

performs all the deferred actions, clears the display surface, and redraws all the segments stored on this workstation unconditionally.

It is anticipated that refresh displays would normally work in the modes (ASAP, ALLOWED) while local storage tubes might work in the mode (BNIL, SUPPRESSED). For an off-line plotter, the mode would most likely be (ASTI, SUPPRESSED).

7.12 INPUT DEVICES

Chapters 5 and 6 have described the logical input devices defined by GKS in the virtual world. Thus the application program will define its output in terms of the output primitives and will define inputs to the program using the logical input devices LOCATOR, STROKE, VALUATOR, CHOICE, PICK and STRING. GKS ensures that the operator of an OUTIN workstation has at least one logical input device of each type available to him. If the operator is using a single workstation, this implies that the workstation must be capable of providing inputs of each type.

A particular installation when it defines workstation types must indicate which logical input devices they support and how they are achieved. It is quite possible for different installations to define the same logical input device on a GKS workstation in significantly different ways. Section 7.2 gave a list of workstations available at the XYZ installation and the logical input devices supported by each workstation.

Whereas most of the OUTIN workstations support all logical input devices, workstations of type 7 and 9 must be used together or in conjunction with one of the other workstations as this is the only way that the operator can have one logical input device of each type available to him. The exact details of how the physical devices available produce logical input values should be described in the installation manual. The available physical devices may be mapped onto one or many logical input devices of each class.

The implementation of the logical input devices is much simpler if the installation only supports REQUEST input (see Section 8.6), since only one input device may be active at any one time. It is then unnecessary for the physical device to include a device identification with the input data.

If XYZ is such an installation, a workstation of type 2 might be defined as follows. This device is a storage tube with keyboard and thumbwheels for controlling the crosshairs. The system can send a signal to the device which causes the crosshairs to appear. The thumbwheels can change the position defined on the display screen by the crosshairs. The input can be sent to the system from the terminal by hitting any key. The key hit and the X, Y coordinates of the crosshairs are sent.

This particular installation has decided to use the crosshairs to produce LOCATOR, STROKE and PICK logical inputs while using the keyboard for VALUATOR, CHOICE and STRING inputs. Only one logical device of each type is supported.

LOCATOR: requesting a LOCATOR value will cause the crosshairs to appear. The locator input value is sent by positioning the crosshairs and hitting a key on the keyboard.

STROKE: requesting a STROKE value will cause the crosshairs to appear. Individual positions of the stroke input are signified by positioning the crosshairs and hitting any key on the keyboard except F. The stroke input is completed by hitting the F key.

VALUATOR: the keyboard is used to input the required value, terminated by the RETURN key.

CHOICE: the keyboard is used to input the required positive integer, terminated by the RETURN key.

PICK: requesting a PICK value will cause the crosshairs to appear. The pick input value is sent by positioning the crosshairs as close as possible to the desired segment and hitting a key on the keyboard.

STRING: the string is typed on the keyboard followed by a RETURN key hit.

If, however, XYZ installation allows all input operating modes (REQUEST, SAMPLE and EVENT), then more sophisticated logical input devices must be defined. Several devices may be active at one time and so extra information to identify the device must be sent (in this case, identifying the class of device is sufficient as the installation is only defining one logical input device of each class). The following changes are needed to the definitions of the logical input devices.

LOCATOR: activating the LOCATOR device will cause the crosshairs to appear if not already visible. A locator value is sent by hitting the L key.

STROKE: activating the STROKE device will cause the crosshairs to appear if not already visible. The S key must be hit to signify the individual positions and the F key to signify completion of the STROKE.

VALUATOR: the value must be preceded by CTRL-V to indicate that it is a valuator input.

CHOICE: the integer must be preceded by CTRL-C to indicate that it is a choice input.

PICK: activating the PICK device will cause the crosshairs to appear if not already visible. The P key must be hit to send a pick input.

STRING: the string must be preceded by CTRL-S to indicate that it is a string input.

Even though it is possible to distinguish between the different logical input devices if several are active at once, it is likely that a workstation of this type would only be used in REQUEST mode.

On a richer real device such as a refresh display with lightpen, keyboard, tablet, potentiometers and button box, the workstation type has a much easier task in mapping real devices to logical ones.

Part II

8 GKS Environment

8.1 INITIALISATION

Chapters 2 to 7 have given an overview of most of the input and output facilities within GKS. However, nothing has been said as to how the user initialises GKS at the start of the program. In fact, none of the GKS functions so far described may be called before GKS is initialised and this is done by the function:

OPEN GKS(EF, SU)

The function OPEN GKS is only called once for an invocation of GKS. The parameter EF specifies the name of a file that will be used by GKS to return error information to the application program. Section 8.5 discusses how GKS handles errors and the use made of the error file. The parameter SU allows the user to specify the size of the internal workspace to be used by GKS if this is meaningful in a particular implementation.

Opening GKS initialises a number of variables to default values, some of which are dependent on the specific implementation. For example the maximum number of workstations that may be open simultaneously may vary from installation to installation. Others are defined as standard for all implementations. For example, GKS always sets the current POLYLINE INDEX and other similar indices to 1. The current normalization transformation is set to 0 and all normalization transformations are initialised so that the window is the unit square and so is the viewport. For example:

```
OPEN GKS(EF, SU)
OPEN WORKSTATION(1, 6, 3)
ACTIVATE WORKSTATION(1)
X(1) = 0.0
X(2) = 1.0
Y(1) = 0.0
Y(2) = 1.0
POLYLINE(2, X, Y)
```

This will draw a single line from the lower left to the top right of the NDC unit square. The line will be drawn in the style specified by polyline index 1.

However, it is important to note that GKS has an alternative attribute handling mechanism, to that used in the earlier chapters, which will be described in Chapter 13. Not all GKS implementations will choose the same default mechanism and it may be necessary to change the mechanism, to that assumed so far by this book, after GKS is opened. How this is done is described in Section 13.4. This is particularly important for readers in the USA.

Just as GKS needs to be initialised before any calls can be made to GKS functions, it is also necessary to close GKS down at the end of the session. This is achieved by calling the function:

CLOSE GKS

The error file is closed and any other housekeeping functions required by the implementation are performed. The program above would be completed by:

```
DEACTIVATE WORKSTATION(1)
CLOSE WORKSTATION(1)
CLOSE GKS
```

Note that it is necessary to deactivate and close all workstations that are open prior to closing GKS down.

8.2 GKS OPERATING STATES

To aid error handling in GKS, a number of operating states are identified. When GKS is in a specified state, certain GKS functions can be called while others are invalid. Before GKS is opened, it is in the state GKS CLOSED. As soon as the function OPEN GKS has been called, GKS is in the state GKS OPEN. The main states of GKS are:

(1) *GKS OPEN*: the function OPEN GKS has been called. GKS leaves this state when CLOSE GKS is called or a workstation is opened.

(2) *WORKSTATION OPEN*: at least one workstation has been opened. In this state, certain attribute setting functions can be called.

(3) *WORKSTATION ACTIVE*: at least one of the open workstations is active. In this state, GKS output primitives can be created and certain segment manipulation functions can be performed.

(4) *SEGMENT OPEN*: a segment is open. Calling CLOSE SEGMENT causes GKS to revert to the state WORKSTATION ACTIVE.

There is a strict ordering to the states. For example, the state WORKS-TATION OPEN cannot be changed to SEGMENT OPEN directly but GKS has first to go through the state WORKSTATION ACTIVE. Effectively, this ensures that a segment cannot be opened unless at least one workstation is active. Similarly, GKS cannot revert directly from the state WORKSTATION ACTIVE to GKS OPEN. This prevents a workstation from being closed if it is still active; the program must first deactivate it.

GKS precisely defines which states each GKS function can be called in and which GKS functions cause the state to change. Most of these are quite obvious as can be seen by the examples above.

8.3 GKS STATE LISTS

Internal to GKS and hidden from the application programmer are a number of state lists (COMMON blocks in a FORTRAN implementation) which contain relevant information about the current state of GKS. We will not go into these in great detail as, to first order, the application programmer does not really need to know that they exist. However, it is useful to get some feel for the underlying structure.

The main state lists are:

(1) *Operating State*: this is a single value giving the state of GKS.

(2) *GKS Description Table*: a table which gives information about the particular implementation of GKS. For example, it contains information as to how many workstations can be open together, the number of different normalization transformations allowed, and the types of workstation available.

(3) *GKS State List*: the main list for the virtual side of GKS. It contains information about all the current settings of attributes, normalization transformations, which segment is open, etc. The input queue is part of this list.

(4) *Workstation Description Table*: these are set up by the installation manager for the site and contain information about the characteristics of the workstations available. There is one table for each workstation type available.

(5) *Workstation State List*: these contain information about the workstations that are open. Each workstation that is open has its own state list and it is initialised to certain values (screen size, for example) from the Workstation Description Table. The Workstation State List contains information concerning the device specific side of GKS. It includes the workstation window and viewport settings and the various tables described in Chapter 7, which control how a particular primitive appears on this workstation.

These tables contain all the current relevant knowledge of GKS and are accessed by the application program via a set of *inquiry* functions.

8.4 INQUIRY FUNCTIONS

Inquiry functions in GKS allow the application programmer to access the information in the various GKS State Lists (see Section 8.3). They are used for a variety of purposes. The major ones are:

(1) To achieve precise results on a specific workstation.

(2) To tailor the application for particular environments.

(3) To produce library functions.

(4) To recover from error.

A typical inquiry function has the form:

INQUIRE NAME OF OPEN SEGMENT(IND, SEGNAME)

The inquiry functions in GKS have been organized so that it is not possible to get a GKS error when calling them. This allows inquiry functions to be called in an error condition without resulting in further GKS errors which could obscure the original error. Also, it allows inquiry functions to be called with no likelihood of them having any impact on the state of GKS.

This is achieved by the inquiry functions all having their initial output parameter as an indication as to whether the information returned by the inquiry is correct or not.

If IND has the value 0 on return, the SEGNAME parameter does contain the name of the open segment. If IND contains a value other than zero, it indicates what error situation has occurred. In the example above, IND could be set to a non-zero value indicating that there is no open segment and, therefore, it is not possible to give the name of the open segment.

The purpose of some inquiry functions is to return a complete list or set from GKS, which can be of unknown size. For example the application may need to scan all the segments so that it can find out if a particular segment exists. In a FORTRAN implementation, the inquiry returns the list one item at a time. Thus the function to return a segment is:

INQUIRE SET MEMBER OF SEGMENT NAMES IN USE(IX, IND, NM, SEG)

Here IX identifies which segment name is to be returned in SEG, IND is the indication of an error as before and NM is the total number of segment names in use.

Suppose we want to discover if segment 62 is in use. We can inquire each segment name and test it in turn. We emerge with a .TRUE. or .FALSE. in the logical variable EXISTS.

```
        EXISTS = .FALSE.
        IX = 1

100     CONTINUE
        INQUIRE SET MEMBER OF SEGMENT NAMES IN USE(IX, IND, NM, SEG)
        IF(IND .NE. 0) GOTO 300
        IF(SEG .EQ. 62) GOTO 200
        IX = IX + 1
        IF(IX .GT. NM) GOTO 300
        GOTO 100

200     EXISTS = .TRUE.
300     CONTINUE
```

As there are around 75 different inquiry functions in GKS, it is not possible to list these all here. It is more sensible for these to be looked up when they are required in the relevant GKS manual for the particular implementation being used.

8.4.1 Precise Results on a Workstation

An application program may require precise alignment with the characteristics of a particular workstation to achieve its aims. For example, the application may require to output to a plotter a scale drawing which will later be used on the assumption that the measurements on the output are precise. Suppose the application defines the picture in NDC space so that the range 0 to 0.5 in the X and Y directions correspond to 400 centimetres on the plotter output. If the application is to be used in a number of different environments, it will be unaware of the sizes of the plotters available or the device coordinates that they use. The inquiry function:

INQUIRE DISPLAY SPACE SIZE(WSTYP, IND, UNITS, RX, RY, IX, IY)

returns the characteristics of the workstation WSTYP. UNITS indicates whether precise measuring is possible on the device or not. The next two parameters give the maximum size of the display either in metres, if precise measurements are possible, or the device coordinates used by the device. The last two parameters give the display space size in terms of addressable positions. To achieve the desired effect above would require:

```
INQUIRE DISPLAY SPACE SIZE(WSTYP, IND, UNITS, RX, RY, IX, IY)
IF(UNITS .NE. METRES) GOTO 100
IF(MIN(RX, RY) .LT. 0.4) GOTO 100
OPEN WORKSTATION(WS, 5, WSTYP)
ACTIVATE WORKSTATION(WS)
SET WORKSTATION WINDOW(WS, 0, 0.5, 0, 0.5)
SET WORKSTATION VIEWPORT(WS, 0, 0.4, 0, 0.4)
```

The code at label 100 will indicate that a precise drawing cannot be obtained with a workstation of this type either because the device does not have precise scaling or is too small.

8.4.2 Tailoring Applications to Particular Environments

An application may expect the device to have a range of representations for a particular primitive. If these are unavailable on a particular device, it may decide to take a different approach to achieve the same results. For example, suppose two sets of points are to be marked by:

```
SET POLYMARKER INDEX(1)
POLYMARKER(N, XA, YA)
SET POLYMARKER INDEX(2)
POLYMARKER(M, XB, YB)
```

At this installation, the five standard markers have been augmented by a sixth marker which outputs ellipses. This particular installation has set representations 1 and 2 to be a dot and ellipse for those devices that can produce markers. However, one device type at the installation only has the ability to output the five standard markers.

In this case, the application could define a function which outputs an ellipse centred at the position specified. The relevant inquiry is:

INQUIRE POLYMARKER FACILITIES(WSTYP, ..., IND, NMK, ...)

This function returns in NMK the number of available marker types.

The other parameters give more information concerning the sizes available and the initial settings to particular representations. To achieve similar results on the limited workstation would require the following:

```
    SET POLYMARKER INDEX(1)
    POLYMARKER(N, XA, YA)
    INQUIRE POLYMARKER FACILITIES(WSTYP, 1, IND, NMK, ...)
    IF (NMK .GT. 5) THEN
    SET POLYMARKER INDEX(2)
    POLYMARKER(M, XB, YB)
    ELSE

    DO 100  I = 1, M
    ELLIPSE(XB(I), YB(I))
100 CONTINUE

    ENDIF
```

There are a large number of attributes of the workstation which an application may wish to inquire. The workstation description table indicates whether the device is a vector or raster display, which output functions require an implicit regeneration of the output, whether the display is monochrome or colour and many other facts. An application can use this information to change its approach. However, significant use of this information may cause the application to be less portable.

8.4.3 Library Functions

In Section 3.6, an example was given of a program which output the New York temperature given by the array MAXPR. It uses normalization transformations 1 to 3 to specify the position of the graph in NDC space and the associated annotations. To achieve its results, it resets a number of text and marker attributes.

If this was to be defined as a function, NEW YORK, it should be defined in such a way that the application using it is unaware that it has changed any attributes. To do this, the values need to be stored on entry to the function and reset before exit:

    SUBROUTINE NEW YORK(MAXPR)

    INQUIRE CURRENT NORMALIZATION TRANSFORMATION
        NUMBER(IND, CURRENT)
    INQUIRE NORMALIZATION TRANSFORMATION(1, IND,
        WIND1, VIEW1)
    INQUIRE NORMALIZATION TRANSFORMATION(2, IND,
        WIND2, VIEW2)
    INQUIRE NORMALIZATION TRANSFORMATION(3, IND,
        WIND3, VIEW3)
    INQUIRE CURRENT POLYMARKER INDEX(IND, PMKINDX)
    INQUIRE CURRENT CHARACTER HEIGHT(IND, CHRHT)
    INQUIRE CURRENT CHARACTER UP VECTOR(IND,
        CHARUPX, CHARUPY)

    (Program as in Section 3.6)

    SET WINDOW(1, WIND1(1), WIND1(2), WIND1(3), WIND1(4))
    SET VIEWPORT(1, VIEW1(1), VIEW1(2), VIEW1(3), VIEW1(4))
    SET WINDOW(2, WIND2(1), WIND2(2), WIND2(3), WIND2(4))
    SET VIEWPORT(2, VIEW2(1), VIEW2(2), VIEW2(3), VIEW2(4))
    SET WINDOW(3, WIND3(1), WIND3(2), WIND3(3), WIND3(4))
    SET VIEWPORT(3, VIEW3(1), VIEW3(2), VIEW3(3), VIEW3(4))
    SELECT NORMALIZATION TRANSFORMATION(CURRENT)
    SET POLYMARKER INDEX(PMKINDX)
    SET CHARACTER HEIGHT(CHRHT)
    SET CHARACTER UP VECTOR(CHARUPX, CHARUPY)

All the attributes reset by the function are returned to their original values before exiting. If there was any danger that the inquiry functions would generate errors, the values of IND returned by the individual inquiries would also need to be checked.

Inquiry functions may differ from language to language as the style of the language differs. The functions given here correspond to the ones available in the FORTRAN binding.

8.5 ERROR HANDLING

GKS has a well defined set of errors which will be reported back to the application program. The philosophy adopted is that all errors are reported by putting details of the error in the *error file* which was specified when GKS was opened. A typical error will record the following information:

(1) *Error Number*: a number indicating which error has occurred.

(2) *GKS Function*: the name of the GKS function that was being obeyed when the error was detected.

There is a full set of error numbers so that a particular error can be precisely identified. What happens when an error has been recognized depends on the application program. If no special action has been specified, GKS calls the installation supplied error handling procedure:

ERROR HANDLING(NMBR, FCTID, EF)

The parameters supplied to it are the error number (NMBR), function name in which the error was detected (FCTID) and the name of the error file (EF). The action of this procedure is to record the error information in the error file by calling the procedure:

ERROR LOGGING(NMBR, FCTID, EF)

and then return to the GKS function where the error has been detected. Normally a GKS function causing an error has no effect on GKS. On return from the GKS function, the state of GKS is as if the function had not been called. In some cases, GKS may not be able to take the clean up action to achieve this and then the effects are unpredictable.

This rather cumbersome way of organizing the error handling has been set up to allow the application program to specify its own error handling procedure which takes a specific action. For example:

```
OPEN GKS(ERRFLE, SU)
OPEN WORKSTATION(1, 6, 3)
ACTIVATE WORKSTATION(1)
CLOSE SEGMENT                 ILLEGAL!!
```

This program would cause an error as the GKS State would be WORKSTATION ACTIVE (see Section 8.2) when CLOSE SEGMENT was called rather than SEGMENT OPEN. As a result, the installation supplied error handling procedure would be called. If the application program required to know whether any workstations were active when the error occurred, it could substitute its own error handling procedure as follows:

```
SUBROUTINE ERROR HANDLING(NMBR, FCTID, ERRFLE)

IF(NMBR .EQ. 4) THEN
INQUIRE OPERATING STATE VALUE(OP)
IF(OP .EQ. WSAC) WRITE(6,*) 'GKS is in the state WORKSTATION ACTIVE'
  - - -

  - - -
ENDIF
ERROR LOGGING(NMBR, FCTID, ERRFLE)
RETURN
END
```

The main point to note is that the user supplied error handling routine should still call ERROR LOGGING before returning. In this example, error number 4 is one indicating that a segment was not open. It has been singled out for special treatment. The inquiry function returns the current value of the GKS Operating State in OP. A suitable message is put out if the Operating State is WORKSTATION ACTIVE. The user supplied error handling procedure could inquire other information and might write this information to the error file or it might store the information in a COMMON block for use by the application program.

The only GKS functions which can be invoked in the error handling procedure are:

> ERROR LOGGING
> Inquiry functions
> EMERGENCY CLOSE GKS

There will be occasions when it is not possible to recover from an error and then the requirement is to save as much of the graphical information produced as possible, for example ensuring that any output information buffered within GKS is transmitted to the device. GKS provides the function:

EMERGENCY CLOSE GKS

for this purpose. GKS itself will invoke this function in response to some classes of error. This function may be invoked by a user supplied error handling procedure.

8.6 LEVELS

It is clear from the previous sections that GKS is a comprehensive graphics system containing most of the features required by the application programmer. This in itself will mean that GKS is quite large and, for simple applications, it is feasible that a great deal of unnecessary complexity is available in GKS. In this case, the user would like to use only a subset of the facilities available in GKS. This is achieved in GKS through the *level structure*.

GKS has nine valid levels defined by three different choices on each of two axes. The two axes are approximately input and all the other functions.

The definitions of the input choices are:

(a)   No input functions allowed.

(b)   Only REQUEST input allowed.

(c)   REQUEST, SAMPLE, and EVENT input are all allowed.

The definitions of the choices on the other axis are:

(0)   Minimal output - all the output primitives are available but the meaning of primitive index values cannot be changed. The installation default settings must be used. There is at least one settable normalization transformation. Only one output workstation is allowed at a time.

(1)   The main additions over (0) are the ability to specify the primitive index representations, the ability to have more than one output workstation active at a time, the ability to use segments, and multiple normalization transformations.

(2)   This allows the workstation independent segment storage facilities described in Chapter 10 to be used.

The simplest GKS implementation is, therefore, Level 0a which only allows output to a single workstation at a time. Level 1b gives most of the functions described in Chapters 2 to 7 excluding Chapter 6. Level 1c adds approximately the input facilities described in Chapter 6.

9 Control of Input Devices

9.1 INTRODUCTION

Chapters 5 and 6 have introduced graphical input in GKS. When an application program requires input data from an operator, it asks a logical input device to obtain it and, using the operating mode, controls the style by which the operator interacts with that logical input device. A particular logical input device can supply to the program values corresponding to one of the six types of input data available in GKS.

This chapter defines an interaction in GKS more precisely and shows how a logical input device can be controlled by sending it an initial value and control parameters which are used when an interaction starts. The other main topic is further control of the input queue.

9.2 AN INTERACTION IN GKS

Implicit in Chapters 5 and 6 has been the *interaction*. An interaction involves an operator and a logical input device. While the interaction is underway, the operator controls the current value (or *measure*) held by the logical input device. It is this measure that is returned to the application program by GKS. While no interaction with a logical input device is underway, the operator has no control over the measure and the program has no way of finding out its value. In effect it does not exist. For example, an operator can move the pen of a tablet across the tablet surface at any time. But if no interaction is underway, the movements of the pen have no effect on the measure and, hence, also have no effect on the application program. If the application program has specified that echoing is to occur, the echo only appears when an interaction starts and disappears when it stops.

In REQUEST mode, a single call to a GKS REQUEST function contains an entire interaction. Otherwise no interaction with that device is underway. In SAMPLE and EVENT modes, an interaction is underway the whole time. It starts when either mode is selected by a GKS function of the form SET XXX MODE and finishes when the same GKS function is next called with the same device specified by its parameters (note that another interaction may start with the next call).

The following (slightly artificial) example demonstrates which GKS functions start and stop an interaction:

SET VALUATOR MODE(WS, DV, SAMPLE, EC)	Interaction starts
SAMPLE VALUATOR(WS, DV, VALUE)	
SET VALUATOR MODE(WS, DV, REQUEST, EC)	Interaction stops
REQUEST VALUATOR(WS, DV, STAT, VALUE)	Entire interaction
SET VALUATOR MODE(WS, DV, EVENT, EC)	Interaction starts
AWAIT EVENT(T, W, C, D)	
GET VALUATOR(VALUE)	
SET VALUATOR MODE(WS, DV, EVENT, EC)	Interaction stops and new one starts
SET VALUATOR MODE(WS, DV, REQUEST, EC)	Interaction stops

9.3 INITIALISING AN INPUT DEVICE

A logical input device may be initialised by calling the appropriate INITIALISE XXX function, where XXX is the class of the device, which is of the form:

INITIALISE XXX(WS, DV, initial value, PE,
    XMN, XMX, YMN, YMX, ..., LDR, DR)

The first two parameters give the workstation identifier and device number. Next follows one or more parameters defining the initial value for that type of device. PE defines the prompt and echo types which will be described in Section 9.3.2. The four parameters XMN, XMX, YMN, YMX define the echo area described in Section 9.3.3. Finally, DR(1) to DR(LDR) is an input data record described in Section 9.3.4.

9.3.1 The Initial Value

During an interaction, the measure of a logical input device is controlled by the operator. However, we have not described how the measure is initialised.

In GKS, an *initial value* associated with the device, initialises the measure when the interaction starts. Therefore, unless the initial value is altered by the application program, the measure is the same at the start of each interaction. For example, if REQUEST LOCATOR is being used and echoing is selected, the echo appears initially in the same place on each call to REQUEST LOCATOR.

For the operator, this method gives the advantage of predictability. However, the initial value may be so unsuitable that the interaction becomes stilted and inefficient. The initial value can be altered by the appropriate GKS function INITIALISE XXX given above. XXX denotes one of the six classes of input data. WS and DV are the workstation identifier and the device number, which together with the data type XXX identify the logical input device whose initial value is to be set. The format of the new initial value depends on the data type XXX and in each case corresponds to the format which would be delivered by the GKS input functions. The remaining parameters have nothing to do with the initial value itself and will be described later.

Two of the GKS INITIALISE functions are:

INITIALISE VALUATOR(WS, DV, VALUE, PE,
    XMN, XMX, YMN, YMX, LOVAL, HIVAL, LDR, DR)
INITIALISE LOCATOR(WS, DV, N, X, Y, PE,
    XMN, XMX, YMN, YMX, LDR, DR)

A good use of INITIALISE is to ensure that the input resulting from one interaction is used as the initial value for the next. For example:

```
100   CONTINUE
      REQUEST LOCATOR(WS, DV, ST, N, X, Y)
      DRAW DUCK AT(X, Y)
      INITIALISE LOCATOR(WS, DV, N, X, Y, PE, XMN, XMX,
          YMN, YMX, LDR, DR)
      GOTO 100
```

Supposing that echoing has been selected, the operator sees an echo appear in a particular position, manipulates a physical device to control the measure and, hence, the echo, terminates the interaction, and then the duck moves to the chosen position. On the next call to REQUEST LOCATOR, the echo appears in the position last input by the operator, who can now engage in another interaction. If the chosen positions are likely to be close together, this extra call by the program can considerably assist the operator.

In general it is a good idea to use an INITIALISE function if the program can make a reasonable prediction of the next input value. For example, an operator's response to a REQUEST CHOICE may cause a particular initial value to be suitable for the next interaction. In the following example, suitable initial locator values are stored in the arrays NT, XP and YP:

```
REQUEST CHOICE(WS, DV1, STAT, N)
IF(STAT .NE. OK) STOP
INITIALISE LOCATOR(WS, DV2, NT(N), XP(N), YP(N), PE,
    XMN, XMX, YMN, YMX, LDR, DR)
```

Note that the initial value used by the program must be legal at the time that the INITIALISE function is called. It must be a value that the operator is able to input. In particular, when setting the initial value of a locator device, the specified point must lie within the window of the specified transformation and for a pick device the specified segment name must exist and be detectable and visible. For example, the following sequence of GKS calls is illegal even though clipping is disabled:

```
SET WINDOW(1, 0, 60, 0, 60)
SET CLIPPING INDICATOR(NOCLIP)
INITIALISE LOCATOR(WS, DV, 1, 70, 70, PE, XMN, XMX, YMN, YMX,
    LDR, DR)                                           ILLEGAL!!
```

It is possible for an initial value to be valid when set up by an INITIALISE function, but to become invalid later when, for example, a normalization transformation changes. In this situation, an interaction starts with a fall-back initial value determined by the implementation of the logical input device. For example:

```
SET WINDOW(1, 0, 60, 0, 60)
INITIALISE LOCATOR(WS, DV, 1, 50, 50, PE, XMN, XMX, YMN, YMX,
    LDR, DR)
SET WINDOW(1, 0, 40, 0, 40)
REQUEST LOCATOR(WS, DV, ST, NT, X, Y)
```

The call to REQUEST LOCATOR causes the fall-back initial value to be used since the specified initial point is now outside the window of the specified normalization transformation.

It is also important to note that some devices may be unable to use the initial value properly. For example, on some input hardware, the crosshairs cannot be initialised at all. GKS accepts input from such a device, but the operator sees the initial echo of a value determined by the hardware and not by the application program.

9.3.2 Prompt and Echo Type

So far echoing has been mentioned as desirable because from it the operator can deduce the current measure: the value that would pass to the program if it were to be delivered now. However, the form of the echo has only been hinted at.

A simple logical input device might only have one method of echoing. Another might have several and each of these may have advantages in different situations. For example, a crosshair cursor usually extends to the edges of a display surface and allows horizontal and vertical alignments to be perceived by the operator. A locator echoed by one corner of a rectangle allows an operator to perceive what lies inside and what lies outside. It seems sensible to permit the application program to select the most appropriate method. In GKS, this selection can be made using the *prompt and echo type* in the INITIALISE function. This is the PE parameter which appeared in all the references to INITIALISE in the last section.

On any logical input device, the PE parameter can take the value 1. For example:

> INITIALISE VALUATOR(WS, DV, VL, 1, XMN, XMX, YMN, YMX,
> LOVAL, HIVAL, LDR, DR)

The form of the echo corresponding to the value 1 is device dependent and is the usual echo for the device. Values of PE other than 1 might be available on some devices but not on others. Some values of PE are defined in GKS and have a particular meaning. The meanings of these are described later. The ISO Registration Authority will assign standard meanings to positive values beyond the range defined by GKS. There will be a different set of registered prompt and echoes for each input class. Negative values are device dependent.

The use of prompt and echo types that are not in the standard set makes a program less portable than if a program confines itself to prompt and echo type 1, but does take advantage of special echoes available on some devices. The program tuned for a particular special echo can be made more adaptable if it inquires what prompt and echo types are available on a logical input device. The GKS function for this purpose is the appropriate INQUIRE DEFAULT XXX DEVICE DATA where XXX is one of the six input classes.

The prompt and echo types that are standardized in GKS are grouped by input class.

LOCATOR prompt and echo types

1 device dependent technique which must be available

2 crosshair cursor intersecting at the current measure

3 tracking cross with its centre at the current measure

4   rubber band line connecting the initial value to the current measure

5   rectangle with one corner at the initial value and the opposite corner at the current measure

6   a digital representation of the coordinates of the current measure

PICK prompt and echo type

1   highlight the picked primitive for a short period of time using a device dependent technique which must be available

2   highlight in some way those primitives in the segment with the same pick identifier; this can be either the contiguous group containing the picked primitive or all primitives with that pick identifier

3   highlight in some way the whole segment

VALUATOR prompt and echo types

1   device dependent technique which must be available

2   any graphical technique (for example: a dial, a pointer or a sliding scale)

3   a digital representation of the value

CHOICE prompt and echo types

1   device dependent technique which must be available

2   prompt using hardware built into the physical device: for example, lights associated with buttons

3   the prompt is a display of character strings, representing a menu; the operator selects a string

4   similar to 3, but operator types in the character string

5   prompt using a segment; the choice numbers correspond to the pick identifiers in the segment

STRING prompt and echo types

1   display the current STRING value which must be available

STROKE prompt and echo types

1   display the current STROKE using a device dependent technique which must be available

2   display a digital representation of the current stroke position

3   echo the stroke points using markers

4   echo the stroke points by joining them with lines

On a particular installation, one locator device might only be able to display a tracking cross. Since prompt and echo type 1 must be available and is the usual type, it would be implemented as a tracking cross on this device and so would prompt and echo type 3. A locator device with a variety of echoes including crosshair and adjustable rectangle might make available prompt and echo types 1, 2 and 4. Initialising these devices might look like:

> INITIALISE LOCATOR(WS1, DV1, NT, X, Y, 1, XMN, XMX, YMN, YMX,
>   LDR, DR)
> INITIALISE LOCATOR(WS2, DV2, NT, X, Y, 4, XMN, XMX, YMN, YMX,
>   LDR, DR)

9.3.3 Echo Area

For some prompt and echo types, both the prompt and the echo can be anywhere on that part of the display surface currently in use (for example, most of the locator prompt and echo types) or is not displayed at all (for example, choice prompt and echo type 2 which puts the lights on). For many prompt and echo types however, the prompt and echo is displayed in a particular place and does not move from there, even though it may change shape. The program can control where such a display goes, by altering the *echo area,* which is a rectangle with sides parallel to the X and Y axes. In each INITIALISE function:

> INITIALISE XXX(WS, DV, initial value, PE,
>   XMN, XMX, YMN, YMX, ..., LDR, DR)

XMN and XMX are the left and right bounds of the echo area and YMN and YMX are the bottom and top bounds. The coordinates are in device coordinates.

For example, a locator value may be echoed by using digits in the top right corner of a 500×500 display surface or a valuator may be echoed using a dial in the top left:

> INITIALISE LOCATOR(WS, DV1, N, X, Y, 6, 450, 500, 450, 500, LDR, DR)
> INITIALISE VALUATOR(WS, DV2, VAL, 2, 0, 40, 450, 500, L, H, LDR, DR)

Since the coordinates are in device coordinates, the echo area can be separate from the area used by GKS output if this is wanted. In the following example, a choice device has an echo area containing a menu. The echo area is distinct from the workstation viewport:

SET WORKSTATION VIEWPORT(WS, 100, 500, 0, 500)
INITIALISE CHOICE(WS, DV, OK, 1, 3, 0, 99, 0, 500, LDR, DR)

9.3.4 Input Data Record

Some logical input devices allow further control over the way they interact with the operator. For example, several sizes of tracking cross might be allowed. Other devices may vary the method by which the value delivered to the program is calculated. For example, if a pick device is emulated by a physical device which only returns an (X,Y) coordinate (a tablet perhaps), the closeness with which the point has to approach a segment before a hit is registered might be a settable parameter.

These quantities are not defined in GKS. However the *input data record* provides a method by which quantities like these and also some compulsory quantities are sent to the logical input device. This is the final pair of parameters of the INITIALISE function. In FORTRAN, it is a CHARACTER*80 array (DR), preceded by the size of the array (LDR). For example:

INITIALISE VALUATOR(WS, DV, VAL, 1, XMN, XMX, YMN, YMX,
    LOVAL, HIVAL, LDR, DR)

The format and contents of the input data record are allowed by the standard to vary from one device to another. In FORTRAN, the array may include integers, reals and characters. Somehow this information has to be passed via the single array DR and to do this a special FORTRAN routine is available. It is not a GKS function, but is available with any FORTRAN implementation of GKS in order to construct data records. It is:

PACK DATA RECORD(NIA, IA, NRA, RA, NS, LSA, SA,
    MDR, ERRIND, NDR, DR)

In this routine, DR is the CHARACTER*80 array into which the data record is put by PACK DATA RECORD. MDR is the size of DR and NDR is the number of entries in DR actually occupied by the data record after being packed. ERRIND indicates whether an error has occurred in the packing. IA, RA and SA contain data (integers, reals, and character strings) to be packed in the data record and, for integers and reals, the preceding parameter is the number of entries to be packed. For character strings, there is a parameter containing the number of them (NS), the number of significant characters in each one (array LSA) and the array of strings themselves (SA). Other uses exist for data records and these will be described in Chapter 12. A routine performing the opposite task, UNPACK DATA RECORD, is also available.

For example, LOCATOR might require 10 integers and 2 real numbers to define its action. This would be achieved as follows:

    PACK DATA RECORD(10, IA, 2, RA, 0, LSA, SA, 100, ERRIND, NDR, DR)

For some input classes, certain entries in the data record have specific meanings. These cases are noted in the following list:

VALUATOR: two values are compulsory, lowest value and highest value. These two values provide a range within which data from a valuator lies.

CHOICE: *For prompt and echo type 2*: an array of logical values specifying which lights to turn on.

For prompt and echo types 3 and 4: an array of character strings to display.

For prompt and echo type 5: segment name.

STRING: Maximum number of characters, initial cursor position (position of first character to be input).

STROKE: Maximum number of points.

In a FORTRAN implementation, the quantities which are always present, are separate parameters which precede the CHARACTER*80 array and its size. Thus INITIALISE VALUATOR contains parameters to set the lowest and highest values. For example, the program may require valuator input to be in the range 4.2 to 8.7:

    PACK DATA RECORD(0, IAR, 0, RA, 0, LS, S, 1, ERRIND, NDR, DR)
    INITIALISE VALUATOR(WS, DV, VAL, 1, XMN, XMX, YMN, YMX,
        4.2, 8.7, NDR, DR)

If a prompt and echo type is set for choice input, the input device requires a menu of character strings. Suppose that the menu is to appear on the left side of the screen. Then we might use:

    DATA LS/4, 3, 4, 5, 4/
    DATA S/'MOVE', 'NEW', 'FILL', 'SCALE', 'QUIT'/
    PACK DATA RECORD(0, IA, 0, RA, 5, LS, S, 10, ERRIND, LDR, DR)
    INITIALISE CHOICE(WS, DV, OK, CH, 3, 0, 50, 0, 400, LDR, DR)

This would make a menu on the left consisting of the five words MOVE, NEW, FILL, SCALE, QUIT.

Other entries in the input data records may vary from one device to another even within the same input class. A variety of quantities is possible. For example, for locator input there might be an entry in the data record controlling the size of the tracking cross or an entry which sends pixels defining the shape of a tracking cross. For valuator, an entry might control the valuator resolution or a linear/logarithmic switch. Increasing the former gives the effect of a valuator which has distinct steps. For stroke, an entry might control the time interval, between separate successive points of the stroke input.

9.3.5 Portability of the INITIALISE Functions

Some of the parameters of the INITIALISE function are device dependent; prompt and echo type is chosen from a device dependent list of possibilities, echo area is in device coordinates and the input data record is in a non-standard form. By contrast the meaning of initial value is workstation independent.

A program, which is to be transported easily, might only use the initial value and ensure that the others are unchanged. It is necessary to use an inquiry function to find the values which are to be unchanged, for example:

INQUIRE VALUATOR DEVICE STATE(WS, DV, MXDR, ERRIND, OPMODE,
    EC, INITVAL, PE, EA, LOVAL, HIVAL, LDR, DR)
INITIALISE VALUATOR(WS, DV, NEWINITVALUE, PE,
    EA(1), EA(2), EA(3), EA(4), LOVAL, HIVAL, LDR, DR)

9.4 FURTHER CONTROL OF THE INPUT QUEUE

Event reports are added to the input queue by logical input devices operating in EVENT mode and removed independently by the application program. This section deals with the possibility of more than one event entering the queue as a result of a single operator action and also the detection and handling of input queue overflow.

9.4.1 Simultaneous Events

When an operator presses a button to trigger an event for a locator input device, it is possible that any of several buttons could have been chosen. In some situations, it is desirable that the program should find out which button was pressed, so extracting the maximum information about the operator's action. Whether this is possible in a particular implementation of GKS depends on how the logical input devices are associated with the physical devices.

Suppose that on a workstation, there is a tablet T capable of generating (X,Y) coordinates and that with it there is a group of buttons B1, B2, B3 and B4 possibly on a puck associated with the tablet. It is possible in GKS for more than one logical input device to be associated with the buttons B1 to B4. In fact the less sophisticated the input hardware, the more likely this is to happen, in order to provide the full six logical input devices.

The following example shows two logical input devices sharing the same group of buttons:

(1) *locator device 1*: the current locator value is generated by the tablet T and any of the four buttons can trigger an event.

(2) *Choice device 1*: the current choice value is the number (1 to 4) of the button most recently pressed while an interaction with the device is taking place. Any of the four buttons can trigger an event.

If any of the four buttons are pressed in EVENT mode, two event reports enter the input queue: one from each logical input device. In GKS, these are referred to as *simultaneous events*. The two events enter the input queue consecutively, but in no particular order.

The application program reads the events one at a time using the GET XXX and AWAIT EVENT functions described in Section 6.6. If it is necessary to discover which events originated from the same operator action, the function:

INQUIRE MORE SIMULTANEOUS EVENTS(ERRIND, ANYMORE)

would be used. The parameter ANYMORE contains the required information. If the input queue still contains any events simultaneous with an event already removed, ANYMORE contains the value MORE, otherwise it contains NOMORE.

The following example illustrates how this inquiry function might be used. The program requires locator input values NT, X, Y and a choice value NCH, which are passed to the application subroutine USE INPUT DATA. Part of the example consists of a loop which collects the input data and ensures that input values are obtained from both logical input devices. It also ensures that simultaneous events are not separated.

```
        SET LOCATOR MODE(WS, DVL, EVENT, ECHO)
        SET CHOICE MODE (WS, DVC, EVENT, ECHO)

100     LOC = .FALSE.
        CHO = .FALSE.

200     CONTINUE
        AWAIT EVENT(600, QWS, CLASS, QDV)
        IF(CLASS .EQ. NONE) GOTO 300
        IF(CLASS .EQ. LOCATOR) GET LOCATOR(NT, X, Y)
        IF(CLASS .EQ. LOCATOR) LOC = .TRUE.
        IF(CLASS .EQ. CHOICE) GET CHOICE(ST, NCH)
        IF(CLASS .EQ. CHOICE) CHO = .TRUE.
        IF( .NOT. (CHO .AND. LOC)) GOTO 200
        INQUIRE MORE SIMULTANEOUS EVENTS(ERRIND, ANYMORE)
        IF(ANYMORE .EQ. MORE) GOTO 200

        USE INPUT DATA(NT, X, Y, ST, NCH)
        GOTO 100

300     CONTINUE
```

Note that, if in an implementation the two logical input devices are not associated in this way, the program still works. The operator would have to trigger two events: one for each device, but in either order. The program would ensure that an event from each logical input device arrived before using the input data. If any repeat occurred, any old value would be thrown away.

9.4.2 Input Queue Overflow

With a logical input device in EVENT mode, it may happen that the operator adds events to the queue faster than the application program removes them. Since the input queue is likely to be of limited size, it can easily overflow in this situation. A consequence of the queue overflowing is that some input data is lost. This section shows how it is possible to find out that loss of input data has occurred.

When the input queue overflows, no more event reports are added until the application program empties the queue in a particular way. The operator would normally perceive that the input actions were no longer being acknowledged.

A GKS error (number 147) is reported, when the program next attempts to remove an event from the queue. The program can trap the error by replacing the ERROR HANDLING procedure as described in Section 8.5.

Alternatively the program can use an inquiry function:

INQUIRE INPUT QUEUE OVERFLOW(ERRIND, EWS,
    ECLASS, EDV)

to detect input queue overflow. If the error indicator ERRIND is returned as 0, the queue has overflowed. If ERRIND is 148, the queue has not overflowed. The inquiry would normally be called immediately after a call to AWAIT EVENT. If overflow has occurred, the other parameters indicate which logical input device was attempting to add the event report that caused the overflow.

Event reports remaining on the queue are valid and repeated calls to AWAIT EVENT remove them and allow them to be examined by the appropriate GET XXX function. However, only when the application program calls AWAIT EVENT with the queue empty (i.e. when the device class parameter is returned with the value NONE), can further event reports be added by the operator. It is at this stage that the application program can assume that the loss of input data occurred.

In the following example, events are taken off the queue and dealt with. This is the loop that starts at statement 100. In the loop, the condition of input queue overflow is tested and, if it has occurred, control passes to statement 200. There the device that caused the overflow is put into REQUEST mode which stops further events being generated. Remaining events in the queue are passed to the application subroutine USE INPUT DATA as if the overflow had not occurred. However when the queue has been emptied, the program jumps to statement 400 to deal with the situation of lost data.

```
      SET LOCATOR MODE(WS, DVL, EVENT, ECHO)
      SET CHOICE MODE(WS, DVC, EVENT, ECHO)

100   AWAIT EVENT(600, WST, CLASS, DEV)
      IF (CLASS .EQ. NONE) GOTO 500
      INQUIRE INPUT QUEUE OVERFLOW(ERRIND, EWS, ECLASS, EDV)
      IF(ERRIND .EQ. 0) GOTO 200
      USE INPUT DATA(WST, CLASS, DEV)
      GOTO 100

200   CONTINUE
      IF(ECLASS .EQ. CHOICE) SET CHOICE MODE(EWS, EDV, REQUEST, ECHO)
      IF(ECLASS .EQ. LOCATOR) SET LOCATOR MODE(EWS, EDV, REQUEST,
          ECHO)
```

```
300    AWAIT EVENT(0, WST, CLASS, DEV)
       IF(CLASS .EQ. NONE) GOTO 400
       USE INPUT DATA(WST, CLASS, DEV)
       GOTO 300

400    CONTINUE
       ...
500    CONTINUE
```

At the statement 400, the queue has been emptied and the program has reached the point where data has been lost.

10 Segment Storage

10.1 INTRODUCTION

The segment concept in GKS has been described in Chapter 4 and its relation to the workstation concept in Chapter 7.

As described in Chapter 7, GKS allows more than one workstation to be active simultaneously. Let us consider now how multiple workstations might be used in practice, by extending the simple animation program developed in Chapter 4. A common requirement for this type of program is the ability to construct a picture on an interactive workstation and to take a 'snap shot' of that picture using some other device. For example the operator may use a colour refresh display to compose each frame of a film; when each frame is satisfactory, he may then wish to make a hardcopy on a plotter. With our present knowledge of GKS, the only way to do this is to have the refresh display and plotter workstations active simultaneously, so all segments created will be created on both workstations. The snag with this technique is that not only are all segments created on both workstations, but also all changes to these segments are also reproduced on both workstations. For example, SET SEGMENT TRANSFORMATION applies to instances of the segment on all workstations on which the segment is stored. We really want to be selective and not output any but the 'final' version of each frame on the plotter workstation. The problem would be overcome if we could move segments from one workstation to another. GKS provides a mechanism for this through a special type of segment storage known as *Workstation Independent Segment Storage* (abbreviated to WISS). The segment storage with which we are already familiar from Chapters 4 and 7 is known as *Workstation Dependent Segment Storage* (abbreviated to WDSS).

10.2 WORKSTATION INDEPENDENT SEGMENT STORAGE

A GKS implementation can provide at most one workstation independent segment storage. It is, as the name implies, a system wide segment store to which all workstations have access. Segments stored in WISS have exactly the same segment attributes as segments stored in workstation dependent segment storage, and are manipulated by the same GKS functions. How for example are segments created in WISS?

WISS is treated by GKS as a workstation. If WISS is active when a segment is created, then the segment will be stored in WISS as well as in the WDSS of each of the other active workstations. Suppose the WISS for a particular implementation of GKS is a workstation of type 11. Then, using the workstation types defined in Chapter 7, consider the following program:

```
OPEN WORKSTATION(1, 5, 11)
OPEN WORKSTATION(2, 6, 4)
ACTIVATE WORKSTATION(1)
ACTIVATE WORKSTATION(2)
CREATE SEGMENT(DK)
DUCK
CLOSE SEGMENT
```

This will create instances of segment DK, the duck, on both the WISS (workstation 1), and the refresh display (workstation 2).

In other respects also, the segments stored on WISS behave like segments on other workstations. For example, the segment created in the last example may be deleted from WISS by:

```
DELETE SEGMENT FROM WORKSTATION(1, DK)
```

The functions for manipulating segment attributes apply to all copies of the specified segment within GKS. Thus:

```
SET SEGMENT TRANSFORMATION(DK, MAT)
```

sets the transformation of segment DK to be the matrix MAT and this applies to all workstations on which segment DK is stored, including WISS.

10.3 WISS FUNCTIONS

We have seen how segments may be stored in WISS, deleted from WISS and how their segment attributes may be changed. We will now see the particular manipulations that are possible for segments in WISS, but not for segments in WDSS. These are the manipulations that make WISS useful. GKS provides three functions to manipulate segments in WISS:

ASSOCIATE SEGMENT WITH WORKSTATION, COPY SEGMENT TO WORKSTATION and INSERT SEGMENT. The simplest to describe is:

ASSOCIATE SEGMENT WITH WORKSTATION(WS, ID)

This function copies the segment ID from the WISS to the WDSS of the workstation WS. The effect is as if workstation WS had been active when the segment was created. This function cannot be invoked if a segment is open.

With this function, we can allow the operator to compose the background of a picture on an interactive workstation (workstation DISPLAY below). When satisfactory, the segment containing the background is associated with the plotter workstation. This is only possible because all changes on the interactive workstation are made in parallel in WISS (workstation SS in the example). In this example and the succeeding ones in this chapter, the workstations and the segments are referred to by variables preset with the appropriate integer values.

```
OPEN WORKSTATION(SS, 5, 11)
OPEN WORKSTATION(DISPLAY, 6, 4)
OPEN WORKSTATION(PLOTTER, 7, 5)
ACTIVATE WORKSTATION(SS)
ACTIVATE WORKSTATION(DISPLAY)
```

compose background interactively in segment BKGND

ASSOCIATE SEGMENT WITH WORKSTATION(PLOTTER, BKGND)

The invocation of ASSOCIATE SEGMENT WITH WORKSTATION causes the segment containing the background (segment BKGND) to be stored in the WDSS of the plotter. After the association takes place, the background will appear on every frame on the plotter, until the segment is changed in some way. This function may cause an implicit regeneration (see Section 7.11).

The next function has two parameters:

COPY SEGMENT TO WORKSTATION(WS, ID)

The primitives in the segment ID (stored in the WISS) are sent to the workstation WS after the segment transformation and clipping have been applied. Workstation WS must not be the WISS. This function cannot be invoked when a segment is open. The major difference between this function and ASSOCIATE SEGMENT WITH WORKSTATION is that as a result of the COPY function, segment ID does not exist *as a segment* on workstation WS. The primitives contained in the segment can no longer be manipulated as a segment on the workstation. It is as if the output primitives in the segment had been called directly.

The example above could be continued using the COPY SEGMENT TO WORKSTATION function. Successive frames are output, consisting of the duck in various locations chosen interactively, drawn against the background that we have already constructed. To force a change to a new frame, we need the GKS function REDRAW ALL SEGMENTS ON WORKSTATION that was described in Chapter 7. In this program, the LOGICAL variable HC is set if a hardcopy is required; how this variable is set is not shown. The example is as follows:

```
        CREATE SEGMENT(DK)
        DUCK
        CLOSE SEGMENT

100     CONTINUE
        position the duck (segment DK) interactively
        IF(HC) THEN
        COPY SEGMENT TO WORKSTATION(PLOTTER, DK)
        REDRAW ALL SEGMENTS ON WORKSTATION(PLOTTER)
        ENDIF
        GOTO 100
```

One effect of the REDRAW ALL SEGMENTS ON WORKSTATION function in this instance is to clear the display surface and then redraw segment BKGND, the background. In a real example in which segment priority is important, care may be necessary to achieve the desired results.

The third function provided to manipulate segments in the WISS is:

INSERT SEGMENT(ID, MAT)

The segment ID must exist in the WISS. Unlike the ASSOCIATE and COPY functions, this function may be invoked when a segment is open, but segment ID cannot be the open segment. The function copies the primitives in segment ID to all the active workstations. If a segment is open, the primitives will become part of that segment, on all workstations that are active (the WISS could be one of them). If there is no segment open, the primitives are copied to all the active workstations, but are not a part of any segment on those workstations.

The transformation specified by the matrix MAT is applied to the contents of segment ID after the segment transformation of segment ID itself. This function may cause an implicit regeneration (see Section 7.11).

To illustrate the differences between the three WISS functions, consider the following example:

```
OPEN WORKSTATION(SS, 5, 11)
OPEN WORKSTATION(DISPLAY, 6, 4)

SET WINDOW(1, 0, 70, 0, 70)
SET VIEWPORT(1, 0, 0.5, 0.5, 1)
SET WINDOW(2, 0, 30, 0, 30)
SET VIEWPORT(2, 0, 0.5, 0, 0.5)

ACTIVATE WORKSTATION(SS)
CREATE SEGMENT(TR)
SELECT NORMALIZATION TRANSFORMATION(1)
TREE
CLOSE SEGMENT
CREATE SEGMENT(DK)
SELECT NORMALIZATION TRANSFORMATION(2)
DUCK
CLOSE SEGMENT
```

WISS (workstation SS) contains two segments, the tree and duck. Consider the effect of:

```
ASSOCIATE SEGMENT WITH WORKSTATION(DISPLAY, TR)
ASSOCIATE SEGMENT WITH WORKSTATION(DISPLAY, DK)
```

Segments TR and DK will now be stored on workstation DISPLAY. The effect is as if workstation DISPLAY had been active when the segments were created.

If, instead of invoking ASSOCIATE SEGMENT WITH WORKSTATION, the following statements had been executed:

```
COPY SEGMENT TO WORKSTATION(DISPLAY, TR)
COPY SEGMENT TO WORKSTATION(DISPLAY, DK)
```

the picture displayed on workstation DISPLAY would be superficially the same, except that the tree and duck are not stored in segment storage.

To show how INSERT SEGMENT differs, consider the statements:

```
ACTIVATE WORKSTATION(DISPLAY)
EVALUATE TRANSFORMATION MATRIX(0, 0, 0, 0, 0, 1, 1, WC, MATI)
CREATE SEGMENT(NEW)
INSERT SEGMENT(TR, MATI)
INSERT SEGMENT(DK, MATI)
CLOSE SEGMENT
```

The transformation matrix defined by EVALUATE TRANSFORMATION MATRIX is the identity transformation, which leaves all points unchanged. The segment store of workstation DISPLAY will now contain a single segment, NEW, which contains both tree and duck. This segment will also, as it happens, be stored on workstation SS since that workstation is also active.

Now let us extend the example to illustrate clipping. In each segment we introduce a shift of 0.25 in the Y direction as follows:

> SET CLIPPING INDICATOR(CLIP)
> EVALUATE TRANSFORMATION MATRIX(0, 0, 0, 0.25, 0, 1, 1, NDC, MAT)
>
> ACTIVATE WORKSTATION(SS)
> CREATE SEGMENT(TR)
> SET SEGMENT TRANSFORMATION(TR, MAT)
> SELECT NORMALIZATION TRANSFORMATION(1)
> TREE
> CLOSE SEGMENT
> CREATE SEGMENT(DK)
> SET SEGMENT TRANSFORMATION(DK, MAT)
> SELECT NORMALIZATION TRANSFORMATION(2)
> DUCK
> CLOSE SEGMENT

WISS contains the segments represented by:

Segment TR
> Clipping Rectangle [0,0.5] × [0.5,1]
> Tree

Segment DK
> Clipping Rectangle [0,0.5] × [0,0.5]
> Duck

Now let us consider the effects of:

> ASSOCIATE SEGMENT WITH WORKSTATION(DISPLAY, TR)
> ASSOCIATE SEGMENT WITH WORKSTATION(DISPLAY, DK)

The segment store of workstation DISPLAY will contain the same segments as WISS, retaining the same clipping rectangles. The appearance of these two segments on workstation DISPLAY is shown in Figure 10-1.

Consider instead:

> COPY SEGMENT TO WORKSTATION(DISPLAY, TR)
> COPY SEGMENT TO WORKSTATION(DISPLAY, DK)

This example does not cause the segments to be stored on workstation DISPLAY, but causes the primitives in the segments to be output there. As with ASSOCIATE SEGMENT WITH WORKSTATION, the primitives in the segments are clipped against the clipping rectangles stored with them, before being output on workstation DISPLAY. The

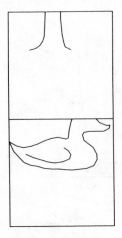

Figure 10-1

appearance of the resulting display is therefore also as shown in Figure
10-1.

For INSERT SEGMENT, consider:

    ACTIVATE WORKSTATION(DISPLAY)
    SET VIEWPORT(3, 0, 0.5, 0, 1)
    EVALUATE TRANSFORMATION MATRIX(0, 0, 0, 0, 0, 1, 1, WC, MATI)

    CREATE SEGMENT(NEW)
    SELECT NORMALIZATION TRANSFORMATION(3)
    INSERT SEGMENT(TR, MATI)
    INSERT SEGMENT(DK, MATI)
    CLOSE SEGMENT

Segment NEW contains primitives corresponding to the picture shown in
Figure 10-2. Note that the polyline representing the tree goes outside the
$[0,1] \times [0,1]$ region of NDC space, but the segment storage in GKS can
handle data in at least the region $[-7,7] \times [-7,7]$. The clipping rectangles
associated with the primitives in segments TR and DK are discarded by
INSERT SEGMENT. The primitives are reassigned the clipping rectangle $[0,0.5] \times [0,1]$, the viewport of the currently selected normalization
transformation (number 3). The appearance of the segment as displayed
on workstation DISPLAY is shown in Figure 10-3. This should be con-
trasted with the appearance of segments TR and DK in Figure 10-1.

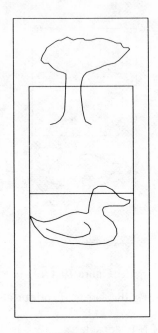

Figure 10-2

Figure 10-3

11 Metafiles

11.1 INTRODUCTION

When GKS is closed, all the information stored in GKS segments is lost. Segments only provide a mechanism for storing graphical information within a single invocation of GKS. A mechanism for long-term storage of graphical information is provided by GKS, the GKS *metafile*. A metafile may be written by one invocation of GKS and reused by subsequent invocations which may be the same program, a different program, a different user, a program at a different site etc.

The format and content of metafiles is a separate project within ISO. The CGM specifies a file and data format for the description of pictures (see Section 1.6). GKS *specifies* how metafiles are to be written and read and *suggests* one method for storing the metafile. This format is an interim measure until the CGM becomes an International Standard. However, there are occasions when this metafile will still be required. The format will not be discussed in this book.

Metafiles are treated by GKS as special categories of workstation. Metafiles are opened and closed by the same functions as other workstations. More than one metafile output workstation can be active simultaneously, to allow for different metafile formats (or media) being written simultaneously. Similarly, more than one metafile input workstation can be open simultaneously for reading. An installation will define particular workstation types belonging to categories GKS metafile input and GKS metafile output.

11.2 METAFILE OUTPUT

A GKS metafile output workstation has the following characteristics:

(1)   Output functions are stored if the workstation is active.

(2)   Attribute functions are stored.

(3)   Segments are stored if the workstation is active.

(4)   Geometric data is stored in a form equivalent to NDC.

(5)   Non-GKS data may be written using the special function WRITE ITEM TO GKSM.

A metafile is regarded by GKS as a sequence of *items,* each of which has three components:

(1)   Item type

(2)   Item data record length

(3)   Item data record

One or more items are generated for each GKS function call.

Suppose workstation type 12 is a GKS metafile output workstation. A trivial program creating output on a display and storing the information in a metafile is as follows:

```
OPEN GKS(ERFILE, SU)

OPEN WORKSTATION(1, 1, 3)
OPEN WORKSTATION(2, 2, 12)
ACTIVATE WORKSTATION(1)
ACTIVATE WORKSTATION(2)

DUCK

DEACTIVATE WORKSTATION(1)
DEACTIVATE WORKSTATION(2)
CLOSE WORKSTATION(1)
CLOSE WORKSTATION(2)

CLOSE GKS
```

The duck will appear on the display and will also be stored on the metafile. The routine DUCK outputs two polylines and they will be stored as separate items on the metafile with their type set to indicate that they represent polylines.

GKS provides a function to allow an application program to store non-graphical data in the metafile:

WRITE ITEM TO GKSM(WS, TYPE, LENGTH, LDRA, DRA)

The particular values of TYPE (item type) that the application program may use and the maximum value of LENGTH (length of item data record) allowed are implementation dependent quantities and will be documented in the local installation handbook. In FORTRAN, DRA is the CHARACTER*80 array containing the information to be sent and LDRA is the dimension of the array. A typical use of this function would be to store alphanumeric descriptions of objects along with their graphical descriptions in the metafile.

11.3 METAFILE INPUT

When a GKS metafile input workstation is opened, the first item becomes the *current item*. There are three GKS functions for use in getting input from a GKS metafile input workstation: GET ITEM TYPE FROM GKSM, READ ITEM FROM GKSM and INTERPRET ITEM. The first is:

GET ITEM TYPE FROM GKSM(WS, TYPE, LENGTH)

This returns the type and data record length of the current item. TYPE is used to decide what action needs to be taken. The major differentiation is between the item type defining the end of the file, the item types defining non-graphical data, and the graphical item types. LENGTH may be used by the application program to check that it has sufficient space to store the metafile item and is also used by INTER-PRET ITEM if the record is to be interpreted.

READ ITEM FROM GKSM(WS, MAXLEN, LDRA, DRA)

This returns the current item data record in the array DRA, which is of dimension LDRA, and MAXLEN is the maximum value of the item data record length. If the LENGTH returned by GET ITEM TYPE FROM GKSM is greater than MAXLEN, the excess parts of the data record are lost. Specifying a zero MAXLEN value, gives an efficient way of skip-ping records. The next item in the metafile becomes the current item.

INTERPRET ITEM(TYPE, LENGTH, LDRA, DRA)

This interprets the last data item read by READ ITEM FROM GKSM. The parameters to INTERPRET ITEM are the ones obtained by calling GET ITEM TYPE FROM GKSM and READ ITEM FROM GKSM. Interpreting an item may lead to an implicit regeneration (see Section 7.11).

The use of these three functions is illustrated in the following program where workstation type 13 is assumed to be a metafile input workstation and workstation type 3 is a refresh display:

```
      OPEN WORKSTATION(1, 5, 13)
      OPEN WORKSTATION(2, 6, 3)
      ACTIVATE WORKSTATION(2)

100   CONTINUE

      GET ITEM TYPE FROM GKSM(1, TYPE, LENGTH)
      IF(TYPE .EQ. EOF) GOTO 200
      IF(LENGTH .GT. MAXLEN) STOP
      READ ITEM FROM GKSM(1, MAXLEN, LDRA, DRA)
      INTERPRET ITEM(TYPE, LENGTH, LDRA, DRA)

      GOTO 100

200   CONTINUE

      DEACTIVATE WORKSTATION(2)
      CLOSE WORKSTATION(1)
      CLOSE WORKSTATION(2)
```

Note that it is not necessary to activate the metafile input workstation. If this program were given the metafile created by the example program in the previous section, the effect on the display from the two programs would be the same. If non-graphical output had been included in the metafile, the program would need to process these specially rather than allow them to be treated by INTERPRET ITEM.

12 Further Facilities

12.1 INTRODUCTION

Chapter 2 described in detail the major output primitives of GKS that may be familiar to users of other graphics systems. This chapter describes the more specialized output primitives. Cell array allows images to be output. Generalized drawing primitive allows special hardware drawing capabilities to be used. This chapter also describes the escape function, which allows special hardware to be used, but does not contain coordinate information.

12.2 CELL ARRAY

For colour raster displays, there is often a need to specify images containing a variety of colours or grey levels which specify a picture. Effectively, the user wishes to associate a particular colour or grey scale with each pixel of the raster display. For sophisticated raster displays, this will normally be done by associating a number with the pixel which identifies a position in the colour look-up table associated with the frame buffer of the display.

In GKS, the primitive used to specify images of this type is called *cell array*. It differs from the pixel image described above in a number of ways. The major one is that the individual cells are rectangular areas in world coordinates and may map on to one or more pixels in the coordinate space of a particular device. It can be thought of as a virtual pixel array. The cell array function is specified by:

CELL ARRAY(XL, YL, XR, YR, DIMX, DIMY, SX, SY, DX, DY, CA)

The two points in world coordinates (XL,YL) and (XR,YR) specify the opposite corners of a rectangular area which is to be divided into DX cells in the X direction and DY cells in the Y direction. Associated with each cell is a colour specified by the entry in the array CA(I,J) where I takes values from SX to (SX+DX-1) and J takes values from SY to (SY+DY-1). The corner cell at (XL,YL) corresponds to the array element CA(SX,SY) and the one at (XR,YR) corresponds to CA(SX+DX-1,SY+DY-1). The entry CA(I,J) contains the position in the workstation colour table where the RGB values of the colour are specified (see Figure 12-1).

Note that the area of the pixel array and the colour numbers associated with the cells are specified in the virtual side of GKS. The colour look-up table on the other hand is specific to a particular workstation. Thus, it is quite easy to specify a cell array which can be viewed quite differently on two different workstations. One could, for example, have a colour table specifying the picture as a grey scale image while a second specifies it as a pseudo colour one.

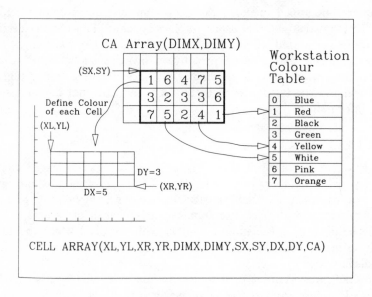

Figure 12-1

As the cell array is specified in world coordinates, it is subject to all the transformations that can be applied to other primitives. In particular, segment transformations and differential scaling in the transformation from world coordinates to normalized device coordinates allow the cell array's border to deform to a parallelogram and possibly get clipped by the window boundary. When this is mapped on to the pixels of a raster display, the pixel takes the colour specified by the cell in which the pixel's centre is contained.

Normally, cell arrays will be used to map images directly on to pixels. By carefully mapping the world coordinate window so that it maps precisely on to the complete viewport of the display, it is possible to ensure that a raster image is mapped 1:1 on to the pixels of the display. For example, suppose an image is specified by IMAGE(512,512) where IMAGE(I,J) is the colour table entry for the required colour. To map this on to a 512×512 raster workstation (RW) would require:

```
SET WINDOW(1, 0, 10, 0, 10)
SET VIEWPORT(1, 0, 1, 0, 1)
SELECT NORMALIZATION TRANSFORMATION(1)
OPEN WORKSTATION(RW, 3, 8)

SET WORKSTATION WINDOW(RW, 0, 1, 0, 1)
SET WORKSTATION VIEWPORT(RW, 0, 512, 0, 512)
ACTIVATE WORKSTATION(RW)
CELL ARRAY(0, 0, 10, 10, 512, 512, 1, 1, 512, 512, IMAGE)
```

The workstation type is specified as 8, which in Section 7.2 indicated a raster display of resolution 512×512 at the installation described there.

It may happen that the user wants to check the cell array output on a device other than a raster display. In this case, the implementation is not forced to produce a complete pixel image. Instead, it can approximate the cell array as best it can. In the very worst case, it is allowed just to draw the boundary of the cell array. On a plotter, a reasonable representation might be to draw a point of the nearest colour to the one required at the centre of each cell of the cell array.

The inquiry function INQUIRE DISPLAY SPACE SIZE described in Section 8.4.1 can be used to map a cell array precisely onto a raster display of any size greater than 512 by 512. The UNITS parameter will either return a value METRES or OTHER. In the first case, the display area is defined by RX and RY in metres. However, IX and IY give the addressable positions on the display in each direction. If IX and IY are greater than 512, to map the cell array onto the lower left corner covering 512 raster positions in each direction requires:

SET WORKSTATION WINDOW(RW, 0, 1, 0, 1)
SET WORKSTATION VIEWPORT(RW, 0, RX*512/IX, 0, RY*512/IY)

If the UNITS parameter returns a value of OTHER, it is likely on a raster display that the installation has defined the device coordinates as in the example given above.

12.3 GENERALIZED DRAWING PRIMITIVE

There exist on the market displays which have hardware capabilities to draw circles, ellipses, arcs and even spline curves. As the most complex line drawing primitive is the polyline, it would be difficult for such hardware to be used in GKS unless there was some mechanism provided in GKS to allow the full capabilities of each workstation to be exploited. The output primitive provided in GKS for this purpose is the *Generalized Drawing Primitive* or GDP for short.

The GDP function takes the form:

GENERALIZED DRAWING PRIMITIVE(N, PX, PY, ID, LDR, DR)

The parameter ID specifies the type of GDP to be output. The two arrays PX and PY of length N specify a set of positions in world coordinates that will be used in the definition of the GDP. As the GDP can have considerably different parameters depending on its type, an array DR of LDR elements is provided to give additional non-coordinate information. This is the GDP *data record*. Section 9.3.4 describes how data records can be constructed. The precise contents of the data record for each type of GDP will be described in the local installation handbook.

It is quite possible for a workstation not to support any GDP types at all, as they are not standardized; a program using a GDP might work on one workstation but not on another. Positive GDP numbers are the subject of registration. Registering a GDP will have the effect of adding an output capability to GKS, but even so a workstation does not have to support it. Negative GDP numbers are defined by the local GKS installation.

However a GDP is defined, certain properties are guaranteed by GKS. The major point is that the GDP specifies a shape or curve in world coordinates and this must appear as the correctly transformed shape on the device. For example, a GDP specifying a circle might be transformed by the normalization transformation into an ellipse. In this case, the workstation is expected to display it correctly.

A possible GDP might be one where N is set to 3 and the three points specify a circular arc whose centre is the first point and the last two points specify the start and end points of the arc. The parameter LDR could be set to indicate a single data value DR(1) which specifies whether the arc is to be drawn clockwise or anticlockwise.

As a GDP could be similar to any one of the other output primitives, it is allowed to use the most appropriate primitive attributes, possibly from more than one primitive. For example, the arc specified above would probably use the polyline index value to specify the type of line to be used.

The exact form of the GDPs on a particular site should be looked up in the local installation handbook. It is possible that the GDP will only be implemented on a subset of workstations with the others returning a minimal interpretation.

12.4 ESCAPE

The ESCAPE function provides another way of specifying non-standard activities in GKS. Although GDP specifies non-standard output primitives, it is constrained to deal with geometric output and it is expected to do the correct conversion from world to device coordinates.

The ESCAPE function, on the other hand, gives an installation the ability to control facilities on a device which would be impossible by the standard GKS functions. It also allows information on non-standard quantities to be read back to the application program. The only constraints on the ESCAPE function are that it should not violate the general design concept of GKS, does not change the state of GKS and does not produce geometric output. An example might be the output of voice or sound annotations to some graphical output (or simply sounding the bell). The form of the GKS function is:

ESCAPE(FCTID, INL, INDR, OUTDIM, OUTL, OUTDR)

The first parameter specifies the type of escape function. The array INDR is the ESCAPE *input data record* (of dimension INL), which is input from the application program to ESCAPE. The array OUTDR is the ESCAPE *output data record* (of dimension OUTDIM) which is output to the application program by ESCAPE; OUTL is the number of array elements actually used. Section 9.3.4 describes a function that can be used to construct data records. The precise contents of the data record for each type of escape function will be described in the local installation handbook.

13 Individual Attributes

13.1 INTRODUCTION

As we saw in Chapter 2, the actual appearance (or aspects) of primitives are controlled by attributes. In GKS, the aspects of primitives belong to two classes:

(1) *Global aspects* are applicable on all workstations. These are controlled directly by attributes.

(2) *Workstation dependent aspects* may vary from workstation to workstation so that the same primitive may be displayed quite differently on different workstations. These are controlled by a single attribute per primitive, the primitive index.

For example, the polyline primitive has no global aspects but has three workstation dependent aspects that are controlled by the polyline index. Polylines may be differentiated by using different values of the polyline index that access different combinations of these workstation dependent aspects or different representations, as we called them earlier. Thus:

```
SET POLYLINE INDEX(1)
POLYLINE(N, XA, YA)
SET POLYLINE INDEX(2)
POLYLINE(M, XB, YB)
```

will output two polylines which should appear different on any workstation. The workstation dependent aspects that are controlled by the polyline index are linetype, linewidth scale factor and polyline colour index.

Other primitives, however, have several global aspects. For example, the text primitive has character height, character up vector, text path and text alignment as its global aspects. Each global aspect is controlled directly by an attribute of the same name. Of course, the text primitive also has a text index which controls the workstation dependent aspects: text font and precision, character expansion factor, character spacing and text colour index.

In general, GKS defines aspects as global if they affect the geometry of the picture being described. Thus, linetype, which does not have any effect on the shape of the line or where it starts and finishes, is defined as workstation dependent. Conversely, character height, which affects the size of the text primitive, and text alignment, which affects the start and finish points of the text primitive, are both defined as global. As character spacing and width are specified relative to character height in GKS, they are defined as workstation dependent. For both text and polyline primitives, the colour indices do not affect the geometry of the picture and so are defined as workstation dependent.

In Chapter 2, output primitives and their attributes were described. In Chapter 7, we saw the means of differentiating the two polylines in the example above, on a workstation and, more importantly, how specific styles of line could be chosen to achieve the differentiation on different workstations. We can choose specific values of the three workstation aspects to associate with a polyline index value on a particular workstation. For example:

    SET POLYLINE REPRESENTATION(WS, 1, LT, LW, PLCI)

would specify that polyline index 1 on workstation WS would be represented by a line of linetype LT with a linewidth scale factor of LW and a colour specified by the entry PLCI in the colour table of the workstation (see Sections 7.5 and 7.6).

The main reason for this method of specifying aspects is to achieve portability of application packages from one environment to another. Only the workstation dependent parts of the program need be changed when it is moved from one installation to another or from one workstation to another. The workstation independent parts of the program do not need to be changed at all. In a similar manner, libraries of high level graphics routines may be written independently of the workstations on which they will run, and the workstation dependent settings incorporated in the application program which invokes the library routines.

This is clearly useful and important for large application packages designed to run on a range of different workstations and systems, especially when the workstation dependent aspects are being used as a means of differentiating particular primitives from others. However, there are disadvantages to this mode of working for certain applications and so, to ensure GKS also caters for their needs, GKS provides another way of controlling the workstation dependent aspects, that is like that used for controlling the global aspects. The former is referred to as *bundled specification* and the latter as *individual specification*.

13.2 DYNAMIC BINDING OF ASPECTS

Another difference between global aspects and workstation dependent aspects is how they are bound to the primitive. A global aspect is controlled directly by an attribute of the same name. For example, the character height aspect is controlled by the character height attribute and so:

SET CHARACTER HEIGHT(2)
TEXT(X, Y, STRING)

will output the text with a character height of 2. A subsequent call of SET CHARACTER HEIGHT cannot change the height of this text. The character height attribute is bound to the primitive when it is output and cannot be changed. The character height aspect is said to be *statically bound*.

Conversely, workstation dependent aspects are controlled in groups (or bundles) by a single attribute called a primitive index. For example, the linetype, linewidth scale factor and polyline colour index aspects are controlled in a bundle by the polyline index attribute and so:

SET POLYLINE REPRESENTATION(WS, 1, LT1, LW1, PLCI1)
SET POLYLINE INDEX(1)
POLYLINE(N, XA, YA)

will output the polyline with a polyline index of 1, statically bound to the polyline. As with the character height for text above, this polyline index is always associated with the polyline and cannot be changed. On workstation WS, the workstation dependent aspects are specified by LT1, LW1 and PLCI1. If this is followed later in the program by:

SET POLYLINE REPRESENTATION(WS, 1, LT2, LW2, PLCI2)
SET POLYLINE INDEX(1)
POLYLINE(M, XB, YB)

it is clear that this latter polyline is also output with a polyline index of 1 and on workstation WS, the workstation dependent aspects are specified by LT2, LW2 and PLCI2. However, in GKS there are further consequences. On workstation WS, all polylines with a polyline index of 1 will now have their workstation dependent aspects specified by LT2, LW2 and PLCI2. At the point where the representation is changed, the workstation is expected to change the aspects of all polylines which have a polyline index of 1, but this is only guaranteed for polylines inside segments. The polyline index of a polyline may not be changed after a polyline has been output but the workstation dependent aspects of a polyline may be changed at any time after it has been output. The linetype, linewidth scale factor and polyline colour index workstation dependent aspects are said to be *dynamically bound*. The workstation may not be able to execute the changes in the picture immediately; Section 7.11 describes when the picture changes will take place and how this may be controlled.

Thus an important distinction between global aspects and workstation dependent aspects is that the former are statically bound while the latter are dynamically bound.

13.3 INDIVIDUAL ATTRIBUTES

So far, this book has concentrated on the bundled specification of workstation dependent aspects. The primitive index for a primitive points into a bundle table which contains the values of the workstation dependent aspects for that primitive. In the case of polyline described above, the polyline index points into the polyline bundle table which contains the values of linetype, linewidth scale factor and polyline colour index. Entries in the table may be altered by the SET POLYLINE REPRESEN-TATION function (and similar functions for other primitives) to provide dynamic binding of the workstation dependent aspects.

However, some applications require features of global aspects for these workstation dependent aspects; they require static binding and applicability on all workstations. GKS provides an alternative mode of working, called individual specification, which allows the workstation dependent aspects to be treated as global aspects.

For individual specification, the workstation dependent aspects are each controlled directly by attributes of the same name (called individual attributes). Thus, polyline has the individual attributes linetype, linewidth scale factor and polyline colour index. These attributes are bound to the primitive when it is output and cannot be changed. For example,

    SET LINETYPE(LT1)
    SET LINEWIDTH SCALE FACTOR(LW)
    SET POLYLINE COLOUR INDEX(PLCI)
    POLYLINE(N, XA, YA)
    SET LINETYPE(LT2)
    POLYLINE(M, XB, YB)

will output the first polyline with aspects LT1, LW and PLCI and the second polyline with aspects LT2, LW and PLCI on all workstations on which they appear. These aspects are statically bound.

An advantage of this mode of working is that lines may be specified as dashed, for example, and will appear dashed on all workstations. In addition, changing aspect values (by setting the corresponding attributes) will not affect primitives that have already been output.

The individual mode of working can also be very useful when the number of different forms of a primitive to be output is potentially very large. For example, if polylines need to be output in possibly five different linetypes, ten linewidths and 256 colours, this would require 12,800 bundle table entries on the workstation. In the individual mode of working, no bundle table entries are needed at all.

Conversely, since the aspects are set globally, it may only be possible to output a primitive with an approximation to its aspects on a particular workstation. In contrast to bundled specification, where a representation may be checked for availability by the specific workstation, it is not possible with individual specification for GKS to check that the specified value of an aspect is available on the required workstation when it is set, as the set of workstations may change while the value is in use. This means that the user has to be more aware of his environment when writing the program. Consider:

```
SET LINEWIDTH SCALE FACTOR(3.0)
POLYLINE(N, XA, YA)
SET LINEWIDTH SCALE FACTOR(1.0)
POLYLINE(M, XB, YB)
```

The user is attempting to differentiate the two polylines by drawing the first one thicker than the second. If the workstation he is using can only draw lines at one thickness, the differentiation will not be visible. A similar problem arises if colour is being used for differentiation when the workstation is a monochrome display!

GKS provides the following functions for individual specification of workstation dependent aspects:

```
SET LINETYPE(LT)
SET LINEWIDTH SCALE FACTOR(LW)
SET POLYLINE COLOUR INDEX(PLCI)
SET MARKER TYPE(MT)
SET MARKER SIZE SCALE FACTOR(MS)
SET POLYMARKER COLOUR INDEX(PMCI)
SET TEXT FONT AND PRECISION(TF, TP)
SET CHARACTER EXPANSION FACTOR(CEF)
SET CHARACTER SPACING(CS)
SET TEXT COLOUR INDEX(TCI)
SET FILL AREA INTERIOR STYLE(FAI)
SET FILL AREA STYLE INDEX(SI)
SET FILL AREA COLOUR INDEX(FACI)
```

The use of individual attributes is illustrated by rewriting the example in

Section 2.8 using individual specification:

```
REAL XNEWDK(44), YNEWDK(44), XNEWW(10), YNEWW(10)

PI = 4*ATAN(1)
XC = 45
YC = 45
R = 30

MOVE DUCK(XC, YC, R, 5*PI/6, XNEWDK, YNEWDK, XNEWW, YNEWW)
SET LINETYPE(1)
SET LINEWIDTH SCALE FACTOR(1)
SET POLYLINE COLOUR INDEX(1)
POLYLINE(44, XNEWDK, YNEWDK)
POLYLINE(10, XNEWW, YNEWW)

MOVE DUCK(XC, YC, R, PI/2, XNEWDK, YNEWDK, XNEWW, YNEWW)
SET LINETYPE(2)
POLYLINE(44, XNEWDK, YNEWDK)
POLYLINE(10, XNEWW, YNEWW)

MOVE DUCK(XC, YC, R, PI/6, XNEWDK, YNEWDK, XNEWW, YNEWW)
SET MARKER TYPE(3)
SET MARKER SIZE SCALE FACTOR(1)
SET POLYMARKER COLOUR INDEX(1)
POLYMARKER(44, XNEWDK, YNEWDK)
SET MARKER TYPE(2)
POLYMARKER(10, XNEWW, YNEWW)

MOVE DUCK(XC, YC, R, -PI/6, XNEWDK, YNEWDK, XNEWW, YNEWW)
SET FILL AREA INTERIOR STYLE(SOLID)
SET FILL AREA COLOUR INDEX(1)
FILL AREA(44, XNEWDK, YNEWDK)

MOVE DUCK(XC, YC, R, -PI/2, XNEWDK, YNEWDK, XNEWW, YNEWW)
SET FILL AREA INTERIOR STYLE(HATCH)
SET FILL AREA STYLE INDEX(-4)
FILL AREA(44, XNEWDK, YNEWDK)
SET LINETYPE(1)
POLYLINE(44, XNEWDK, YNEWDK)
```

```
MOVE DUCK(XC, YC, R, -5*PI/6, XNEWDK, YNEWDK, XNEWW, YNEWW)
FILL AREA(44, XNEWDK, YNEWDK)
SET LINETYPE(2)
POLYLINE(44, XNEWDK, YNEWDK)

SET TEXT FONT AND PRECISION(-104, STROKE)
SET CHARACTER EXPANSION FACTOR(1)
SET CHARACTER SPACING(0)
SET TEXT COLOUR INDEX(1)
SET CHARACTER HEIGHT(7.5)
SET TEXT ALIGNMENT(RIGHT, HALF)
TEXT(23.5, 45, 'G')
SET CHARACTER HEIGHT(3)
SET TEXT ALIGNMENT(LEFT, HALF)
TEXT(23.5, 45, 'RAPHICAL')
SET TEXT ALIGNMENT(RIGHT, HALF)
TEXT(59, 45, 'DUC')
SET CHARACTER HEIGHT(7.5)
SET TEXT ALIGNMENT(LEFT, HALF)
TEXT(59, 45, 'KS')
```

The output produced is the same as that shown in Figure 2-30. The same colour index is used for all primitives and so the output will be in one colour.

It should be noted that although the colour aspects are statically bound, the colour aspects are themselves indices into the colour table of the workstation. The entries in the colour table may be changed and the changes may affect the primitives that have already been output. Thus, to ensure that a primitive appears with the same colour on two workstations, it is necessary to make the colour table entry, pointed to by the colour index, the same on the two workstations.

13.4 SWITCHING MODES

It is clear that both modes of working cannot be in use at the same time. GKS provides a function which allows the user to switch between the two modes of working. This function is:

SET ASPECT SOURCE FLAGS(LST)

The array LST specifies for *each aspect* whether it is to be specified globally (INDIVIDUAL) or through a bundle (BUNDLED). Each element is termed an *aspect source flag* (ASF). The order of elements in this array is the same as the order in which the corresponding functions appear

above. Most installations are likely to define higher level routines on top
of this function to specify the mode of working for each primitive's
aspects. Although it is possible for the mode setting to be changed during
the program's execution, it is more normal for one mode to be set at the
start of the program for the complete program run.

A particular installation will specify one mode of working as the
default. Bundled specification will normally be set as the default although
it is possible in some installations where a small number of similar devices
exist that the default will be individual specification. Implementations in
the USA are likely to have individual specification as the default.

The examples in this book (in Chapter 2 in particular) assume that the
default mode of working is bundled. For these examples to work
correctly on an implementation of GKS for which the default is individual attributes, the following function call needs to be made after GKS
has been opened:

```
INTEGER LST(13)
DATA LST/13*BUNDLED/

SET ASPECT SOURCE FLAGS(LST)
```

Similarly, for the example in Section 13.3 to work correctly on an implementation for which the default is bundled, the following is required:

```
INTEGER LST(13)
DATA LST/13*INDIVIDUAL/

SET ASPECT SOURCE FLAGS(LST)
```

13.5 USER DEFINED BUNDLES

As each of the aspect source flags can be set independently, it is possible
to use mixed mode working and specify that some aspects are global and
statically bound while others are workstation dependent and dynamically
bound. It is useful to think of this as giving the user the ability to define
the contents of the bundles for each primitive. For example, if we consider that the text bundle should consist of only the text font and precision and text colour index aspects and that the character expansion factor
and character spacing should be global and should not vary between
workstations, we can achieve this by:

```
INTEGER LST(13)
DATA LST/13*BUNDLED/

LST(8) = INDIVIDUAL
LST(9) = INDIVIDUAL
SET ASPECT SOURCE FLAGS(LST)
```

Let us use these settings in an example:

```
SET TEXT REPRESENTATION(WS1, 4, 3, STROKE, 0, 1, 1)
SET TEXT REPRESENTATION(WS2, 4, 1, CHAR, 0, 1, 3)

SET TEXT INDEX(4)
SET CHARACTER HEIGHT(CH)
SET CHARACTER EXPANSION FACTOR(1.5)
SET CHARACTER SPACING(0.2)
TEXT(X, Y, LABEL)
```

The text will be output in font 3 at STROKE precision and colour 1 on workstation WS1 (maybe a monochrome high quality hardcopy device) and in font 1 at CHAR precision and colour 3 on workstation WS2 (maybe a colour raster display for preview). On both workstations a character expansion factor of 1.5 and a character spacing of 0.2 will be used (so that the characters are placed in the same positions on the preview device and the hardcopy device, for instance). The corresponding parameters in the SET TEXT REPRESENTATION functions have been specified as standard values, reflecting that these parameters are not used. They could equally well have been set to any other valid values as they are not used when the corresponding aspect source flags are set to INDIVIDUAL. However, the workstation will still check that a valid representation has been defined.

As has been shown, GKS provides a very versatile method of specifying how aspects should be associated with primitives. Novices are recommended to use either the bundled mode or the individual mode of working initially and only venture into mixed mode working, defining their own bundles, when they fully understand all the consequences.

Appendix A   Abbreviations

ACM	Association for Computing Machinery
ANSI	American National Standards Institute
ANSI X3H3	ANSI Computer Graphics Working Group
ASF	Aspect Source Flag
BSI	British Standards Institution
CGI	Computer Graphics Interface techniques for dialogues with graphical devices
CGM	Computer Graphics Metafile for transfer and storage of picture description information
DC	Device Coordinates
DIN	Deutsches Institute fur Normung, the West German Standards Organization
DIN UA5.9	DIN Computer Graphics Working Group
DIS	Draft International Standard
DP	Draft Proposal
GDP	Generalized Drawing Primitive
GINO	Graphical Input/Output (graphics package)
GKS	Graphical Kernel System
GKSM	GKS Metafile
GPGS	General Purpose Graphic System
GSPC	Graphic Standards Planning Committee
IDIGS	Interactive Device Independent Graphic System
IFIP	International Federation for Information Processing
IFIP WG5.2	IFIP CAD/CAM Working Group
IS	International Standard
ISO	International Organization for Standardization
ISO/TC97/SC5	Programming Languages Subcommittee of ISO (until 1984)
ISO/TC97/SC21	Open Systems Subcommittee of ISO (since 1985)
ISO/TC97/SC5/WG2	Computer Graphics Working Group of ISO (until 1984)

ISO/TC97/SC21/WG2	Computer Graphics Working Group of ISO (since 1985)
NDC	Normalized Device Coordinates
NWI	New Work Item
PHIGS	Programmers' Hierarchical Interactive Graphics System
SC5	Contraction of ISO/TC97/SC5
SC21	Contraction of ISO/TC97/SC21
SIGGRAPH	ACM Special Interest Group on Computer Graphics
WC	World Coordinates
WDSS	Workstation Dependent Segment Storage
WG2	Contraction of ISO/TC97/SC5/WG2 (until 1984) Contraction of ISO/TC97/SC21/WG2 (since 1985)
WISS	Workstation Independent Segment Storage
X3H3	Contraction of ANSI X3H3

Appendix B Language Binding

GKS, itself, is defined independently of a programming language. Before it can be used from a particular language, a *language binding* must be defined for that language. At the time of writing, the FORTRAN (77) language binding is being submitted for registration as a Draft International Standard. Details of the language binding are listed in this appendix and this is the binding used throughout the book. INQUIRY functions are excluded from this appendix.

Corresponding to some GKS functions, the language binding contains two subroutines; one is for full FORTRAN 77, the other is for the FORTRAN 77 subset. This occurs whenever the GKS function contains a string parameter, because it is not possible in the FORTRAN 77 subset for a CHARACTER variable to have an unknown length. Throughout the book and in this appendix, only the full FORTRAN 77 version is shown.

In the examples in the book, the GKS names were substituted for the subroutine names in the language binding. In this appendix, the GKS names are listed on the left hand side and the FORTRAN 77 subroutine names on the right hand side. The functions are grouped according to their type in the same manner as in the GKS document. Tables 1 and 2 contain alphabetical lists of each set of names together with their corresponding names in the other set.

The parameters of each subroutine are listed with an indication of whether they are input (In) or output (Out), their type and their meaning. Some parameters specify a number of options, which in Pascal would be of enumeration type. In the FORTRAN 77 language binding, these are expressed as integers. The correspondence between the names used in the text and the integers in the language binding is given in Table 3. The FORTRAN 77 language binding defines names for these values, that should be made available, by means of PARAMETER or DATA statements, for inclusion in application programs (in an installation dependent manner). These names are listed in Table 4. Names used exclusively in INQUIRY functions are omitted.

Table 1

GKS Name	FORTRAN 77 Name
ACCUMULATE TRANSFORMATION MATRIX	GACTM
ACTIVATE WORKSTATION	GACWK
ASSOCIATE SEGMENT WITH WORKSTATION	GASGWK
AWAIT EVENT	GWAIT
CELL ARRAY	GCA
CLEAR WORKSTATION	GCLRWK
CLOSE GKS	GCLKS
CLOSE SEGMENT	GCLSG
CLOSE WORKSTATION	GCLWK
COPY SEGMENT TO WORKSTATION	GCSGWK
CREATE SEGMENT	GCRSG
DEACTIVATE WORKSTATION	GDAWK
DELETE SEGMENT	GDSG
DELETE SEGMENT FROM WORKSTATION	GDSGWK
EMERGENCY CLOSE GKS	GECLKS
ERROR HANDLING	GERHND
ERROR LOGGING	GERLOG
ESCAPE	GESC
EVALUATE TRANSFORMATION MATRIX	GEVTM
FILL AREA	GFA
FLUSH DEVICE EVENTS	GFLUSH
GENERALIZED DRAWING PRIMITIVE	GGDP
GET CHOICE	GGTCH
GET ITEM TYPE FROM GKSM	GGTITM
GET LOCATOR	GGTLC
GET PICK	GGTPK
GET STRING	GGTST
GET STROKE	GGTSK
GET VALUATOR	GGTVL
INITIALISE CHOICE	GINCH
INITIALISE LOCATOR	GINLC
INITIALISE PICK	GINPK
INITIALISE STRING	GINST
INITIALISE STROKE	GINSK
INITIALISE VALUATOR	GINVL
INSERT SEGMENT	GINSG
INTERPRET ITEM	GIITM
MESSAGE	GMSG
OPEN GKS	GOPKS

OPEN WORKSTATION	GOPWK
PACK DATA RECORD (Language Binding)	GPREC
POLYLINE	GPL
POLYMARKER	GPM
READ ITEM FROM GKSM	GRDITM
REDRAW ALL SEGMENTS ON WORKSTATION	GRSGWK
RENAME SEGMENT	GRENSG
REQUEST CHOICE	GRQCH
REQUEST LOCATOR	GRQLC
REQUEST PICK	GRQPK
REQUEST STRING	GRQST
REQUEST STROKE	GRQSK
REQUEST VALUATOR	GRQVL
SAMPLE CHOICE	GSMCH
SAMPLE LOCATOR	GSMLC
SAMPLE PICK	GSMPK
SAMPLE STRING	GSMST
SAMPLE STROKE	GSMSK
SAMPLE VALUATOR	GSMVL
SELECT NORMALIZATION TRANSFORMATION	GSELNT
SET ASPECT SOURCE FLAGS	GSASF
SET CHARACTER EXPANSION FACTOR	GSCHXP
SET CHARACTER HEIGHT	GSCHH
SET CHARACTER SPACING	GSCHSP
SET CHARACTER UP VECTOR	GSCHUP
SET CHOICE MODE	GSCHM
SET CLIPPING INDICATOR	GSCLIP
SET COLOUR REPRESENTATION	GSCR
SET DEFERRAL STATE	GSDS
SET DETECTABILITY	GSDTEC
SET FILL AREA COLOUR INDEX	GSFACI
SET FILL AREA INDEX	GSFAI
SET FILL AREA INTERIOR STYLE	GSFAIS
SET FILL AREA REPRESENTATION	GSFAR
SET FILL AREA STYLE INDEX	GSFASI
SET HIGHLIGHTING	GSHLIT
SET LINETYPE	GSLN
SET LINEWIDTH SCALE FACTOR	GSLWSC
SET LOCATOR MODE	GSLCM
SET MARKER SIZE SCALE FACTOR	GSMKSC
SET MARKER TYPE	GSMK
SET PATTERN REFERENCE POINT	GSPARF
SET PATTERN REPRESENTATION	GSPAR

SET PATTERN SIZE	GSPA
SET PICK IDENTIFIER	GSPKID
SET PICK MODE	GSPKM
SET POLYLINE COLOUR INDEX	GSPLCI
SET POLYLINE INDEX	GSPLI
SET POLYLINE REPRESENTATION	GSPLR
SET POLYMARKER COLOUR INDEX	GSPMCI
SET POLYMARKER INDEX	GSPMI
SET POLYMARKER REPRESENTATION	GSPMR
SET SEGMENT PRIORITY	GSSGP
SET SEGMENT TRANSFORMATION	GSSGT
SET STRING MODE	GSSTM
SET STROKE MODE	GSSKM
SET TEXT ALIGNMENT	GSTXAL
SET TEXT COLOUR INDEX	GSTXCI
SET TEXT FONT AND PRECISION	GSTXFP
SET TEXT INDEX	GSTXI
SET TEXT PATH	GSTXP
SET TEXT REPRESENTATION	GSTXR
SET VALUATOR MODE	GSVLM
SET VIEWPORT	GSVP
SET VIEWPORT INPUT PRIORITY	GSVPIP
SET VISIBILITY	GSVIS
SET WINDOW	GSWN
SET WORKSTATION VIEWPORT	GSWKVP
SET WORKSTATION WINDOW	GSWKWN
TEXT	GTX
UNPACK DATA RECORD (Language Binding)	GUREC
UPATE WORKSTATION	GUWK
WRITE ITEM TO GKSM	GWITM

Table 2

FORTRAN 77 Name	GKS Name
GACTM	ACCUMULATE TRANSFORMATION MATRIX
GACWK	ACTIVATE WORKSTATION
GASGWK	ASSOCIATE SEGMENT WITH WORKSTATION
GCA	CELL ARRAY
GCLKS	CLOSE GKS
GCLRWK	CLEAR WORKSTATION
GCLSG	CLOSE SEGMENT
GCLWK	CLOSE WORKSTATION
GCRSG	CREATE SEGMENT
GCSGWK	COPY SEGMENT TO WORKSTATION
GDAWK	DEACTIVATE WORKSTATION
GDSG	DELETE SEGMENT
GDSGWK	DELETE SEGMENT FROM WORKSTATION
GECLKS	EMERGENCY CLOSE GKS
GERHND	ERROR HANDLING
GERLOG	ERROR LOGGING
GESC	ESCAPE
GEVTM	EVALUATE TRANSFORMATION MATRIX
GFA	FILL AREA
GFLUSH	FLUSH DEVICE EVENTS
GGDP	GENERALIZED DRAWING PRIMITIVE
GGTCH	GET CHOICE
GGTITM	GET ITEM TYPE FROM GKSM
GGTLC	GET LOCATOR
GGTPK	GET PICK
GGTSK	GET STROKE
GGTST	GET STRING
GGTVL	GET VALUATOR
GIITM	INTERPRET ITEM
GINCH	INITIALISE CHOICE
GINLC	INITIALISE LOCATOR
GINPK	INITIALISE PICK
GINSG	INSERT SEGMENT
GINSK	INITIALISE STROKE
GINST	INITIALISE STRING
GINVL	INITIALISE VALUATOR
GMSG	MESSAGE
GOPKS	OPEN GKS

GOPWK	OPEN WORKSTATION
GPL	POLYLINE
GPM	POLYMARKER
GPREC	PACK DATA RECORD (language binding)
GRDITM	READ ITEM FROM GKSM
GRENSG	RENAME SEGMENT
GRQCH	REQUEST CHOICE
GRQLC	REQUEST LOCATOR
GRQPK	REQUEST PICK
GRQSK	REQUEST STROKE
GRQST	REQUEST STRING
GRQVL	REQUEST VALUATOR
GRSGWK	REDRAW ALL SEGMENTS ON WORKSTATION
GSASF	SET ASPECT SOURCE FLAGS
GSCHH	SET CHARACTER HEIGHT
GSCHM	SET CHOICE MODE
GSCHSP	SET CHARACTER SPACING
GSCHUP	SET CHARACTER UP VECTOR
GSCHXP	SET CHARACTER EXPANSION FACTOR
GSCLIP	SET CLIPPING INDICATOR
GSCR	SET COLOUR REPRESENTATION
GSDS	SET DEFERRAL STATE
GSDTEC	SET DETECTABILITY
GSELNT	SELECT NORMALIZATION TRANSFORMATION
GSFACI	SET FILL AREA COLOUR INDEX
GSFAI	SET FILL AREA INDEX
GSFAIS	SET FILL AREA INTERIOR STYLE
GSFAR	SET FILL AREA REPRESENTATION
GSFASI	SET FILL AREA STYLE INDEX
GSHLIT	SET HIGHLIGHTING
GSLCM	SET LOCATOR MODE
GSLN	SET LINETYPE
GSLWSC	SET LINEWIDTH SCALE FACTOR
GSMCH	SAMPLE CHOICE
GSMK	SET MARKER TYPE
GSMKSC	SET MARKER SIZE SCALE FACTOR
GSMLC	SAMPLE LOCATOR
GSMPK	SAMPLE PICK
GSMSK	SAMPLE STROKE
GSMST	SAMPLE STRING
GSMVL	SAMPLE VALUATOR
GSPA	SET PATTERN SIZE
GSPAR	SET PATTERN REPRESENTATION

GSPARF	SET PATTERN REFERENCE POINT
GSPKID	SET PICK IDENTIFIER
GSPKM	SET PICK MODE
GSPLCI	SET POLYLINE COLOUR INDEX
GSPLI	SET POLYLINE INDEX
GSPLR	SET POLYLINE REPRESENTATION
GSPMCI	SET POLYMARKER COLOUR INDEX
GSPMI	SET POLYMARKER INDEX
GSPMR	SET POLYMARKER REPRESENTATION
GSSGP	SET SEGMENT PRIORITY
GSSGT	SET SEGMENT TRANSFORMATION
GSSKM	SET STROKE MODE
GSSTM	SET STRING MODE
GSTXAL	SET TEXT ALIGNMENT
GSTXCI	SET TEXT COLOUR INDEX
GSTXFP	SET TEXT FONT AND PRECISION
GSTXI	SET TEXT INDEX
GSTXP	SET TEXT PATH
GSTXR	SET TEXT REPRESENTATION
GSVIS	SET VISIBILITY
GSVLM	SET VALUATOR MODE
GSVP	SET VIEWPORT
GSVPIP	SET VIEWPORT INPUT PRIORITY
GSWKVP	SET WORKSTATION VIEWPORT
GSWKWN	SET WORKSTATION WINDOW
GSWN	SET WINDOW
GTX	TEXT
GUREC	UNPACK DATA RECORD (Language Binding)
GUWK	UPDATE WORKSTATION
GWAIT	AWAIT EVENT
GWITM	WRITE ITEM TO GKSM

Table 3

Aspect Source
    0 BUNDLED   1 INDIVIDUAL
Clear Control Flag
    0 CONDITIONALLY 1 ALWAYS
Clipping Indicator
    0 NOCLIP   1 CLIP
Coordinate Switch
    0 WC   1 NDC
Deferral Mode
    0 ASAP   1 BNIG   2 BNIL   3 ASTI
Detectability
    0 UNDETECTABLE 1 DETECTABLE
Echo Switch
    0 NOECHO   1 ECHO
Fill Area Interior Style
    0 HOLLOW   1 SOLID   2 PATTERN   3 HATCH
Highlighting
    0 NORMAL   1 HIGHLIGHTED
Implicit Regeneration Mode
    0 SUPPRESSED   1 ALLOWED
Input Class
    0 NONE   1 LOCATOR   2 STROKE   3 VALUATOR
    4 CHOICE   5 PICK   6 STRING
Input Device Status
    0 NONE   1 OK   2 NOPICK
                                      2 NOCHOICE
Operating Mode
    0 REQUEST   1 SAMPLE   2 EVENT
Relative Viewport Input Priority
    0 HIGHER   1 LOWER
Simultaneous Events Flag
    0 NOMORE   1 MORE
Text Alignment Horizontal
    0 NORMAL   1 LEFT   2 CENTRE   3 RIGHT
Text Alignment Vertical
    0 NORMAL   1 TOP   2 CAP   3 HALF
    4 BASE   5 BOTTOM
Text Path
    0 RIGHT   1 LEFT   2 UP   3 DOWN
Text Precision
    0 STRING   1 CHAR   2 STROKE
Type of Returned Values
    0 SET   1 REALIZED
Update Regeneration Flag
    0 POSTPONE   1 PERFORM
Visibility
    0 INVISIBLE   1 VISIBLE

Table 4

Aspect Source			
0 GBUNDL	1 GINDIV		
Clear Control Flag			
0 GCONDI	1 GALWAY		
Clipping Indicator			
0 GNCLIP	1 GCLIP		
Coordinate Switch			
0 GWC	1 GNDC		
Deferral Mode			
0 GASAP	1 GBNIG	2 GBNIL	3 GASTI
Detectability			
0 GUNDET	1 GDETEC		
Echo Switch			
0 GNECHO	1 GECHO		
Fill Area Interior Style			
0 GHOLLO	1 GSOLID	2 GPATTR	3 GHATCH
Highlighting			
0 GNORML	1 GHILIT		
Implicit Regeneration Mode			
0 GSUPPD	1 GALLOW		
Input Class			
0 GNCLAS	1 GLOCAT	2 GSTROK	3 GVALUA
4 GCHOIC	5 GPICK	6 GSTRIN	
Input Device Status			
0 GNONE	1 GOK	2 GNPICK	
		2 GNCHOI	
Operating Mode			
0 GREQU	1 GSAMPL	2 GEVENT	
Relative Viewport Input Priority			
0 GHIGHR	1 GLOWER		
Simultaneous Events Flag			
0 GNMORE	1 GMORE		
Text Alignment Horizontal			
0 GAHNOR	1 GALEFT	2 GACENT	3 GARITE
Text Alignment Vertical			
0 GAVNOR	1 GATOP	2 GACAP	3 GAHALF
4 GABASE	5 GABOTT		
Text Path			
0 GRIGHT	1 GLEFT	2 GUP	3 GDOWN
Text Precision			
0 GSTRP	1 GCHARP	2 GSTRKP	
Type of Returned Values			
0 GSET	1 GREALI		
Update Regeneration Flag			
0 GPOSTP	1 GPERFO		
Visibility			
0 GINVIS	1 GVISI		

CONTROL FUNCTIONS

OPEN GKS   GOPKS

SUBROUTINE GOPKS(ERRFIL, BUFA)

In   INTEGER ERRFIL   error message file
In   INTEGER BUFA   amount of memory units for buffer area

Start working with GKS

CLOSE GKS   GCLKS

SUBROUTINE GCLKS

None

Stop working with GKS

OPEN WORKSTATION   GOPWK

SUBROUTINE GOPWK(WKID, CONID, WTYPE)

In   INTEGER WKID   workstation identifier
In   INTEGER CONID   connection identifier
In   INTEGER WTYPE   workstation type

Create a connection between the specified workstation and GKS

CLOSE WORKSTATION   GCLWK

SUBROUTINE GCLWK(WKID)

In   INTEGER WKID   workstation identifier

Release the connection between the specified workstation and GKS

ACTIVATE WORKSTATION   GACWK

SUBROUTINE GACWK(WKID)

In   INTEGER WKID   workstation identifier

Output is routed to the specified workstation

DEACTIVATE WORKSTATION   GDAWK

SUBROUTINE GDAWK(WKID)
In   INTEGER WKID   workstation identifier

Output is no longer routed to the specified workstation

CLEAR WORKSTATION   GCLRWK

SUBROUTINE GCLRWK(WKID, COFL)
In   INTEGER WKID   workstation identifier
In   INTEGER COFL   control flag

Perform all deferred actions and clear display space on the specified
workstation. All segments stored on the workstation are deleted

REDRAW ALL SEGMENTS ON WORKSTATION   GRSGWK

SUBROUTINE GRSGWK(WKID)
In   INTEGER WKID   workstation identifier

Redraw all visible segments stored on the specified workstation

UPDATE WORKSTATION   GUWK

SUBROUTINE GUWK(WKID, REGFL)
In   INTEGER WKID   workstation identifier
In   INTEGER REGFL   update regeneration flag

Perform all deferred actions and redraw all visible segments stored on
the specified workstation

SET DEFERRAL STATE   GSDS

SUBROUTINE GSDS(WKID, DEFMOD, REGMOD)
In   INTEGER WKID   workstation identifier
In   INTEGER DEFMOD   deferral mode
In   INTEGER REGMOD   implicit regeneration mode

Set deferral state for the specified workstation

MESSAGE   **GMSG**

SUBROUTINE GMSG(WKID, MESS)
In   INTEGER WKID   workstation identifier
In   CHARACTER*(*) MESS   message

Send a message to the specified workstation

ESCAPE   **GESC**

SUBROUTINE GESC(FCTID, LIDR, IDR, MODR, LODR, ODR)
In   INTEGER FCTID   function identification
In   INTEGER LIDR   dimension of escape input data record
In   CHARACTER*80 IDR(LIDR)   escape input data record
In   INTEGER MODR   maximum length of escape output data record
Out INTEGER LODR   number of array elements occupied in ODR
Out CHARACTER*80 ODR(MODR)   escape output data record

A standard way of invoking non-standard features

OUTPUT FUNCTIONS

POLYLINE   **GPL**

SUBROUTINE GPL(N, PX, PY)
In   INTEGER N   number of points
In   REAL PX(N)   X coordinates of points in WC
In   REAL PY(N)   Y coordinates of points in WC

Generate a polyline defined by points in world coordinates

POLYMARKER   **GPM**

SUBROUTINE GPM(N, PX, PY)
In   INTEGER N   number of points
In   REAL PX(N)   X coordinates of points in WC
In   REAL PY(N)   Y coordinates of points in WC

Generate markers of a given type at specified points in world coordinates

TEXT   **GTX**

SUBROUTINE GTX(PX, PY, CHARS)

In	REAL PX	X coordinate of text position in WC
In	REAL PY	Y coordinate of text position in WC
In	CHARACTER*(*) CHARS	string of characters

Generate a text string at the given position in world coordinates

FILL AREA   **GFA**

SUBROUTINE GFA(N, PX, PY)

In	INTEGER N	number of points
In	REAL PX(N)	X coordinates of points in WC
In	REAL PY(N)	Y coordinates of points in WC

Generate a polygon which may be filled with a colour, a hatch or a pattern, or may be hollow

CELL ARRAY   **GCA**

SUBROUTINE GCA(PX, PY, QX, QY, DIMX, DIMY,
        ISC, ISR, DX, DY, CLA)

In	REAL PX	
In	REAL PY	two points (P, Q) in WC
In	REAL QX	
In	REAL QY	
In	INTEGER DIMX	dimension of CLA in x
In	INTEGER DIMY	dimension of CLA in y
In	INTEGER ISC	index of starting column
In	INTEGER ISR	index of starting row
In	INTEGER DX	number of columns in colour index array
In	INTEGER DY	number of rows in colour index array
In	INTEGER CLA(DIMX, DIMY)	colour index array

Map the given array of colour indices onto the display surface

GENERALIZED DRAWING PRIMITIVE   GGDP

SUBROUTINE GGDP(N, PX, PY, PRIMID, LDR, DR)

In	INTEGER N	number of points
In	REAL PX(*)	X coordinates of points in WC
In	REAL PY(*)	Y coordinates of points in WC
In	INTEGER PRIMID	GDP identifier
In	INTEGER LDR	dimension of GDP data record
In	CHARACTER*80 DR(LDR)	GDP data record

Generate a generalized drawing primitive defined by a sequence of points in world coordinates and a data record

OUTPUT ATTRIBUTES

Workstation Independent Primitive Attributes

SET POLYLINE INDEX   GSPLI

SUBROUTINE GSPLI(INDEX)

In	INTEGER INDEX	polyline index

Select a bundle index for polylines

SET LINETYPE   GSLN

SUBROUTINE GSLN(LTYPE)

In	INTEGER LTYPE	linetype

Set the linetype for use when the corresponding ASF is INDIVIDUAL

SET LINEWIDTH SCALE FACTOR   GSLWSC

SUBROUTINE GSLWSC(LWIDTH)

In	REAL LWIDTH	linewidth scale factor

Set the linewidth scale factor for use when the corresponding ASF is INDIVIDUAL

SET POLYLINE COLOUR INDEX   GSPLCI

SUBROUTINE GSPLCI(COLI)

In   INTEGER COLI   polyline colour index

Set the polyline colour index for use when the corresponding ASF is INDIVIDUAL

SET POLYMARKER INDEX   GSPMI

SUBROUTINE GSPMI(INDEX)

In   INTEGER INDEX   polymarker index

Select a bundle index for polymarkers

SET MARKER TYPE   GSMK

SUBROUTINE GSMK(MTYPE)

In   INTEGER MTYPE   marker type

Set the marker type for use when the corresponding ASF is INDIVIDUAL

SET MARKER SIZE SCALE FACTOR   GSMKSC

SUBROUTINE GSMKSC(MSZSF)

In   REAL MSZSF   marker size scale factor

Set the marker size scale factor for use when the corresponding ASF is INDIVIDUAL

SET POLYMARKER COLOUR INDEX   GSPMCI

SUBROUTINE GSPMCI(COLI)

In   INTEGER COLI   polymarker colour index

Set the polymarker colour index for use when the corresponding ASF is INDIVIDUAL

SET TEXT INDEX   GSTXI

SUBROUTINE GSTXI(INDEX)

In   INTEGER INDEX   text index

Select a bundle index for text

SET TEXT FONT AND PRECISION   GSTXFP

SUBROUTINE GSTXFP(FONT, PREC)

In   INTEGER FONT   text font
In   INTEGER PREC   text precision

Set the text font and precision for use when the corresponding ASF is INDIVIDUAL

SET CHARACTER EXPANSION FACTOR   GSCHXP

SUBROUTINE GSCHXP(CHXP)

In   REAL CHXP   character expansion factor

Set the character expansion factor as a fraction of the character height for use when the corresponding ASF is INDIVIDUAL

SET CHARACTER SPACING   GSCHSP

SUBROUTINE GSCHSP(CHSP)

In   REAL CHSP   character spacing

Set the character spacing as a fraction of the character height for use when the corresponding ASF is INDIVIDUAL

SET TEXT COLOUR INDEX   GSTXCI

SUBROUTINE GSTXCI(COLI)

In   INTEGER COLI   text colour index

Set the text colour index for use when the corresponding ASF is INDIVIDUAL

SET CHARACTER HEIGHT   GSCHH

SUBROUTINE GSCHH(CHH)

In   REAL CHH   character height in WC

Set the character height in world coordinates

SET CHARACTER UP VECTOR   GSCHUP

SUBROUTINE GSCHUP(CHUX, CHUY)

| In | REAL CHUX | X component of character up vector in WC |
| In | REAL CHUY | Y component of character up vector in WC |

Set the character up vector in world coordinates

SET TEXT PATH   GSTXP

SUBROUTINE GSTXP(TXP)

| In | INTEGER TXP | text path |

Set the text path

SET TEXT ALIGNMENT   GSTXAL

SUBROUTINE GSTXAL(TXALH, TXALV)

| In | INTEGER TXALH | text alignment horizontal |
| In | INTEGER TXALV | text alignment vertical |

Set the horizontal and vertical alignment of text strings

SET FILL AREA INDEX   GSFAI

SUBROUTINE GSFAI(INDEX)

| In | INTEGER INDEX | fill area index |

Select a bundle index for fill area

SET FILL AREA INTERIOR STYLE   GSFAIS

SUBROUTINE GSFAIS(INTS)

| In | INTEGER INTS | fill area interior style |

Set the fill area interior style for use when the corresponding ASF is INDIVIDUAL

SET FILL AREA STYLE INDEX   GSFASI

SUBROUTINE GSFASI(STYLI)

| In | INTEGER STYLI | fill area style index |

Set the fill area style index for use when the corresponding ASF is IN-DIVIDUAL

SET FILL AREA COLOUR INDEX   GSFACI

SUBROUTINE GSFACI(COLI)

In   INTEGER COLI   fill area colour index

Set the fill area colour index for use when the corresponding ASF is INDIVIDUAL

SET PATTERN SIZE   GSPA

SUBROUTINE GSPA(SZX, SZY)

In   REAL SZX   pattern size (X) in WC
In   REAL SZY   pattern size (Y) in WC

Set the pattern size in world coordinates for use in the display of fill area primtives with interior style PATTERN

SET PATTERN REFERENCE POINT   GSPARF

SUBROUTINE GSPARF(RFX, RFY)

In   REAL RFX   X coordinate of pattern reference point in WC
In   REAL RFY   Y coordinate of pattern reference point in WC

Set the pattern reference point in world coordinates for use in the display of fill area primitives with interior style PATTERN

SET ASPECT SOURCE FLAGS   GSASF

SUBROUTINE GSASF(LASF)

In   INTEGER LASF(13)   list of aspect source flags

Define whether the value of each non-geometric aspect is obtained from the corresponding individual attribute or from the appropriate bundle on the workstation

SET PICK IDENTIFIER   GSPKID

SUBROUTINE GSPKID(PKID)

In   INTEGER PKID   pick identifier

Set pick identifier

Workstation Attributes (Representations)

SET POLYLINE REPRESENTATION   GSPLR

SUBROUTINE GSPLR(WKID, PLI, LTYPE, LWIDTH, COLI)

In	INTEGER WKID	workstation identifier
In	INTEGER PLI	polyline index
In	INTEGER LTYPE	linetype
In	REAL LWIDTH	linewidth scale factor
In	INTEGER COLI	colour index

Define the representation of polylines on the specified workstation

SET POLYMARKER REPRESENTATION   GSPMR

SUBROUTINE GSPMR(WKID, PMI, MTYPE, MSZSF, COLI)

In	INTEGER WKID	workstation identifier
In	INTEGER PMI	polymarker index
In	INTEGER MTYPE	marker type
In	REAL MSZSF	marker size scale factor
In	INTEGER COLI	colour index

Define the representation of polymarkers on the specified workstation

SET TEXT REPRESENTATION

SUBROUTINE GSTXR(WKID, TXI, FONT, PREC, CHXP, CHSP, COLI)

In	INTEGER WKID	workstation identifier
In	INTEGER TXI	text index
In	INTEGER FONT	text font
In	INTEGER PREC	text precision
In	REAL CHXP	character expansion factor
In	REAL CHSP	character spacing
In	INTEGER COLI	colour index

Define the representation of text on the specified workstation

SET FILL AREA REPRESENTATION   GSFAR

SUBROUTINE GSFAR(WKID, FAI, INTS, STYLI, COLI)

In	INTEGER WKID	workstation identifier
In	INTEGER FAI	fill area index
In	INTEGER INTS	interior style
In	INTEGER STYLI	style index
In	INTEGER COLI	colour index

Define the representation of fill area primitives on the specified workstation

SET PATTERN REPRESENTATION   GSPAR

SUBROUTINE GSPAR(WKID, PAI, DIMX, DIMY,
    ISC, ISR, DX, DY, CLA)

In	INTEGER WKID	workstation identifier
In	INTEGER PAI	pattern index
In	INTEGER DIMX	dimension of CLA in x
In	INTEGER DIMY	dimension of CLA in y
In	INTEGER ISC	index of start column
In	INTEGER ISR	index of start row
In	INTEGER DX	number of columns in pattern array
In	INTEGER DY	number of rows in pattern array
In	INTEGER CLA(DIMX, DIMY)	pattern array

Define the pattern to be associated with a pattern index (i.e. a fill area style index) on the specified workstation

SET COLOUR REPRESENTATION   GSCR

SUBROUTINE GSCR(WKID, CI, CR, CG, CB)

In	INTEGER WKID	workstation identifier
In	INTEGER CI	colour index
In	REAL CR	red intensity
In	REAL CG	green intensity
In	REAL CB	blue intensity

Define the colour to be associated with a colour index on the specified workstation

TRANSFORMATION FUNCTIONS

Normalization Transformation

SET WINDOW   **GSWN**

SUBROUTINE GSWN(TNR, XMIN, XMAX, YMIN, YMAX)
In	INTEGER TNR	transformation number
In	REAL XMIN	window limits in WC
In	REAL XMAX	XMIN < XMAX
In	REAL YMIN	YMIN < YMAX
In	REAL YMAX	

Set the window in world coordinates of the specified normalization transformation

SET VIEWPORT   **GSVP**

SUBROUTINE GSVP(TNR, XMIN, XMAX, YMIN, YMAX)
In	INTEGER TNR	transformation number
In	REAL XMIN	viewport limits in NDC
In	REAL XMAX	XMIN < XMAX
In	REAL YMIN	YMIN < YMAX
In	REAL YMAX	

Set the viewport in normalized device coordinates of the specified normalization transformation

SET VIEWPORT INPUT PRIORITY   **GSVPIP**

SUBROUTINE GSVPIP(TNR, RTNR, RELPRI)
In	INTEGER TNR	transformation number
In	INTEGER RTNR	reference transformation number
In	INTEGER RELPRI	relative priority

Set the input priority of the specified viewport for locator and stroke input

SELECT NORMALIZATION TRANSFORMATION   **GSELNT**

SUBROUTINE GSELNT(TNR)
| In | INTEGER TNR | transformation number |

Select a normalization transformation for output

SET CLIPPING INDICATOR   GSCLIP

SUBROUTINE GSCLIP(CLSW)

In   INTEGER CLSW   clipping indicator

Set the clipping indicator for the current normalization transformation

Workstation Transformation

SET WORKSTATION WINDOW   GSWKWN

SUBROUTINE GSWKWN(WKID, XMIN, XMAX, YMIN, YMAX)

In	INTEGER WKID	workstation identifier
In	REAL XMIN	workstation window limits in NDC
In	REAL XMAX	XMIN < XMAX
In	REAL YMIN	YMIN < YMAX
In	REAL YMAX	

Set the workstation window in normalized device coordinates

SET WORKSTATION VIEWPORT   GSWKVP

SUBROUTINE GSWKVP(WKID, XMIN, XMAX, YMIN, YMAX)

In	INTEGER WKID	workstation identifier
In	REAL XMIN	workstation viewport limits in DC
In	REAL XMAX	XMIN < XMAX
In	REAL YMIN	YMIN < YMAX
In	REAL YMAX	

Set the workstation viewport in device coordinates

SEGMENT FUNCTIONS

Segment Manipulation Functions

CREATE SEGMENT   GCRSG

SUBROUTINE GCRSG(SGNA)

In   INTEGER SGNA   segment name

The specified segment is created and becomes the open segment

CLOSE SEGMENT GCLSG

SUBROUTINE GCLSG
None

Close the open segment

RENAME SEGMENT GRENSG

SUBROUTINE GRENSG(OLD, NEW)
In   INTEGER OLD   old segment name
In   INTEGER NEW   new segment name

Change the name of the specified segment

DELETE SEGMENT GDSG

SUBROUTINE GDSG(SGNA)
In   INTEGER SGNA   segment name

Delete the specified segment

DELETE SEGMENT FROM WORKSTATION GDSGWK

SUBROUTINE GDSGWK(WKID, SGNA)
In   INTEGER WKID   workstation identifier
In   INTEGER SGNA   segment name

Delete the specified segment from the specified workstation

ASSOCIATE SEGMENT WITH WORKSTATION GASGWK

SUBROUTINE GASGWK(WKID, SGNA)
In   INTEGER WKID   workstation identifier
In   INTEGER SGNA   segment name

Associate the specified segment, present in workstation independent segment storage, with the specified open workstation

COPY SEGMENT TO WORKSTATION   GCSGWK

SUBROUTINE GCSGWK(WKID, SGNA)

| In | INTEGER WKID | workstation identifier |
| In | INTEGER SGNA | segment name |

Copy the primitives of the specified segment, present in workstation independent segment storage, to the specified workstation

INSERT SEGMENT   GINSG

SUBROUTINE GINSG(SGNA, M)

| In | INTEGER SGNA | segment name |
| In | REAL M(2, 3) | transformation matrix |

Insert the specified segment, present in workstation independent segment storage, (after the segment transformation and the insert transformation have been applied) into the open segment or the stream of primitives outside segments

Segment Attributes

SET SEGMENT TRANSFORMATION   GSSGT

SUBROUTINE GSSGT(SGNA, M)

| In | INTEGER SGNA | segment name |
| In | REAL M(2, 3) | transformation matrix |

Set the segment transformation attribute for the specified segment

SET VISIBILITY   GSVIS

SUBROUTINE GSVIS(SGNA, VIS)

| In | INTEGER SGNA | segment name |
| In | INTEGER VIS | visibility |

Set the visibility attribute for the specified segment

SET HIGHLIGHTING   GSHLIT

SUBROUTINE GSHLIT(SGNA, HIL)

In   INTEGER SGNA   segment name
In   INTEGER HIL   highlighting

Set the highlighting attribute for the specified segment

SET SEGMENT PRIORITY   GSSGP

SUBROUTINE GSSGP(SGNA, PRIOR)

In   INTEGER SGNA   segment name
In   REAL PRIOR   segment priority

Set the segment priority attribute for the specified segment

SET DETECTABILITY   GSDTEC

SUBROUTINE GSDTEC(SGNA,DET)

In   INTEGER SGNA   segment name
In   INTEGER DET   detectability

Set the segment detectability attribute for the specified segment

INPUT FUNCTIONS

Initialisation of Input Devices

INITIALISE LOCATOR   GINLC

SUBROUTINE GINLC(WKID, LCDNR, TNR, IPX, IPY, PET,
    XMIN, XMAX, YMIN, YMAX, LDR, DR)

In	INTEGER WKID	workstation identifier
In	INTEGER LCDNR	locator device number
In	INTEGER TNR	initial normalization transformation number
In	REAL IPX	X coordinate of initial locator position in WC
In	REAL IPY	Y coordinate of initial locator position in WC
In	INTEGER PET	prompt and echo type
In	REAL XMIN	echo area limits in DC
In	REAL XMAX	XMIN < XMAX
In	REAL YMIN	YMIN < YMAX
In	REAL YMAX	
In	INTEGER LDR	length of locator data record
In	CHARACTER*80 DR(LDR)	locator data record

Initialise the specified locator device

INITIALISE STROKE   GINSK

SUBROUTINE GINSK(WKID, SKDNR, TNR, N, IPX, IPY, PET,
    XMIN, XMAX, YMIN, YMAX, BUFLEN, LDR, DR)

In	INTEGER WKID	workstation identifier
In	INTEGER SKDNR	stroke device number
In	INTEGER TNR	initial normalization transformation number
In	INTEGER N	number of points in initial stroke (may be ≥ 0)
In	REAL IPX(*)	X coordinates of points in initial stroke
In	REAL IPY(*)	Y coordinates of points in initial stroke
In	INTEGER PET	prompt and echo type
In	REAL XMIN	echo area limits in DC
In	REAL XMAX	XMIN < XMAX
In	REAL YMIN	YMIN < YMAX
In	REAL YMAX	
In	INTEGER BUFLEN	buffer length for stroke
In	INTEGER LDR	length of stroke data record
In	CHARACTER*80 DR(LDR)	stroke data record

Initialise the specified stroke device

INITIALISE VALUATOR   **GINVL**

SUBROUTINE GINVL(WKID, VLDNR, IVAL, PET,
   XMIN, XMAX, YMIN, YMAX, LOVAL, HIVAL, LDR, DR)

In	INTEGER WKID	workstation identifier
In	INTEGER VLDNR	valuator device number
In	REAL IVAL	initial value
In	INTEGER PET	prompt and echo type
In	REAL XMIN	echo area limits in DC
In	REAL XMAX	XMIN < XMAX
In	REAL YMIN	YMIN < YMAX
In	REAL YMAX	
In	REAL LOVAL	low limit of valuator range
In	REAL HIVAL	high limit of valuator range
In	INTEGER LDR	length of valuator data record
In	CHARACTER*80 DR(LDR)	valuator data record

Initialise the specified valuator device

INITIALISE CHOICE   **GINCH**

SUBROUTINE GINCH(WKID, CHDNR, ISTAT, ICH, PET,
   XMIN, XMAX, YMIN, YMAX, LDR, DR)

In	INTEGER WKID	workstation identifier
In	INTEGER CHDNR	choice device number
In	INTEGER ISTAT	initial status
In	INTEGER ICH	initial choice number
In	INTEGER PET	prompt and echo type
In	REAL XMIN	echo area limits in DC
In	REAL XMAX	XMIN < XMAX
In	REAL YMIN	YMIN < YMAX
In	REAL YMAX	
In	INTEGER LDR	length of choice data record
In	CHARACTER*80 DR(LDR)	choice data record

Initialise the specified choice device

INITIALISE PICK   GINPK

SUBROUTINE GINPK(WKID, PKDNR, ISTAT, ISGNA, IPKID,
PET, XMIN, XMAX, YMIN, YMAX, LDR, DR)

In	INTEGER WKID	workstation identifier
In	INTEGER PKDNR	pick device number
In	INTEGER ISTAT	initial status
In	INTEGER ISGNA	initial segment name
In	INTEGER IPKID	initial pick identifier
In	INTEGER PET	prompt and echo type
In	REAL XMIN	echo area limits in DC
In	REAL XMAX	$XMIN < XMAX$
In	REAL YMIN	$YMIN < YMAX$
In	REAL YMAX	
In	INTEGER LDR	length of pick data record
In	CHARACTER*80 DR(LDR)	pick data record

Initialise the specified pick device

INITIALISE STRING   GINST

SUBROUTINE GINST(WKID, STDNR, LSTR, ISTR, PET,
XMIN, XMAX, YMIN, YMAX, BUFLEN, INIPOS, LDR, DR)

In	INTEGER WKID	workstation identifier
In	INTEGER STDNR	string device number
In	INTEGER LSTR	length of initial string (must be ≥ 0)
In	CHARACTER*(*) ISTR	initial string
In	INTEGER PET	prompt and echo type
In	REAL XMIN	echo area limits in DC
In	REAL XMAX	$XMIN < XMAX$
In	REAL YMIN	$YMIN < YMAX$
In	REAL YMAX	
In	INTEGER BUFLEN	buffer length of string
In	INTEGER INIPOS	initial cursor position
In	INTEGER LDR	length of string data record
In	CHARACTER*80 DR(LDR)	string data record

Initialise the specified string device

Setting Mode of Input Devices

SET LOCATOR MODE   GSLCM

SUBROUTINE GSLCM(WKID, IDNR, MODE, ESW)
In	INTEGER WKID	workstation identifier
In	INTEGER IDNR	locator device number
In	INTEGER MODE	operating mode
In	INTEGER ESW	echo switch

Set operating mode of the specified locator device

SET STROKE MODE   GSSKM

SUBROUTINE GSSKM(WKID, IDNR, MODE, ESW)
In	INTEGER WKID	workstation identifier
In	INTEGER IDNR	stroke device number
In	INTEGER MODE	operating mode
In	INTEGER ESW	echo switch

Set operating mode of the specified stroke device

SET VALUATOR MODE   GSVLM

SUBROUTINE GSVLM(WKID, IDNR, MODE, ESW)
In	INTEGER WKID	workstation identifier
In	INTEGER IDNR	valuator device number
In	INTEGER MODE	operating mode
In	INTEGER ESW	echo switch

Set operating mode of the specified valuator device

SET CHOICE MODE   GSCHM

SUBROUTINE GSCHM(WKID, IDNR, MODE, ESW)
In	INTEGER WKID	workstation identifier
In	INTEGER IDNR	choice device number
In	INTEGER MODE	operating mode
In	INTEGER ESW	echo switch

Set operating mode of the specified choice device

SET PICK MODE   **GSPKM**

SUBROUTINE GSPKM(WKID, IDNR, MODE, ESW)

In	INTEGER WKID	workstation identifier
In	INTEGER IDNR	pick device number
In	INTEGER MODE	operating mode
In	INTEGER ESW	echo switch

Set operating mode of the specified pick device

SET STRING MODE   **GSSTM**

SUBROUTINE GSSTM(WKID, IDNR, MODE, ESW)

In	INTEGER WKID	workstation identifier
In	INTEGER IDNR	string device number
In	INTEGER MODE	operating mode
In	INTEGER ESW	echo switch

Set operating mode of the specified string device

Request Input Functions

REQUEST LOCATOR   **GRQLC**

SUBROUTINE GRQLC(WKID, LCDNR, STAT, TNR, PX, PY)

In	INTEGER WKID	workstation identifier
In	INTEGER LCDNR	locator device number
Out	INTEGER STAT	status
Out	INTEGER TNR	normalization transformation number
Out	REAL PX	X coordinate of locator position in WC
Out	REAL PY	Y coordinate of locator position in WC

Request position in world coordinates and normalization transformation number from the specified locator device

REQUEST STROKE   GRQSK

SUBROUTINE GRQSK(WKID, SKDNR, N, STAT, TNR,
NP, PX, PY)

In	INTEGER WKID	workstation identifier
In	INTEGER SKDNR	stroke device number
In	INTEGER N	maximum number of points
Out	INTEGER STAT	status
Out	INTEGER TNR	normalization transformation number
Out	INTEGER NP	number of points
Out	REAL PX(N)	X coordinates of points in stroke in WC
Out	REAL PY(N)	Y coordinates of points in stroke in WC

Request sequence of points in world coordinates and normalization
transformation number from the specified stroke device

REQUEST VALUATOR   GRQVL

SUBROUTINE GRQVL(WKID, VLDNR, STAT, VAL)

In	INTEGER WKID	workstation identifier
In	INTEGER VLDNR	valuator device number
Out	INTEGER STAT	status
Out	REAL VAL	value

Request real value from the specified valuator device

REQUEST CHOICE   GRQCH

SUBROUTINE GRQCH(WKID, CHDNR, STAT, CHNR)

In	INTEGER WKID	workstation identifier
In	INTEGER CHDNR	choice device number
Out	INTEGER STAT	status
Out	INTEGER CHNR	choice number

Request non-negative integer, representing a selection from a number
of choices, and choice status from the specified choice device

REQUEST PICK   **GRQPK**

SUBROUTINE GRQPK(WKID, PKDNR, STAT, SGNA, PKID)
In   INTEGER WKID   workstation identifier
In   INTEGER PKDNR   pick device number
Out INTEGER STAT   status
Out INTEGER SGNA   segment name
Out INTEGER PKID   pick identifier

Request segment name, pick identifier and pick status from the specified pick device

REQUEST STRING   **GRQST**

SUBROUTINE GRQST(WKID, STDNR, STAT, LSTR, STR)
In   INTEGER WKID   workstation identifier
In   INTEGER STDNR   string device number
Out INTEGER STAT   status
Out INTEGER LSTR   length of string (in characters)
Out CHARACTER*(*) STR   character string

Request character string from the specified string device

Sample Input Functions

SAMPLE LOCATOR   **GSMLC**

SUBROUTINE GSMLC(WKID, LCDNR, TNR, PX, PY)
In   INTEGER WKID   workstation identifier
In   INTEGER LCDNR   locator device number
Out INTEGER TNR   normalization transformation number
Out REAL PX   X coordinate of locator position in WC
Out REAL PY   Y coordinate of locator position in WC

Sample the specified locator device, delivering a point in world coordinates and a normalization transformation number

SAMPLE STROKE   **GSMSK**

SUBROUTINE GSMSK(WKID, SKDNR, N, TNR, NP, PX, PY)

In	INTEGER WKID	workstation identifier
In	INTEGER SKDNR	stroke device number
In	INTEGER N	maximum number of points
Out	INTEGER TNR	normalization transformation number
Out	INTEGER NP	number of points
Out	REAL PX(N)	X coordinates of points in stroke in WC
Out	REAL PY(N)	Y coordinates of points in stroke in WC

Sample the specified stroke device, delivering a sequence of points in world coordinates and a normalization transformation number

SAMPLE VALUATOR   **GSMVL**

SUBROUTINE GSMVL(WKID, VLDNR, VAL)

In	INTEGER WKID	workstation identifier
In	INTEGER VLDNR	valuator device number
Out	REAL VAL	value

Sample the specified valuator device, delivering a real value

SAMPLE CHOICE   **GSMCH**

SUBROUTINE GSMCH(WKID, CHDNR, STAT, CHNR)

In	INTEGER WKID	workstation identifier
In	INTEGER CHDNR	choice device number
Out	INTEGER STAT	status
Out	INTEGER CHNR	choice number

Sample the specified choice device, delivering a non-negative integer, which represents a selection from a number of choices, and choice status

SAMPLE PICK   **GSMPK**

SUBROUTINE GSMPK(WKID, PKDNR, STAT, SGNA, PKID)

In	INTEGER WKID	workstation identifier
In	INTEGER PKDNR	pick device number
Out	INTEGER STAT	status
Out	INTEGER SGNA	segment name
Out	INTEGER PKID	pick identifier

Sample the specified pick device, delivering a segment name, pick identifier and pick status

SAMPLE STRING   **GSMST**

SUBROUTINE GSMST(WKID, STDNR, LSTR, STR)

In	INTEGER WKID	workstation identifier
In	INTEGER STDNR	string device number
Out	INTEGER LSTR	length of string (in characters)
Out	CHARACTER*(*) STR	character string

Sample the specified string device, delivering a character string

Event Input Functions

AWAIT EVENT   **GWAIT**

SUBROUTINE GWAIT(TOUT, WKID, ICL, IDNR)

In	REAL TOUT	timeout in seconds
Out	INTEGER WKID	workstation identifier
Out	INTEGER ICL	input class
Out	INTEGER IDNR	logical input device number

If the input queue is empty, wait for an input item until the specified time has elapsed. Read the workstation identifier, input class, and logical input device number of the oldest entry in the input queue and make the values available for subsequent interrogation by the GET functions.

FLUSH DEVICE EVENTS   **GFLUSH**

SUBROUTINE GFLUSH(WKID, ICL, IDNR)

In	INTEGER WKID	workstation identifier
In	INTEGER ICL	input class
In	INTEGER IDNR	logical input device number

Delete all the events from the specified logical input device in the input queue

GET LOCATOR   **GGTLC**

SUBROUTINE GGTLC(TNR, PX, PY)

Out	INTEGER TNR	normalization transformation number
Out	REAL PX	X coordinate of locator position in WC
Out	REAL PY	Y coordinate of locator position in WC

Transfer position in world coordinates and normalization transformation number from the current event report to the application program

GET STROKE   **GGTSK**

SUBROUTINE GGTSK(N, TNR, NP, PX, PY)

In	INTEGER N	maximum number of points
Out	INTEGER TNR	normalization transformation number
Out	INTEGER NP	number of points
Out	REAL PX(N)	X coordinates of points in stroke in WC
Out	REAL PY(N)	Y coordinates of points in stroke in WC

Transfer sequence of points in world coordinates and normalization transformation number from the current event report to the application program

GET VALUATOR   **GGTVL**

SUBROUTINE GGTVL(VAL)

| Out | REAL VAL | value |

Transfer real value from the current event report to the application program

GET CHOICE   **GGTCH**

SUBROUTINE GGTCH(STAT, CHNR)

Out INTEGER STAT   status
Out INTEGER CHNR   choice number

Transfer non-negative integer, representing a selection from a number of choices, and choice status from the current event report to the application program

GET PICK   **GGTPK**

SUBROUTINE GGTPK(STAT, SGNA, PKID)

Out INTEGER STAT   status
Out INTEGER SGNA   segment name
Out INTEGER PKID   pick identifier

Transfer segment name, pick identifier and pick status from the current event report to the application program

GET STRING   **GGTST**

SUBROUTINE GGTST(LSTR, STR)

Out INTEGER LSTR   length of string (in characters)
Out CHARACTER*(*) STR   character string

Transfer character string from the current event report to the application program

METAFILE FUNCTIONS

WRITE ITEM TO GKSM   **GWITM**

SUBROUTINE GWITM(WKID, TYPE, IDRL, LDR, DR)

In INTEGER WKID   workstation identifier
In INTEGER TYPE   item type
In INTEGER IDRL   item data record length
In INTEGER LDR   dimension of data record array
In CHARACTER*80 DR(LDR)   data record array

Pass non-graphical data from the application program to the GKS metafile

GET ITEM TYPE FROM GKSM   GGTITM

SUBROUTINE GGTITM(WKID, TYPE, IDRL)

In	INTEGER WKID	workstation identifier
Out	INTEGER TYPE	item type
Out	INTEGER IDRL	item data record length

Pass the item type and item data record length of the current item back to the application program

READ ITEM FROM GKSM   GRDITM

SUBROUTINE GRDITM(WKID, MIDRL, MLDR, DR)

In	INTEGER WKID	workstation identifier
In	INTEGER MIDRL	maximum item data record length
In	INTEGER MLDR	dimension of data record array
Out	CHARACTER*80 DR(MLDR)	data record array

Pass the current item to the application program (graphical or nongraphical item)

INTERPRET ITEM   GIITM

SUBROUTINE GIITM(TYPE, IDRL, LDR, DR)

In	INTEGER TYPE	item type
In	INTEGER IDRL	item data record length
In	INTEGER LDR	dimension of data record array
In	CHARACTER*80 DR(LDR)	data record array

Interpret the item read in by **READ ITEM FROM GKSM**. The interpretation causes appropriate changes in the set of GKS state variables and generates appropriate graphical output as determined by the metafile specification

UTILITY FUNCTIONS

Functions Defined in GKS

EVALUATE TRANSFORMATION MATRIX   GEVTM

SUBROUTINE GEVTM(XO, YO, DX, DY, PHI, FX, FY,
    SW, MOUT)

In	REAL XO	X coordinate of fixed point in WC or NDC
In	REAL YO	Y coordinate of fixed point in WC or NDC
In	REAL DX	X component of shift vector in WC or NDC
In	REAL DY	Y component of shift vector in WC or NDC
In	REAL PHI	rotation angle in radians
In	REAL FX	X scale factor
In	REAL FY	Y scale factor
In	INTEGER SW	coordinate switch specifying WC or NDC
Out	REAL MOUT(2, 3)	output transformation matrix

The transformation specified by fixed point, shift vector, rotation angle and scale factors is evaluated and the result is returned in the output transformation matrix

ACCUMULATE TRANSFORMATION MATRIX   GACTM

SUBROUTINE GACTM(MIN, XO, YO, DX, DY, PHI, FX, FY,
    SW, MOUT)

In	REAL MIN(2, 3)	input transformation matrix
In	REAL XO	X coordinate of fixed point in WC or NDC
In	REAL YO	Y coordinate of fixed point in WC or NDC
In	REAL DX	X component of shift vector in WC or NDC
In	REAL DY	Y component of shift vector in WC or NDC
In	REAL PHI	rotation angle in radians
In	REAL FX	X scale factor
In	REAL FY	Y scale factor
In	INTEGER SW	coordinate switch specifying WC or NDC
Out	REAL MOUT(2, 3)	output transformation matrix

The transformation specified by fixed point, shift vector, rotation angle and scale factors is combined with the input transformation matrix and the result is returned in the output transformation matrix

Functions Defined in this Language Binding

PACK DATA RECORD   GPREC

SUBROUTINE GPREC(IL, IA, RL, RA, NS, LSA, CA,
     IDIL, ERRIND, IDOL, DR)

In	INTEGER IL	length of integer array
In	INTEGER IA(*)	integer array
In	INTEGER RL	length of real array
In	REAL RA(*)	real array
In	INTEGER NS	number of strings
In	INTEGER LSA(*)	length of each string (in characters)
In	CHARACTER*(*) CA (*)	array of strings
In	INTEGER IDIL	maximum length of data record
Out	INTEGER ERRIND	error indicator
Out	INTEGER IDOL	length of data record
Out	CHARACTER*80 DR(IDIL)	data record

Pack a data record into a CHARACTER*80 array

UNPACK DATA RECORD   GUREC

SUBROUTINE GUREC(IDL, DR, IIL, IRL, ISL, ERRIND, IL, IA,
     RL, RA, NS, LSA, CA)

In	INTEGER IDL	length of data record
In	CHARACTER*80 DR(IDL)	data record
In	INTEGER IIL	maximum length of integer array
In	INTEGER IRL	maximum length of real array
In	INTEGER ISL	maximum length of string array
Out	INTEGER ERRIND	error indicator
Out	INTEGER IL	number of integers
Out	INTEGER IA(IIL)	integer array
Out	INTEGER RL	number of reals
Out	REAL RA(IRL)	real array
Out	INTEGER NS	number of strings
Out	INTEGER LSA(ISL)	length of each string (in characters)
Out	CHARACTER*(*) CA(ISL)	array of strings

Unpack a data record from a CHARACTER*80 array

ERROR HANDLING

EMERGENCY CLOSE GKS   GECLKS

SUBROUTINE GECLKS
None

Tries to close GKS in case of an error, saving as much information as possible

ERROR HANDLING   GERHND

SUBROUTINE GERHND(ERRNR, FCTID, ERRFIL)
In   INTEGER ERRNR   error number
In   INTEGER FCTID   function identification
In   INTEGER ERRFIL   error file

A procedure called by GKS when an error is detected. It may be user supplied

ERROR LOGGING   GERLOG

SUBROUTINE GERLOG(ERRNR, FCTID, ERRFIL)
In   INTEGER ERRNR   error number
In   INTEGER FCTID   function identification
In   INTEGER ERRFIL   error file

A procedure called by the standard GKS error handling procedure. It prints an error message and function identification on the error file

Appendix C Complete Program

This appendix contains a complete FORTRAN 77 GKS program, written in strict FORTRAN 77, except for the installation dependent inclusion of a PARAMETER statement.

The program is based on the example in Section 2.8. Introductory and terminating GKS functions have been added to make the example into a complete program and the program comments contain references to the description of these additional functions.

```
      PROGRAM DUCKS
C
      REAL XNEWDK(44), YNEWDK(44), XNEWW(10), YNEWW(10)
C
C     Include FORTRAN 77 PARAMETER definitions of enumeration
C     type parameters (installation dependent)
C
$INSERT SYSCOM > GKS.PAR.INS.F77
C
C     Set up array of aspect source flags
C
      INTEGER LASFS(13)
      DATA LASFS/13*GBUNDL/
C
C     Open GKS, open and activate one workstation, and set aspect source flags
C     (see Chapters 7, 8 and 13)
C
      CALL GOPKS(1, -1)
      CALL GOPWK(1, 1, 5)
      CALL GACWK(1)
      CALL GSASF(LASFS)
```

```
C
C       Set window 1, use default viewport 1 and select
C       normalization transformation 1 (see Chapter 3)
C
        CALL GSWN(1, 0.0, 90.0, 0.0, 90.0)
        CALL GSELNT(1)
C
C       Set required polyline, polymarker, fill area and text representations
C       use values assumed in Chapter 2 - negative values are implementation dependent
C       (see Chapter 7)
C
        CALL GSPLR(1, 1, 1, 1.0, 1)
        CALL GSPLR(1, 2, 2, 1.0, 1)
        CALL GSPMR(1, 1, 3, 1.0, 1)
        CALL GSPMR(1, 2, 4, 1.0, 1)
        CALL GSPMR(1, 3, 2, 1.0, 1)
        CALL GSFAR(1, 1, GHOLLO, 0, 1)
        CALL GSFAR(1, 2, GSOLID, 0, 1)
        CALL GSFAR(1, 3, GHATCH, -4, 1)
        CALL GSTXR(1, 1, -104, GSTRKP, 1.0, 0.0, 1)
C
C       Continue with example from Section 2.8
C
        PI = 4.0*ATAN(1.0)
        XCEN = 45.0
        YCEN = 45.0
        RADIUS = 30.0
C
        THETA = 5.0*PI/6.0
        CALL MOVEDK(XCEN, YCEN, RADIUS, THETA, XNEWDK, YNEWDK,
     1   XNEWW, YNEWW)
        CALL GSPLI(1)
        CALL GPL(44, XNEWDK, YNEWDK)
        CALL GPL(10, XNEWW, YNEWW)
C
        THETA = PI/2.0
        CALL MOVEDK(XCEN, YCEN, RADIUS, THETA, XNEWDK, YNEWDK,
     1   XNEWW, YNEWW)
        CALL GSPLI(2)
        CALL GPL(44, XNEWDK, YNEWDK)
        CALL GPL(10, XNEWW, YNEWW)
```

```
      THETA = PI/6.0
      CALL MOVEDK(XCEN, YCEN, RADIUS, THETA, XNEWDK, YNEWDK,
     1   XNEWW, YNEWW)
      CALL GSPMI(1)
      CALL GPM(44, XNEWDK, YNEWDK)
      CALL GSPMI(3)
      CALL GPM(10, XNEWW, YNEWW)
C
      THETA = -PI/6.0
      CALL MOVEDK(XCEN, YCEN, RADIUS, THETA, XNEWDK, YNEWDK,
     1   XNEWW, YNEWW)
      CALL GSFAI(2)
      CALL GFA(44, XNEWDK, YNEWDK)
C
      THETA = -PI/2.0
      CALL MOVEDK(XCEN, YCEN, RADIUS, THETA, XNEWDK, YNEWDK,
     1   XNEWW, YNEWW)
      CALL GSFAI(3)
      CALL GFA(44, XNEWDK, YNEWDK)
      CALL GSPLI(1)
      CALL GPL(44, XNEWDK, YNEWDK)
C
      THETA = -5.0*PI/6.0
      CALL MOVEDK(XCEN, YCEN, RADIUS, THETA, XNEWDK, YNEWDK,
     1   XNEWW, YNEWW)
      CALL GFA(44, XNEWDK, YNEWDK)
      CALL GSPLI(2)
      CALL GPL(44, XNEWDK, YNEWDK)
C
      CALL GSTXI(1)
      CALL GSCHH(6.0)
      CALL GSTXAL(GARITE, GAHALF)
      CALL GTX(24.0, 45.0, 'G')
      CALL GSCHH(3.0)
      CALL GSTXAL(GALEFT, GAHALF)
      CALL GTX(24.0, 45.0, 'RAPHICAL')
      CALL GSTXAL(GARITE, GAHALF)
      CALL GTX(60.0, 45.0, 'DUC')
      CALL GSCHH(6.0)
      CALL GSTXAL(GALEFT, GAHALF)
      CALL GTX(60.0, 45.0, 'KS')
```

```
C
C        Deactivate and close workstation and close GKS
C        (see Chapters 8 and 7)
C
         CALL GDAWK(1)
         CALL GCLWK(1)
         CALL GCLKS
         END
C
         SUBROUTINE MOVEDK(XC, YC, R, THETA, XNWDK, YNWDK, XNWW, YNWW)
C
C        Calculates coordinates of duck and wing when centre of duck
C        is placed on circle centre (XC, YC) of radius R at angle
C        THETA from horizontal radius.
C
         REAL XNWDK(44), YNWDK(44), XNWW(10), YNWW(10)
         REAL XDK(44), YDK(44), XW(10), YW(10)
C
C        DATA initialise XDK, YDK, XW, YW as earlier
C
         DATA XDK/ 0.0, 2.0, 4.0, 6.0, 8.0,10.0,12.0,14.0,16.4,17.0,17.3,
     1      17.8,18.5,20.0,22.0,24.0,26.0,28.0,29.0,28.8,27.2,25.0,
     2      23.0,21.5,21.1,21.5,22.8,24.1,25.1,25.2,24.2,22.1,20.0,
     3      18.0,16.0,14.0,12.0,10.0, 8.0, 6.1, 4.2, 3.0, 1.3, 0.0/
         DATA YDK/ 8.8, 7.6, 7.1, 7.4, 8.0, 8.9, 9.6, 9.9, 9.4, 9.7,12.0,
     1      14.0,16.1,17.0,17.0,16.0,13.9,13.1,13.2,12.3,11.5,11.5,
     2      11.5,11.2,10.5, 9.0, 8.0, 7.0, 5.1, 3.6, 1.9, 1.1, 0.9,
     3       0.7, 0.8, 1.0, 1.0, 1.2, 1.8, 2.1, 2.9, 4.1, 6.0, 8.8/
         DATA XW/15.7,17.0,17.7,17.3,15.3,13.0,11.0, 9.0, 7.0, 4.7/
         DATA YW/ 7.0, 6.1, 5.0, 3.8, 3.0, 2.7, 3.0, 3.6, 4.2, 5.2/
C
         XPOS = XC + R*COS(THETA)
         YPOS = YC + R*SIN(THETA)
         DO 100 I = 1,44
         XNWDK(I) = XDK(I)-14.5 + XPOS
100      YNWDK(I) = YDK(I)-8.85 + YPOS
         DO 200 I = 1,10
         XNWW(I) = XW(I)-14.5 + XPOS
200      YNWW(I) = YW(I)-8.85 + YPOS
         RETURN
         END
```

Index

abbreviations, 195
Abingdon meeting, 7
ACCUMULATE TRANSFORMA-
    TION MATRIX, 65, 71, 234
acknowledgement, 103
ACM, 195
ACTIVATE WORKSTATION, 120,
    142, 206
ACTIVE, WORKSTATION, GKS state
    143
Ada language binding, 8
alignment, of text, 31, 34
ALLOWED, implicit regeneration, 137,
    204
ALWAYS, clear workstation flag, 121,
    204
angle of rotation, of transformation, 65
annotation, of graphs, 54
    voice, 183
ANSI X3H3, 5, 195
arc, 182
area, filling, 22
ASAP, deferral mode, 136, 204
ASF, 191, 195
aspect ratio, 49, 123
aspect source flag, 191, 192, 204
aspects, 14, 125, 185
ASSOCIATE SEGMENT WITH
    WORKSTATION, 137, 169, 219
ASTI, deferral mode, 136, 204
asynchronous input, 101
attention handling, (see EVENT mode)
attributes, primitive, 14, 41

individual, 185, 188
mode of working, 191
segment, 65
AWAIT EVENT, 108, 163, 165, 230
AXES subroutine, 19

background colour, 127
BASE, text alignment, 36, 204
BCS Standards Committee, 4
Bellinglise meeting, 3, 10
Benodet meeting, 9
blink, 76
BNIG, deferral mode, 136, 204
BNIL, deferral mode, 136, 204
Bologna meeting, 5
BOTTOM, text alignment, 36, 204
boundary, of fill area, 24
break, input, 104
brightness, (see highlighting, colour
    table)
BSI, 6, 195
Budapest meeting, 5
BUNDLED, aspect source flag, 191, 204
bundle table, (see representations)
bundled specification, of aspects, 187
button device, (see CHOICE input)

CAP, text alignment, 36, 204
cartesian coordinates, 45
category, of workstation, 118
Computer Graphics Interface, (see CGI)
Computer Graphics Metafile, (see CGM)
cell, 179

A.P.I.C. Studies in Data Processing
General Editors: Fraser Duncan and M. J. R. Shave

★ Out of print.
† Now published in the Computer Science Classics Series.